D1588480

What Economics is About

What Economics is About

Worker, Consumer, Government
and Corporation

Michael Barratt Brown

Senior Lecturer, Department of Extramural Studies
University of Sheffield

Weidenfeld and Nicolson

5 Winsley Street London W1

SBN 297 00193 0

Printed in Great Britain by
Cox & Wyman Ltd,
London, Fakenham and Reading

Contents

List of Tables

List of Figures

Preface

This book is directed generally to the intelligent man of today whose father was the target of G.D.H. Cole's *Intelligent Man's Guides* to the world of the 1930s. It is directed especially to adult students who are either studying at home or following part-time courses, like those of the Open University. Such students have the disadvantage of limited time and facilities either for detailed instruction or for reading widely in the ever-growing economic literature, much of it in specialized journals. At the same time, they have the advantage of practical experience of economic life. This book is designed to introduce them to the ways of thinking of economists, and attempts at all times to relate theory to practice. It is based on the premise that the purpose of making the abstractions that economists make in their theories is in the end to understand better and so to improve the practical working of the economies we live in.

The book can be used alone as an introductory textbook, but it is designed as a study guide to be used with other books. Each chapter begins with a summary or signpost to what follows, so that students can see what they are being introduced to. Economic terms and concepts are explained and some major economic problems are examined, together with the answers that different economists have given to them, but the reader is referred to other books and parts of books for essential arguments and case studies. Although reference is made in this way to a wide range of specialist books, the guide is designed primarily to introduce the student to a central body of about twenty-five works on different aspects of economics. All these works are written in popular language by leading authorities and may be expected to last as standard works for some time to come. All should be available from any good lending library, but since most are obtainable in paperback editions, students will be well advised to build up their own libraries, especially of the titles which are referred to many times. References appear in the text but full bibliographical details will be found at the end of the book.

Economists are generally derided because they so often disagree in their analysis and in the facts which they regard as important. Other scientists also disagree among themselves in this way, but they have the advantage of being more easily able to isolate particular variable factors in their analysis by controlled experiments. The social scientists cannot interfere in society in this way, but must rely on comparisons between societies at different times and in different places in order to develop general concepts for explaining particular facts. Throughout this book, therefore, there will be found references to Britain's economic history and to other economies at different stages of development from Britain's.

The other distinguishing feature of social scientists is that they are studying societies, in the ordering of which all citizens have an interest. Since the citizens' interests vary, their views about how society should be ordered will also vary, and since economists are also citizens their views too will vary. Students, like other citizens, may be expected to be more sympathetic to economists of their own persuasion and to facts and interpretations that suit their views. But they will not learn to think for themselves unless they are presented with conflicting facts and interpretations to examine.

In this book the author has attempted, as honestly as he can, to state or to refer to differing views on controversial questions; he himself, however, has his own views and believes that it is an essential part of the evidence for any adult student to know where an author stands. The book can be distinguished from most economic textbooks by its inclusion of Marx's economics in the main stream of economic thought. This reflects the author's own conviction of the abiding importance of Marxian concepts. Thus the book might be called a study guide with a viewpoint, which will be made clear at each stage of the work.

The viewpoint is very briefly that the relationship of men (and women) at work is the most important one to be studied. Most economics by contrast concentrates upon the relationship of men (and women) shopping in the market. It is the author's view that the power of the consumer is very small. Indeed this is one of the main reasons for the increasing demand that governments should intervene in the working of the market; the others being to sustain full employment and economic growth and national solvency. Thus of the four categories in the title the organized workers and the giant corporations are seen as the primary powers, each bidding today for influence over the third – the growing power of government; while the power of the consumer, for all the talk of consumer sovereignty, remains essentially weak.

Statistical tables and figurative graphs are used throughout the book to illustrate or provide evidence for the lines of argument. Students should note the sources of the statistics and follow them up to discover changes in trends subsequent to publication of this book. A combined Glossary and Index at the end of the book provides brief definitions of the economic and statistical terms used throughout. The first time one of these terms appears in the text it is printed in small capitals and can be looked up in the Glossary.

The book derives from many years of teaching economics in adult classes, mainly classes for trade unionists – miners, steel-workers, engineers – released from work for one or two days a week on three-year courses under the auspices of the Extramural Department of Sheffield University. It is hoped that it will be of especial value to students like those who are already involved in the Labour Movement, know something of its aims, and wish to devote themselves more effectively to the emancipation of their fellow men. It is dedicated to my students who have taught me so much and have shown me how real that devotion may be.

I have to thank Professor K. J. W. Alexander, Stephen Bodington, and my son Christopher Ronald, for reading the typescript *in toto* and making many valuable suggestions. I have also to thank several of my colleagues in the Sheffield University Extramural Department for reading and commenting on parts of the text at various stages. The book could not even have been attempted without the love and support of my wife. My thanks are due also to Christine Fawcett who typed the book from a well-nigh illegible script.

Michael Barratt Brown

Sheffield, August 1969

'Labour is, in the first place, a process in which both man and Nature participate, and in which man of his own accord starts, regulates, and controls the material re-actions between himself and Nature. He opposes himself to Nature as one of her own forces, setting in motion arms and legs, head and hands, the natural forces of his body, in order to appropriate Nature's productions in a form adapted to his own wants. By thus acting on the external world and changing it, he at the same time changes his own nature. He develops his slumbering powers and compels them to act in obedience to his sway. We are not now dealing with those primitive instinctive forms of labour that remind us of the mere animal. An immeasurable interval of time separates the state of things in which a man brings his labour-power to market for sale as a commodity, from that stage in which human labour was still in its first instinctive stage. We presuppose labour in a form that stamps it as exclusively human. A spider conducts operations that resemble those of a weaver, and a bee puts to shame many an architect in the construction of her cells. But what distinguishes the worst architect from the best of bees is this, that the architect raises his structure in imagination before he erects it in reality. At the end of every labour-process, we get a result that already existed in the imagination of the labourer at its commencement.'

Karl Marx, *Capital* (1867) Chapter VII

'So that in the right Definition of Names, lyes the first use of Speech; which is the Acquisition of Science: And in wrong, or no Definitions, lyes the first abuse; from which proceed all false and senselesse Tenets; which make those men that take their instruction from the authority of books, and not from their own meditation, to be as much below the condition of ignorant men, as men endued with true Science are above it. For between true Science, and erroneous Doctrines, Ignorance is in the middle. Naturall sense and imagination are not subject to absurdity. Nature it selfe cannot erre: and as men abound in copiousnesse of language; so they become more wise, or more mad than ordinary. Nor is it possible without Letters for any man to become either excellently wise, or (unless his memory be hurt by disease, or ill constitution of organs) excellently foolish. For words are wise mens counters, they do but reckon by them: but they are the mony of fooles.'

Thomas Hobbes, *Leviathan* (1651) Chapter IV

'The nature of things is easier to conceive when one sees them evolving little by little than when one sees them as all finished.'

René Descartes, *Discourse on Method* (1637)

The reader may well find the first chapters of this book difficult but taking them 'little by little' and by 'the right definition of names' it is hoped that he may 'raise a structure in imagination' that conforms to reality, without becoming the 'mony of fooles'.

M.B.B.

1 Economics, Economizing, Economists and Economic Science

SUMMARY

The word ECONOMIC[1] is generally used to describe attitudes and relations among human beings that arise from the process of their getting a living. Economics is concerned with studying these relations and discovering how they change and are influenced – for better or worse. The uses of economics range from economical household management to national economic planning. Economics is a practical subject but economic theories differ widely and different economists approach economic questions in many different ways.

These differences can be set out as five groups of alternatives. Most economists can be divided into those who accept the first alternative in each case or those who accept the second; but there are many who might accept the first of some and the second of others:

(1) Some look broadly at the working of the ECONOMY as a whole; others more narrowly at PRICE determination and ECONOMIZING the use of RESOURCES;

(2) Some regard economies as susceptible of MANAGEMENT, others think of them as essentially SELF-REGULATING;

(3) Some include the study of the political and social framework of economic activity; others largely exclude this;

(4) Some work mainly by inference (INDUCTION) of general laws from observed facts; others make DEDUCTIONS from universal truths about human nature;

(5) Some believe that what has happened in the past provides evidence for general PREDICTIONS about the future; others limit themselves to more strictly verifiable statements.

Some of these distinctions, and especially the last one, the economist shares both with historians and with natural

[1] For definitions of words printed in small capitals, see Glossary, page 287.

scientists. All alike acknowledge explicitly or implicitly the need to use some general model of the world they are studying, according to which they select the facts they choose to observe and the theories they choose to test.

1. WHAT ARE ECONOMIC QUESTIONS?

If we list some ways in which we use the term 'economic' we may be helped to define what are economic questions. We speak of economic motives meaning those concerned with getting more money or more goods or services; of the most economic way of producing goods and services meaning the one that uses least resources; of economic pressures meaning forces brought to bear upon our capacity to get goods and services; of economic CLASSES meaning those groups of persons distinguished by their different relationship to the means of producing goods and services; of economic power meaning control over such means of production; of economic PLANNING meaning some conscious direction of the means of production. In all these cases we are talking about the attitudes and relations among human beings in getting a living.

The relationships that men find themselves involved in when they set out to get a living in a society like ours are very complex and they are constantly changing. An older steel-worker or coalminer may look back over his working life and consider how much has changed: the distance he travels to work, the transport he uses, the size of the plant where he works, the numbers of other men he works with, the tools and machines he uses, the organization of his work, the hours of work, the way he is paid, how much he can buy with his money, the kinds of goods and services that are available. He may have seen periods of unemployment and short-time; he may have changed jobs and moved many miles from his original home; he may have saved something for his retirement in addition to his old age pension, and seen rising prices reduce the value of his savings; he may have seen his children take up quite different kinds of work and ways of living; he may have seen his firm nationalized and new management brought in; he may have hoped for even bigger changes; he will certainly wonder what more are to come. These are some of the economic changes that a man may have seen in a lifetime as affecting him most closely. Many must seem to have fallen upon him like natural catastrophes beyond human control. Yet others may seem to have been within his power to influence.

Very close to any man will be the question of how his wages could be raised so that he may increase his command of goods and services. He may take a purely individualistic view, pursuing his own advantage, improving himself by education and training, increasing his output by piece-work and overtime, knowing that others are doing the same. He may take a sectional view, helping to increase the performance and earnings of members of his Union, of his plant or firm or industry, again knowing that others are doing the same. He may take collective action a step further, attempting through the power of his Union and of other Unions to raise the earnings of labour knowing that this will cut into the return to capital. He may take political action to change the general economic situation of employment and security, in which he and others like him are bargaining for their share of income. He may finally despair of all these efforts and build his hopes on changing the whole relationship of capital and labour. In each case his view follows from a general picture or model of the economy which he has at the back of his mind. He will bring this to bear on all the complex economic events that take place around him. If he does not have some such general picture, the events of which he hears and reads will seem disconnected and largely meaningless.

The London newspapers on the day these pages were written carried, among other reports, news of the fall of the value of the pound in the face of demand for German marks on the foreign exchange markets; a warning from the director of the International Monetary Fund that Britain might have to face a tighter credit squeeze; a report of British Government action to enforce TV hire purchase deposits; figures showing a fall in new registration of motor-cars in Britain; growing unrest about their wages among West German public service employees; the announcement by the United States Government that it would provide funds for developing a US supersonic aircraft to rival the Anglo-French Concorde; a suggestion that airline fares might have to be increased; the invitation by the British Ministry of Power to international oil companies to bid for further exploration blocks for natural gas in the North Sea; a statement by the Rank Organization that it would close its ten-pin bowling centres in Britain; a demand from the Trades Union Congress for a government pledge to support equal pay for women; estimates from the Registrar General's office of the population in Britain by 1991 with big increases forecast for the South-East; a leak of a Labour Party draft election manifesto covering proposals for Britain's entry into the Common Market and for reducing the power of private wealth in Britain; rumours of new talks on the future ownership of the *Sun* newspaper.

It was not an exceptional day. This is what we have come to expect on the front page of even the moderately serious daily papers. All these are economic matters. They are connected here just in being reported on the same day, but they may be connected in other deeper ways; some of them are obviously very closely linked. A study of economics will be expected by an intelligent practical man to help him to understand the connections. He will want to know the implications of each of these pieces of news for himself and his family now and in the future. He will suppose that all the government and company decisions and proposals referred to are based on an understanding of these connections and implications – between prices and wages, credit and sales, foreign exchange and the value of the pound, expansion and contraction of INVESTMENT, private and public ownership, and so on. Understanding, moreover, can lead to control and improvement. But for this we have to do more than increase our knowledge of the facts as the papers report them; we have to develop theories, postulates, HYPOTHESES, laws – whatever you like to call them – and build them into MODELS which reveal the basic connection between the facts. That is what economics is about.

2. POLITICAL ECONOMY AND ECONOMIZING

The words, economy, economic, economist and economize all derive from a Greek word meaning 'household management'. The ancient Greeks themselves used the word for the administration of the state as well of a private household. If we think for a moment of what is involved in housekeeping, we can see that an economy must be concerned with organizing and with regulating – what comes into the house, what goes out, the work done in the house, the maintenance, repair and extension of the house itself. Thus economic questions are concerned with the relationship of persons both inside the household and between one household and others. It is these relationships that must be understood through some kind of simplified model of the infinite complexity of actual life, if the study of economics is to be justified to a practical man. Economic theories and models have to be tested by being applied. Economics is essentially a practical subject.

The actual techniques, however, of growing food, or making clothes or housebuilding are not the subjects of economics – these are matters for technologists; it is the forms of organization of human relations in which men and women carry on these techniques which are those we describe as economic. There will, of course, be a close connection between TECHNO- LOGY and economic processes because different techniques will require different types of organization. An economy of hunters and fishermen, like that of the Eskimos, using primitive tools made of bone, will evidently differ greatly from our own economy, in which the production of food, clothing, housing and many other things is carried on by means of large and complicated machines. We shall look in the next chapter at differences in economies based on different technologies.

Side by side with the concept of an economy as a form of organizing human relations to meet man's daily needs, there grew up a second concept from the original Greek word for housekeeping. This was the concept of economizing, of good management which makes the best use of limited resources. Many economists and many economic textbooks for nearly one hundred years have based themselves on the assumption that the most important fact of economic life is SCARCITY. It is scarcity, they say, that gives to goods and services, and to land and capital and labour, their VALUE; and it is because of scarcity that economizing, or getting the best use of our limited resources, becomes the most urgent subject of economic study.

These two concepts – of economies and of economizing – reveal a major difference in emphasis among economists. We shall notice other differences in a moment but this is a crucial one. We can in part relate it to the historical circumstances in which different economists have worked. Up till about a hundred years ago most economists were concerned with economies rather than with economizing; and this concern was symbolized in the title they gave to the subject: POLITICAL ECONOMY. These older, or CLASSICAL, economists were interested in such subjects as *England's Treasure by Forraign Trade*,[1] or the *Nature and Causes of the Wealth of Nations*.[2] In England in the early seventeenth century, and still more in the last quarter of the eighteenth century, the sudden increase of wealth, or economic GROWTH as we should now call it, was evident for all to see and was the central objective of inquiry.

By the 1860s, and still more after the slump of 1870, England had enjoyed a hundred years of economic growth; questions about the distribution of wealth and proper husbanding of resources were being raised. It is not at all surprising that Stanley Jevons, who was among the first to emphasize[3] the central importance of ECONOMIZING in economics, had first written a book on *The Coal Question* in 1865, in which he warned of the early exhaustion of Britain's coal reserves. He concluded that the most important economic question was how to make the best use of our limited resources – what are called the FACTORS OF PRODUCTION – LAND, CAPITAL and LABOUR. He emphasized, as his predecessors had, that this could only be done if there was a free MARKET for each factor and each was therefore allocated to the highest bidder, since that man must for that very reason have the best use for it.

He went further, however, and developed an idea that borrowed heavily from the differential and integral CALCULUS fundamental to the mathematics of physics, that what mattered was the use of the last bit of each factor – MARGINAL land, the last pound of capital laid out, the last worker taken on.

---

[1] Thomas Mun's exposition of so-called MERCANTILIST economics written in 1630.
[2] Adam Smith's great book criticizing mercantilism written in 1776.
[3] In *The Theory of Political Economy*, 1871.

We shall meet this idea when we talk about marginal costs and returns. In the last fifty years, however, the possibility of increasing the resources available as well as of allocating them economically has become important again. UNEM-PLOYED or UNDEREMPLOYED men and other unemployed or underemployed resources have stared us in the face. Economists have turned their attention once more to problems of economic growth and the nature and causes of DEVELOPED and UNDERDEVELOPED economies.

3. A SELF-REGULATING OR A REGULATED ECONOMY

A different distinction must now be drawn between those economists who have thought of the economy as self-regulating and those who have thought of it as being susceptible of human regulation – mainly by government INTERVENTION. Before Adam Smith the mercantilist economists certainly assumed government intervention as necessary to support merchant MONOPOLIES at home and to defend them against foreign merchants and so to build up the national treasure. Smith argued for ending all such government intervention and for freeing trade from monopolies so that the market could become the organizing principle of economic activity. The economizers like Jevons shared with the political economists their faith in FREE TRADE and their view of the economy as essentially self-regulating. Individual choices in the shops and in the markets for labour, capital and land operated through the influence of SUPPLY and DEMAND upon PRICES to produce the best allocation of resources. Adam Smith spoke of an 'invisible hand' and all agreed that no individuals or groups of persons or governments consciously regulated the economy. They looked for a law of VALUE, not so much as a measure of the values of all the factors of production, but as the ultimate determinant of their employment, and of the DISTRIBU-TION of products, through movements in prices. Classical political economy saw this ultimate value in the quantity of labour applied to production (tending, therefore, apparently to exclude the factors of capital and land). Later economists saw only an EQUILIBRIUM of the forces of supply and demand working at the margin to determine prices. More recently,

however, economists like Piero Sraffa[4] have reintroduced concepts of real comparison in terms of DATED LABOUR, i.e.
labour applied to production at different dates in producing the
goods themselves and in producing the capital equipment and
RAW MATERIALS from which to produce the goods.

Joan Robinson[5] has called this whole preoccupation with
laws and theories of value a metaphysical idea – that is to say
one that cannot be tested and proved right or wrong. Value
theory is certainly a very difficult aspect of economic theory
and not one to be tackled by a student until he has mastered
the general ways of thinking of economists. None the less, we
have to notice here that we shall in fact have to measure one
product against another when we speak for example of a
country's GROSS NATIONAL PRODUCT or of PRODUCTIVITY or
of REAL WAGES. We use prices to make these measures but we
often say that something 'isn't really worth it' implying some
'real' comparison.

Marx built this distinction into the very heart of his analysis
of a capitalist economy when he distinguished USE VALUE and
EXCHANGE VALUE. Use value is the value a good has in satisfying human wants. It is useful in fact and the usefulness to
the user can be measured in terms of actual concrete labour
incorporated in it, but the labour might have been wastefully
applied. Exchange value is by contrast the market value of a
good, that in Marx's view incorporates only a kind of abstract
labour – that portion of society's labour that at that time was
necessary to apply to its production. We shall take up this
question again, especially in the last chapter, when we
examine in a PLANNED ECONOMY as opposed to a MARKET
ECONOMY the determination of the ratios in which goods and
services are exchanged. We shall then come back to Sraffa's
concept of 'dated' labour.

One result of the growing doubts of economists about laws
of value and self-regulating equilibria was that the way was
opened for increased interest in the possibilities of conscious
intervention in the regulation of the economy. An ECONOMICS
OF WELFARE was developed in which criteria were examined

[4] P. Sraffa, *Production of Commodities by Means of Commodities,* 1960, p. 38.
[5] A modern economist whose book on *Economic Philosophy,* 1962, is an
essential introduction to these questions.

for discovering how the welfare of the community could in fact be determined, since in the words of A. C. Pigou, 'It now is, or eventually may become, feasible for governments to control the play of economic forces in such wise as to promote the economic welfare, and through that, the total welfare of their citizens as a whole'.[6] It was not, however, until it became obvious that the mechanism of the self-regulating market did not work at all well, and that an economic equilibrium could be established which left millions of men unemployed, that the feasibility of governments' controlling the play of economic forces became an urgent matter. To make such control more feasible required a revolution in economic thinking.

The 'revolution' was supplied by John Maynard Keynes. His *General Theory of Employment, Interest and Money* (1936) followed the great slump of the early 1930s and led to governments' beginning to manage their national economies. Keynes challenged Adam Smith's conviction that to try to CONTROL the economy was to fall into delusion:

I shall argue [said Keynes] 'that the postulates of the classical theory are applicable to a special case only and not to the general case, the situation which it assumed being a LIMITING point of the possible positions of equilibrium. Moreover, the characteristics of the special case assumed by the classical theory happen not to be those of the economic society in which we happen to live with the result that its teaching is misleading and disastrous if we attempt to apply it to the facts of experience.

The revolution consisted mainly, as we shall see in Chapter 6, in Keynes' analysis of the relation between SAVING and spending in the economy and the need for governments to sustain spending in order to maintain full employment.

Today a new gap, the widening gap between the developed economies and the undeveloped, has become only too obvious. Economists like Dudley Seers have been led to write again of the 'Limitations of the Special Case' (OU Institute of Statistics *Bulletin*, 1963). This time they mean the case of the few developed industrial economies, a case which is quite inapplicable to the 'typical case' of the hundred or so 'largely unindustrialized economies . . . covering the great majority of

6 *Economics of Welfare*, 1920.

the world's population'. The new revolution in economic
thinking which is needed could according to Dudley Seers find
a useful guide in the slogan: 'Economics is the study of
Economies.' Paraphrasing a dictum of the historian E. H.
Carr,[7] Seers writes:

> Before you study economics study the economist; before you
> study the economist study his historical and social environ-
> ment. . . . The title of Samuelson's Text (the most popular
> American textbook) should not be *Economics* but *The Economics
> of the United States in the Twentieth Century*. . . . The Soviet
> textbook *Political Economy* should perhaps be called *A Nine-
> teenth-Century Interpretation of Economic and Political change,
> based on Experience in Western Europe*.

Development economics involves once more then, in this view,
the study of economies rather than of economizing.

4. POLITICS, ECONOMICS AND SOCIOLOGY

Associated with the varying concern among economists with
either the self-regulating nature of market economies or with
the possibilities of 'managed' economies lies a difference of
view on the proper range of an economist's interest. Although
Adam Smith was anxious to free the economy from government intervention, his political economy, as the name implied,
was concerned not only with studying economies as a whole
but with the political, or what we would now rather call the
social, structure within which economic activities take place.
Thus in opening his examination of the price of labour, Smith
writes that 'wealth is power'. 'The person who either acquires,
or succeeds to a great fortune does not necessarily acquire or
succeed to any political power either civil or military' but 'the
power of purchasing; a certain command over all the labour,
or over all the produce of labour which is then in the market'.
And again writing of RENT, he speaks of the landlords 'as soon
as the land of any country has all become private property',
loving 'to reap where they never sowed and demand a rent
even for its natural produce'. It is the ownership of wealth in
capital or land that for Adam Smith determines the distribution
of incomes.

[7] Carr examined the study of history in *What is History?*, 1961.

Smith's great successor David Ricardo took the matter further:

> The produce of the earth – all that is derived from its surface by the united application of labour, machinery and capital is divided among three classes of the community, namely the proprietors of the land, the owner of the stock or capital necessary for its cultivation, and the labourers by whose industry it is cultivated. . . . [It is] to determine the laws which regulate this distribution (that) is the principal problem in Political Economy.[8]

Here is the search for a law of value but it is one that must be found within the social framework of landlord, capitalist and labourer, not of abstract factors of production. It was on Ricardo's LABOUR THEORY of value – his emphasis 'that in all countries and at all times profits depend on the quantity of labour requisite to provide necessaries for the labourers on that land' – that Karl Marx built his theory of SURPLUS VALUE. By this Marx meant the value that is extracted by the owner of land and capital from paying for the labour of the labourers only what is necessary for their SUBSISTENCE and perpetuation. This is essentially a social as much as an economic theory. Marx makes fun of the way in which those whom he dubs the 'vulgar economists' talk about economic categories without relating them to the social conditions in which they exist:

> It is an enchanted perverted topsy-turvy world in which Mr Capital and Mistress Land carry on their goblin tricks as social characters and at the same time as mere things. . . . Capital, Land, Labour! But capital is not a thing. It is a definite interrelation in social production belonging to a definite historical formation of society.[9]

It is the insistence on the essential connection between SOCIOLOGY and economics that marks off Marxian from other economists. In Marx's 'vision' of the economic process, as the historian of economic analysis, Joseph Schumpeter, calls it, that is in what economists would now call his model, there stands at the very centre the specific social economic relationship which men enter into in the process of production in societies at different levels of technical development.

[8] *Principles of Poliitcal Economy and Taxation*, 1817, Original Preface.
[9] Karl Marx, *Capital*, Vol. III, 1867, chapter 48.

In the process of production, human beings work not only upon
nature but also upon one another. They produce only by working
together in a specified manner and reciprocally exchanging their
activities. In order to produce they enter into definite connections and relations to one another and only within these actual
connections and relations does their influence upon nature
operate, i.e. does production take place.[10]

Marx, and the classical writers of political economy undoubtedly thought of these relations as being bound together in a
social SYSTEM. We need, therefore, to consider the idea of a
'system' for a moment. Many people talk about a CAPITALIST
system, FEUDAL system, etc. Marx in fact did not use the word
'system'. He spoke of the 'social formation' to describe all the
political, legal, economic and productive STRUCTURES that
make up society at any time; and within that formation of the
MODE OF PRODUCTION to describe the correspondence of the
economic structure of relations in production to what he saw
as the technological BASE, the stage of development of productive forces at the time. This schema is reproduced at Fig. 1.1.

It is necessary then briefly to describe what is meant by a
structure here. As opposed to a heap or a random assemblage,
the parts in a structure are related to each other in a certain
way. In a game of spillikins you may take one piece away
without necessarily disturbing the others, but in a biological,
physical or social structure this is impossible. Thus, in a social
system there will be many different structures at different
levels which have their own internal relations and between
which there are certain relationships that make up the whole.
Marx insisted that the SUPERSTRUCTURE of legal and political
relations was to be thought of as deriving from an economic
structure of property relations which in turn was based on the
forces of production, or what we should call the technology.
Change came from changing technology and from the conflicts
that new technology would create in the structures built upon
the old technology. The structures themselves, including the
economic structure, were self-regulating in Marx's view, but he
allowed that the contradictions between them had to work
themselves out in men's minds – in their consciousness – before
social change could take place. In the models that physicists

[10] Karl Marx, *Wage, Labour and Capital,* 1849, Section III.

make to understand the physical world, they stand outside the system; but in social models the model makers are inside the system.[11]

To speak of an economic or social system, however, can also be seen as a way of isolating one period of the history of a country or countries according to certain elements that the

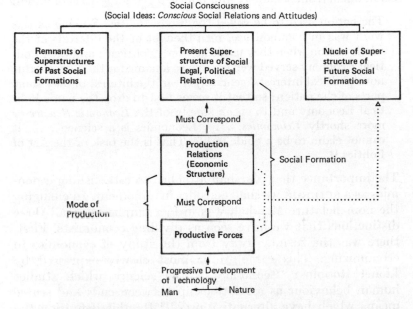

Source: O. Lange, *Political Economy*, p.33, derived from Marx, Preface to a *Contribution to the Critique of Political Economy*.

Figure 1.1. Marx's schema of social structure and development

whole period has in common. From this can be built a conceptually functioning model of the relationships that make-up the whole. The test of the value of the model will then be the extent to which it appears to account for the actual regulation of the economy and society over the period, and enables predictions to be made about its future evolution. This is what Marx referred to in the Preface to *Capital* as 'the ultimate aim of this work' to 'lay bare the economic law of motion of

[11] This is a crude summary of Marx's own statement in his Preface to *A Contribution to the Critique of Political Economy*, 1859, which students should study before looking at Marx's main works. It is printed at the beginning of *Marx on Economics* edited by R. Freedman.

modern society'. We shall consider in the next section how legitimate or useful it may be to isolate periods and construct systems and models of structures in this way. Such grand theorizing was largely rejected by economists after the death of Marx and Mill.

It was above all Alfred Marshall who narrowed the view of economists from sociology and political economy to economics.

> The nation used to be called the 'Body Politic'. So long as this word was in common use, men thought of the interests of the whole nation when they used the word 'Political'; and then Political Economy served well enough as a name for the science. But now 'political interests' generally mean the interest of only some parts of the nation; so that it seems best to drop the name Political Economy and to speak simply of the *Economic Science* or more shortly *Economics*. . . . Economics is a science . . . it cannot claim to be a guide in life. That is the task of the Art of Politics.[12]

The importance that Marshall attached to establishing economics as a SCIENCE we shall consider in a moment. In changing the nomenclature Marshall was in fact emphasizing all three distinctions that we have seen as dividing economists. First, there was the turning away from the study of economies to economizing. This came to be most clearly expressed by Lionel Robbins: 'Economics is the science which studies human behaviour as a relationship between ends and scarce means which have alternative uses.'[13] By this definition the conception is rejected 'of Economics as the study of the causes of material welfare'. The laws of economics are 'of universal applicability', Robbins insists, 'not limited to certain conditions of time and space'.

Secondly, ends are separated from means. This does not prevent Marshall from moralizing about the 'social possibilities of economic chivalry' and appealing for 'a devotion to public well-being on the part of the rich'.[14] But it does mean that politics as well as economics become defined in a certain way –

[12] Alfred Marshall, *Economics of Industry*, 1879, p. 2.
[13] Lionel Robbins. *The Nature and Significance of Economic Science*, 1932, p. 16.
[14] Alfred Marshall, *Principles of Economics*, 1890, Book vi, Ch. xiii, Section 13.

economics becomes a POSITIVE science concerned with reconciling means;[15] politics is NORMATIVE – being concerned with reconciling ends.

This separation led to the abandonment of the concept central to classical political economy of a self-regulating economic 'system'. It had a dual effect on political economy. On the one hand, as we have seen, it opened the way once more to state interference, which Marshall's own interests in industry and trade foreshadowed. If economic laws were concerned with the way human beings behaved regardless of the conditions of time and space, that is of the technology or social structure, then there could be no inherent obstacle in 'the system' to government interference. On the other hand, this splitting of political economy into its two components led to the abandonment of the search for laws regulating a politico- and socio-economic system and from which are generated the growth and the distribution of wealth.

Thirdly, then, this separation of politics and economics involve a narrowing of the range of economic inquiry. Marshall abandoned the term political economy because the 'body politic' became divided after the working class had received the vote in 1867 and 1884. Marshall himself confessed in old age that having at first

> developed a tendency to socialism . . . fortified later on by Mill's essay's in *The Fortnightly Review* in 1879, I ended up in the main occupied with the influences which still make for sectional and class selfishness, with the limited tendencies of self-interest to direct each individual's action on those lines in which it will be most beneficial to others.[16]

Land, Labour and Capital became once more factors of production divorced from their social roots. The distribution of income was to be examined as part of the THEORY OF PRICES, as a FUNCTION of the most efficient return to scarce factors of production. The social distribution of the factors themselves, i.e. whether a man has capital or land or labour to offer on the market, is not questioned nor are the implications of one being scarcer than another.

[15] R. G. Lipsey's *Introduction to Positive Economics* is the standard current textbook in universities.
[16] Alfred Marshall, *Industry and Trade,* 1919, Preface.

The steadily growing demand today for economists to advise governments on the results of interfering in the economy has enormously increased both the interest in the economy as a whole and the development of techniques of measurement of the forces at work – so called ECONOMETRICS. In this field, however, the very refining of the instruments of economic analysis has tended to maintain the separation between politics and economics, although increasingly the interaction of the two becomes crucial for correct solutions to problems. But the separation of political economy into its component parts means that the politicians concern themselves with institutions for reconciling differences about ends; while the economist devote themselves to perfecting techniques of analysis of the means to those ends. Divorced from each other, the economist and the politician must assume that not only can the politician reconcile the ends and the economist the means but that the means and ends chosen are themselves reconcilable. The result is a special kind of politics as well as a special kind of economics. One of 'the conditions for political rule' becomes 'a society in which there are no extremes of wealth'.[17]

Where extremes of wealth persist, political economy is coming back once more into its own in the attempt to explain the persistence of poverty amidst affluence in the developed countries themselves, as well as in the widening gap between developed and underdeveloped. Once again questions of social structure are re-entering economic analysis. Much of the new work of economists in studying DEVELOPING economies has been devoted to the examination of social as well as economic structures and their influence on economic activities. The special case of the social structure of an advanced industrialized economy is, as we saw earlier, having to be set aside in studying the more typical case of an undeveloped economy. Thus the economics of the special case are being abandoned, economies replace economizing as the main subject of study, and the concept of an economic 'system' with certain tendencies built into it is being re-examined. All these changes present difficult scientific problems for economists.

[17] Bernard Crick, *In Defence of Politics*, p. 160.

5. ECONOMICS AS A SCIENCE AND ITS RELATION TO HISTORY

When Alfred Marshall distinguished 'Economic Science' from 'Political Economy', he went on to define a science:

Economics is a science because it collects, arranges and reasons about one particular class of facts. A science brings together a great number of similar facts and finds that they are special cases of some great uniformity which exists in nature. It describes this uniformity in a simple and definite statement or law. *A Law* of science states that a certain result will be produced whenever a certain set of causes are present. . . . Science when obtaining new Laws is said to be Inductive; when reasoning from them and finding how they are connected with one another, it is said to be Deductive; its third task (is) that of verification. . . . There has been a controversy as to whether Economics is an Inductive or a Deductive Science. It is both: its Inductions continually suggest new Deductions; its Deductions continually suggest new Inductions.[18]

This controversy was not entirely concluded by Marshall in 1881. Lionel Robbins was still writing in 1932 that:

The laws of economics . . . are obviously deductions from a series of postulates (about human behaviour) [which] . . . do not need controlled experiments to establish their validity . . . they have only to be stated to be recognized as obvious. . . . They are of universal applicability. . . . Our beliefs in this particular generalization and many others is more complete than belief based upon any number of controlled experiments. . . . On what then does it depend? . . . In the last analysis, therefore our proposition rests upon deductions which are implicit in our initial definition of the subject matter of Economic Science as a whole.[19]

Such a wholesale commitment to what must be largely circular reasoning led one scientist, Lancelot Hogben, to comment: 'This passage briefly summarizes every attitude to knowledge discarded by the natural sciences in reaching the prestige they now enjoy.'[20]

In the next edition of his book Lionel Robbins somewhat modified the phrasing of his commitment to economics as a

[18] Alfred Marshall, *Economics of Industry*, Preface.
[19] Lionel Robbins, *The Nature and Significance of Economic Science*, pp. 79–81.
[20] Lancelot Hogben, *Science and the Citizen*, 1938, p. 217.

wholly deductive science, but he left in that part of his criticism which questioned the appeal to history as any justification
for a science of economics:

> The frequent concomitance of certain phenomena in time may
> suggest a problem to be solved. It cannot by itself be taken to
> imply a definite casual relationship. . . . If there is one thing that
> *is* shown by history, not less than by elementary logic, it is that
> historical induction unaided by analytical judgment is the
> worst possible basis of prophecy. . . . It is one of the great merits
> of the modern philosophy of history that it has repudiated all
> claims of this sort. . . .

What is at issue here is first of all the whole inductive method
of economics, of making generalizations from observations of
particular facts, of finding in Marshall's words the 'great
uniformity' when facts are collected and arranged. Of course,
all modern economic analysis proceeds not only from the
obvious facts of human behaviour, which alone Lionel Robbins
appears to allow as postulates, but also from the growing mass
of STATISTICS which are collected and arranged and corre-
lated for us in our economy today. We shall say more about
the economists' use of statistics in the next chapter. But
Lionel Robbins is aiming his shafts not only at the inductive
principles in economics but also at a second target – that view
of history which implies that laws of social development can
be inferred from history.

It is necessary here to clarify the meaning of the inductive
and deductive principles to which Marshall referred. Many
philosophers and particularly David Hume[21] have been troubled
by the principle of induction, that is that we may infer a universal statement from a singular statement, i.e. generalize
from particular instances. This is partly because the principle
of induction is itself a generalization, partly because we can
have no proof that single instances observed in the past will
recur in the future. In our own century Professor Karl Popper
has questioned whether the inductive process is in any case
one that any scientist proceeds by:

> I do not believe that we ever make inductive generalizations in
> the sense that we start with observations and try to derive our

[21] David Hume, *Treatise on Human Nature*, 1739–40.

theories from them. I believe that the prejudice that we proceed in this way is a kind of optical illusion and that at no stage of scientific development do we begin without something in the nature of a theory, such as a hypothesis, or a prejudice or a problem – often a technological one – which in some way *guides* our observations, and helps us to select from the innumerable objects of observations those which may be of interest. . . . And in the social sciences it is even more obvious that we cannot see and observe our objects before we have thought about them. For most of the objects of social science, if not all of them, are abstract objects; they are *theoretical* constructions (even 'the war' or 'the army' are abstract concepts strange as this may sound to some. What is concrete is the many who are killed; or the men and women in uniform, etc.) These objects, these theoretical constructions used to interpret our experience, are the result of constructing certain *models* (especially of institutions), in order to explain our experiences – a familiar theoretical method in the natural sciences (where we construct our models of atoms, molecules, solids, liquids, etc).[22]

Popper here quotes Einstein as saying of 'the search for those highly universal laws . . . from which a picture of the world can be obtained by pure deduction . . . [that] there is no logical path leading to these . . . laws. They can only be reached by intuition based upon something like an intellectual love of the objects of experience.' Professor Popper, moreover, believes that 'the discovery of instances which confirm a theory means very little if we have not tried and failed, to discover refutations. . . . All tests can be interpreted as attempts to weed out false theories. . . . Only if we cannot falsify them can we say that they have stood up to severe tests'. This means that we cannot ever be finally certain that our theories are true in the natural or the social sciences. Popper concludes:

The demand for scientific objectivity makes it inevitable that every scientific statement must remain *tentative for ever*. It may indeed be corroborated, but every corroboration is relative to other statements which, again, are tentative. Only in our subjective experiences of conviction, in our subjective faith, can we be 'absolutely certain'.[23]

This is rather comforting to the social scientist, because it is

[22] *Poverty of Historicism*, 1944 and 1957 and 1959 editions, p. 135.
[23] Karl Popper, *Logic of Scientific Discovery*, 1934.

often argued that the natural and social sciences are to be distinguished by the greater certainty of the generalization and PREDICTION that may be made in the former. It is said in particular that this is because in the natural sciences we can make use of experiments, which isolate certain features of the real world, so as to reproduce similar conditions and consequently to test the results. But for this very reason the prediction of physical events is limited to such artificially isolated SYSTEMS. Even in the natural sciences says Professor Popper:

> We are very far from being able to predict the precise results of a concrete situation such as a thunderstorm or a fire. . . . (The solar system is an exceptional case – one of natural not artificial isolation; once its isolation is destroyed by the intrusion of a foreign body of sufficient size all our forecasts are liable to break down.) Social situations are no more complex than physical ones. There is indeed an advantage in studying societies in that human beings can be relied upon to behave rationally, though there may be other difficulties in measuring variables that tend in societies to change rather rapidly.

Popper makes light of the difficulty of setting up experiments in the social sciences:

> A grocer who opens up a new shop is conducting a social experiment . . . experiments on a somewhat larger scale would be the decision of a monopolist to change the price of his product; the introduction whether by a private or a public insurance company of a new type of health or employment insurance or the introduction of a new sales tax or of a policy to combat trade cycles.[24]

But he insists that all these are piecemeal experiments from which we learn by our mistakes. What we cannot do is to set up great experiments covering the behaviour of whole societies.

What Popper wishes to warn us against is a belief in the possibility of deriving laws of social development from a study of history. Belief in this possibility is what he terms HISTORICISM. Scientific predictions, he has insisted, must all be conditional, i.e., depending on certain initial conditions, and the basic fact of history is that the conditions change. Even the possibility is challenged of generalizing about certain periods

[24] *Poverty of Historicism*, p. 87.

which appear to share common features, and which we described earlier as having a social system. The attempt to look at societies as a whole cannot, he believed, lead to scientific conclusions about trends of development. For not only are there too many features to look at, but there is a crucial logical difficulty. A prediction is likely to influence subsequent events either making it more likely to occur or leading to attempts by men to prevent it from occurring.

Much of Professor Popper's criticism in this respect is directed at Marx. The title of his book *The Poverty of Historicism*, he tells us, contains a deliberate allusion to Marx's *The Poverty of Philosophy* which in turn was alluding to Proudhon's *Philosophy of Poverty*. Popper's main critique of Marx is that his predictions, even if they were right, not only leave nothing to chance or to the effects of the predictions upon themselves, and overlook the initial conditions on which they were based, but they leave no room for human activity. He quotes Marx's claim not only to 'lay bare the economic law of motion of modern society' but also to 'shorten and lessen the birth pangs of future social development'. Far from our being able to change the world, Popper asserts that in Marx's view we have to accept the inevitability of the changes that are inherent in it. A modern Marxist has tried to put the matter in another way. 'By foreseeing the future we alter it, and thus falsify our prophecies. Marx does this by correctly predicting what would happen to capitalism if it continued on its actual line.'[25] The trouble is that this last is a statement that on Popper's terms is not capable of being refuted or validated. Marx in fact allowed to human consciousness, including consciousness of the past, a much greater role in changing society than Popper supposes. Popper's final answer to those he calls 'historicists' is what he describes as a simple proof:

> If there is such a thing as growing knowledge, then we cannot anticipate today what we shall only know tomorrow, since no scientific predictor ... can possibly predict by scientific methods, his own future results.[26]

This is an argument of real substance, but it is interestingly similar in certain respects to Marx's own view. This is not a

[25] V. G. Kiernan 'Notes on Marxism in 1968', *Socialist Register*, 1968, p. 204.
[26] *Poverty of Historicism*, Prefaces 1957 and 1959.

crude DETERMINISM, that it is the growth of technology, of
man's knowledge and control over his environment that determines everything else, but a view that the models we build of
the world, in which we make technology the determining
factor, help us most in understanding social change.

Much of Popper's argument, that we first classify events into
categories and then test hypotheses to explain their connection, every scientist including the social scientists, will accept.
What is less widely accepted is Popper's doubt about the
large-scale models of the world – physical or social – which we
construct in formulating and testing hypotheses. The clearest
reply to Popper here is to be found in Professor E. H. Carr:
'the assertion that men learn nothing from history', Carr main-
tains, 'is contradicted by a multitude of observable facts.'[27]
The probability of accidents occurring as well as of predictions
destroying their own fulfilment do not invalidate our search
for causes. Nor do they lessen the value of distinguishing what
Carr calls the 'hierarchy of causes' – the more and the less
significant – which the scientist uses in establishing 'not a
photographic copy of the real world but rather a working
model which enables him (the historian like the scientist) more
or less effectively to understand it and control it.' Indeed Carr
discovered in Popper's work itself a confession in parenthesis
that among the 'plurality of interpretations', which Popper
believes to be necessary in looking at history, 'some may be
distinguished by their fertility'.[28] Popper adds that this is 'a
point of some importance', to which Carr replies that 'it is *the*
point which proves that historicism is not so poor after all'.

There are evidently some real differences between the social
sciences and the natural sciences. There is so much in history
that is chance and individual that if 'sociology is theoretical
history' it may seem to be unwise even to speak of hypotheses
which may be rigorously tested. All statements about society
and economies are bound to be only of the conditional type,
which must be prefaced with that old qualification of the
economist 'other things being equal'. It was, as Marshall
insisted, only in the rather narrowly limited definition of
economics that something near to the precision of the natural

[27] E. H. Carr, *What is History?*, p. 101.
[28] Karl Popper, *The Poverty of Historicism*, p. 151.

sciences could be achieved, and then only because economic factors had been isolated from other social and political factors. If this isolating of certain factors, however, fails to give us adequate explanations, for example, of economic development and stagnation, then we shall have to look at society as a whole once more. In the social sciences as in history we cannot abandon the search for trends and the elaboration of systems, dependent though they must be upon explicit conditions. For without them we have no model to work from, no 'organizing insights',[29] in examining the mass of facts at the economist's and the historian's disposal and in testing particular theories and hypotheses which we use to classify these facts.

[29] I owe the phrase to Royden Harrison.

2 The Facts of Economic Life

SUMMARY

In this chapter we examine first the facts of human behaviour which interest those whom we have called the economizing school of economists, and secondly the facts of different economies which are of interest to those who are more political economists. The graphical expression of economic relations is employed in analysing human behaviour and a number of statistical terms and concepts are introduced to describe different economies. Thereafter a selection of facts about our economy is presented, mainly in tabular form. These can be studied now in general and re-examined in detail later in the book where they are referred to again. Finally, there follows a brief description of an undeveloped economy to point the contrast with the advanced industrial condition of our economy. But there is a clear implication in this description which is brought out at the end, that economic facts are not primarily about Robinson Crusoe alone on a desert island, but about relationships of people at work and particularly the relationship between owners and producers at different levels of technology and in different social systems.

1. SOME FACTS OF HUMAN BEHAVIOUR

The economists whom we have described as belonging to the economizing school, start from the facts of human behaviour, or at least from certain postulates or assumptions about human behaviour. These enable them to make deductions that are said to be universally valid – for Robinson Crusoe (a favourite character of theirs), for an Indian peasant and for you and me. As Lionel Robbins put it, 'They have only to be stated, to be recognized as obvious'. It is worthwhile, therefore, to state some of these general facts of human behaviour that are assumed by economists. Later we shall turn to the more specific facts of particular economies, but we may take it that some facts of human behaviour are of almost universal application:

(*a*) In normal circumstances we strive to keep ourselves and our families alive by taking action to avoid starvation, exposure or destruction by natural forces, wild animals and human enemies.

(*b*) We seek more satisfaction rather than less; such satisfactions may not necessarily be physical, and sometimes they may be bad for us; the economist tends to exclude as being too difficult to quantify such psychological satisfactions as a sense of security, self-respect, exercise of power, etc.

(*c*) Other things being equal, we prefer more remuneration to less, whatever form this takes as WAGES, SALARIES, PROFITS, etc.

(*d*) Most of us prefer leisure to work, easy work to hard work, inactivity to activity, at least beyond a certain level of work.

(*e*) We prefer the cheaper to the more expensive among similar goods or services and also among goods or services that are a close SUBSTITUTE for each other, e.g. fish and meat, wool and nylon.

(*f*) As our income and purchasing power increase we prefer variety, and so, as each urgent WANT is satisfied, we move on to satisfying less urgent wants.

(*g*) Most of us do not want money for its own sake, to HOARD like misers, but for what it will buy in goods and services (or perhaps in power over others).

(*h*) As our income rises we are more able and more prepared to use money to make more money, to SAVE for the future in illness or retirement.

It is on such simple facts of human behaviour that the economizers' concepts are built up. Given our limited resources we have to economize so that we get the best out of what we have. The nineteenth-century economists used the word UTILITY to describe the capacity of goods or services to satisfy our wants. Utility according to Jeremy Bentham, the founder of the utilitarian school of philosophy, is the power in actions directly or indirectly to produce pleasure or to prevent pain. All actions can be judged according to this utilitarian measure or calculus, as he called it, and all societies too, according to whether they produce 'the greatest happiness of the greatest number'. Such a condition was to be achieved by LAISSEZ-

FAIRE, by leaving each individual free to make his own choices in the market. This left unsolved some awkward questions. Happiness is not easily measured or the happiness of different people compared. One man's happiness may cause another man misery. Bentham genuinely believed in equal shares of happiness and in equal rights for all to choose as they wished. On this basis the pleasure from 'pushpin was as good as poetry'. Bentham's successors, like John Stuart Mill[1] felt bound to concede that the poetry lover was what George Orwell[2] later called 'more equal' than the pushpin player. The even more awkward question of equality between different persons whatever their interests was shelved, but we shall have to take it up again in the last chapter.

These difficulties with the concept of utility are discussed by Joan Robinson in *Economic Philosophy*. Utility, she argues, is another metaphysical concept like value and it cannot be measured or even defined in a way that can easily be refuted or validated. Economists soon abandoned it for more precise ways of speaking. But before they abandoned it they used it to develop that very important concept in economics – the concept of the MARGIN.

Stanley Jevons concluded that price was the measure of what he called MARGINAL UTILITY. Given our preference for variety, as our need for any particular commodity is satisfied, our desire for that commodity steadily diminishes. The last bite is always less satisfying than the previous bite. The more of a commodity we consume the more satisfaction we are assumed to derive. But the margin by which our satisfaction increases is smaller for each successive bit consumed. This diminishing marginal utility is part of a law of the economists which they call the LAW OF DIMINISHING RETURNS. We should then arrange all our purchases so that the last little bit of every commodity gives us equal satisfaction. For if the last bit of one gave more satisfaction than the last bit of another, we should exchange some of the second for some of the first. We may apply this principle equally to the problem of comparing the satisfaction derived from more leisure with that derived from more goods obtained by extra work. Later

[1] J.S.Mill, *Utilitarianism*, Everyman ed., p. 7.
[2] G. Orwell, *Animal Farm*.

economists avoided the difficulties involved in the concept of utility by speaking simply of marginal PREFERENCES and marginal RATES OF SUBSTITUTION between two classes of goods. This meant abandoning the attempt to measure the intensity of different desires or preferences and of their satisfaction. It became possible therefore only to explain relative prices in general, as they reflect market demand (which we shall study in Chapter 5). A MONEY STANDARD for prices can still be used like the standard weights used on the scales, but standard money or CURRENCY is simply accepted as a convenient measure.

Of course, prices are determined not only by people's preferences but also by costs of production. Once again the concept of the margin provides a useful test. Land and labour and capital – the factors of production – will be laid out by an ENTREPRENEUR in such a way that the advantages derived from the last bit of each will be equal. It is assumed again that factors are homogeneous and there are diminishing returns from applying more of any one factor unless techniques are switched. We can test this principle with an example from agriculture.

Table II.1

Diminishing Marginal Product in Cotton Crop Yields as supplies of Fertilizer and Water are Increased (in lbs of cotton seed per acre)

Sulphate of Ammonia applied per Acre	Rate of Watering				
	Light	MP	Medium	MP	Heavy
None	(414)	48	462	12	474
Marginal Product	180		273		366
300 lbs	(594)	141	(735)	105	840
Marginal Product	80		177		297
600 lbs	684	228	(912)	225	(1137)

Source: Gregory, Crowther and Lambert, *Journal of Agricultural Science*, 22.617, 1932. Quoted in James Fyfe 'Malthus and Malthusiasm', *Modern Quarterly*, Vol. 6, no. 3, 1951.

At any level of fertilizer more water shows a diminishing return (MARGINAL PRODUCT or MP). At any rate of watering extra fertilizer shows a diminishing return. Applying more of one factor gives a diminishing return, but the combination of the two shows a steadily rising yield. We do not know the relative costs of applying extra fertilizer and more water, but if 300 lb of fertilizer costs the same as each extra step up in the rate of watering, then the best path for the farmer to follow is that indicated by the positions that have been bracketed. Following this path there is in fact then no diminishing return from equal marginal increments of the two factors as far as the Table goes.

The choice before an industrialist generally involves deciding between more capital and more labour. If a better result (more profit) can be obtained by using an extra bit of capital and fewer workers, for example, this will be done. Each factor will then be paid according to the return from adding one extra bit. Wages for example will tend to settle around the value of the extra output added by the last worker to be taken on – the marginal worker. Marginal land will tend to set the rent of all land. The price of goods will be the result of both costs and preferences – that is of supply and demand – reaching an *equilibrium* where marginal costs equals marginal revenue. We shall examine in a moment the meaning in economics of an equilibrium and the many qualifications to which this rule is subject.

Once again we have to notice that all this provides an explanation of relative prices only. A special problem arises with capital in that it is not in any real sense homogeneous, but consists of capital equipment introduced at different times, which makes return to capital dependent on rates of interest – a circular argument. Thus problems of 'real' costs or value or utility were left on one side for the philosophers to speculate about, but we shall return to them. The final stage in this process was reached in the work of the Austrian school of economists (Fredrich von Wieser 1851–1926, and Eugen von Böhm-Bawerk, 1851–1914) who invented the OPPORTUNITY-COST principle which an English economist, P. H. Wickstead, developed. This principle states simply that the cost of anything is the opportunity forgone of having something else. Thus the cost of an hour's leisure to me is the return I could have had from an extra hour's work at that time. The cost of buying more food is the lost opportunity of buying more of something else. The cost of any factor of production is to be measured in opportunities forgone of its use for other purposes. We do not need to bring money values into our description of costs. We can speak simply of CURVES OF INDIFFERENCE as a Swiss economist, Pareto, called them. These are explained later in the chapter – see Figs. 2.5 and 2.6. What we can say now is that there will be many mixes of goods and services, between which we shall be indifferent how we lay out our resources. According to this school of thought relativity is complete and when we have determined relative prices we have gone as far as deductions from human behaviour will take us. This comes as we shall see from considering human beings in isolation like Robinson Crusoe.

Attempts to determine principles of economic policy for a whole society, such as we shall examine in the last chapter are obviously rendered impossible by this school of thought. The welfare economists who followed Pigou have attempted to rescue something from the relativities of Pareto. The so-called pareto optimum was a position from which no one could be made better off without making someone else worse off. The happiness of Bentham's greatest number must then be weighted against the misery of one man. Two modern economists, N. Kaldor and J. R. Hicks, have suggested that a COM-PENSATION principle can be introduced here by which we should ask whether those made better off could afford to compensate those made worse off by a redistribution of factors and still have something left over. Then we could speak of an improved allocation of resources. They are careful of course not to speak of happiness but only of money benefits and losses; and we shall take up this whole question again in the last chapter when we look at COST-BENEFIT analysis.[3]

Before we go back from the world of the economizers to the world of economies, however, we must look at the concept of an equilibrium in economics and at the graphical representation of functional relations which are used by economists to reveal so called equilibrium positions and to draw their deductions about relative prices from the postulates of human behaviour.

[3] All these different economists can be studied in M. Blaug's *Economic Theory in Retrospect*, 1962.

2. THE GRAPHICAL EXPRESSION OF HUMAN WANTS

Let us now consider the idea of an equilibrium. When two pounds of sugar and a two-pound weight are on opposite pans of a pair of scales they are in equilibrium. As you pour the sugar gradually on to one side, with the weight already on the other, they move towards equilibrium. On the scales we can only weigh two things at a time, but by using a standard weight we can weigh and compare many different things. In economics it would be possible to try to analyse the relations of all prices moving towards a GENERAL EQUILIBRIUM; but economists mainly content themselves with isolating particular products or factors and their prices and taking these as the VARIABLES, while all others are assumed to remain constant. Such PARTIAL EQUILIBRIUM ANALYSIS makes up nearly all of economic analysis. But it must be remembered that such analysis by isolation can give only conditional results. The conditions that are assumed, that is to say those features of a total situation that are assumed to be constant, so that the relation of certain other variables may be studied, are called PARAMETERS. In another analysis some of the parameters may be studied as variables, while the previous variables are assumed to be constant.

Evidently the whole concept of an equilibrium is a STATIC or stable one. The scales are in balance, and the system is one which tends to a position of balance. In economics, that is to say that there is no economic motive for change. But this is bound to be a very SHORT-RUN situation. Ever since Alfred Marshall, economists have been distinguishing short-run from LONG-RUN results – in STATIC and DYNAMIC EQUILIBRIUM. The distinction is a valuable one, although the actual limits of time involved may be hard to determine. What is more of a problem, the idea of a situation having forces in it that will lead to a long-run or dynamic equilibrium implies peculiarly unreal assumptions about all the other things that have to remain constant while this is happening. 'In the long run,' as Keynes put it, 'we are all dead'; 'but not all of us at once', as Joan Robinson adds in her discussion of this problem.[4] All economists, however, including Marx have used the tool of

[4] In *Economic Philosophy*, pp. 81–3.

equilibrium analysis. It provides the basis for the mathematical equations that economists use; for when they work with equations they are in fact making movements that will preserve a balance, as on either side of a pair of scales.

We may return to our facts or postulates of human behaviour and the deductions that can be made from them. Taking two of them together – the disinclination of man for work and our preference for variety as our income rises – we can make two statements: on the one hand, to obtain more of any particular product a consumer may have to pay a higher price for an extra UNIT (in the short run) in order to overcome the producers' disinclination to produce more; on the other hand, as the consumer obtains more of any particular product, his preparedness to pay a higher price is reduced with each additional unit. We can think of price in terms of opportunity cost if we like; but what matters is that the production cost of each additional unit, i.e. the MARGINAL COST or supply price, rises and the sales price of each additional unit falls, i.e. the MARGINAL REVENUE or demand price falls. This is the heart of all the economizing types of economics and should be re-read until fully understood.

We may represent these rises and falls on a graph. A graph is only a diagrammatic picture that shows the relations between different movements, marked off as CO-ORDINATES from two AXES set at right angles as in the crosses in Fig. 2.1. These can be equally described in mathematical equations, and the relation between graphs and equations can be studied in mathematics textbooks.[5] To describe the rise and fall of the costs and prices we have been talking about we can show units of price of the product on one axis and units of the quantity produced on the other.

The schedules of supply and demand are assumed to be independent of each other. In each case both for the consumer and the producer, quantity is related to price – directly in the case of the producer, inversely in the case of the consumer. These relations are said to be functional relations. Either way demand and supply may be said to be a function of the price. The demand curve (it may be a straight line) shows that, with each increase in quantity offered, the consumer is

[5] See also R. J. Gillings, *Graphs.*

c

prepared to pay less and less in price. It will be noted that the curves are steeper at the top end. This is because on the demand side the consumer will be prepared to give up more money for the product when he only has a little of it than when he has a lot. Similarly, on the supply side, the producer will be harder and harder put to it to produce more, the greater the

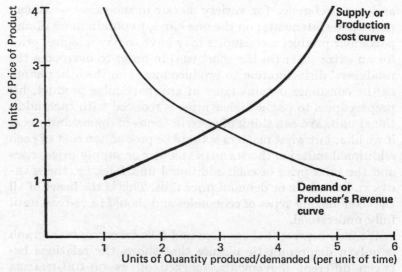

Figure 2.1. Supply and demand curves

quantity he produces. The shapes of the curves follow from the law of diminishing returns. We have introduced units of price into Fig. 2.1, but it may help to think of these in terms of opportunity cost, that is, of things forgone to obtain this particular product. Thus for one unit of product a consumer will pay four units of price but for five units of product only one unit of price each. The supply curve (or line) shows that with each increase of quantity produced the price is raised. One unit of product is produced for one unit of price but it takes four units of price each to extract from the producer five units of product. The point at which the two curves of consumer and producer intersect we may call the point of equilibrium. This is where the price reflecting the consumer's preparedness to buy and the producer's preparedness to sell is the same. The consumer will increase his purchases up to this point and the producer his output, but if either goes beyond this point he will tend to come back to it, like a pendulum coming to rest.

Prices and choices are thus dependent on both supply and demand. The equilibrium price we may say is a function of supply *and* demand. Of course in actual fact, goods are produced with tools and machines; and unit costs will not simply reflect the inclination or disinclination of human beings for work. This matter of supply costs will be considered in the next chapters. Here we may explore a little further the demand side of the story and particularly the relationship between the demand for different products. We start by assuming, as usual with the economizers, that we have limited resources and that the cost of producing any goods can be measured in terms of opportunities forgone for producing other goods.

This concept of opportunity cost may be very simply expressed in a graphical form by using two axes on a diagram to measure the different mixes of two goods that are available at any time. For the purposes of the diagram we limit the mix to two goods only – food and clothing – and assume that these are the only two classes of goods available between which existing resources can be divided. With the same resources, then, we can have either all food and no clothing, all clothing and no food, or a mixture of the two in certain proportions – say two units of food and two units of clothing. These are fixed by the production possibilities and by the units we have chosen to measure in.

To make the example more concrete it may help to think of Robinson Crusoe with his very limited resources. The units could then be a week's supply of food and a week's supply of food and clothing (to stand for shelter as well). The choice for him over a certain period of time, or his production possibilities, could be (as in Fig. 2.2) that six weeks' supply of clothing costs him the equivalent of three weeks' food supply. We shall leave aside the question of hours of Crusoe's labour because of the difficulties of assigning the time he spent in making the tools and preparing the land prior to the stage of control over his environment that he has reached. These were the difficulties that we saw led economists to look only at relative prices at any one time, but we shall return to the question later in discussing 'dated' labour.

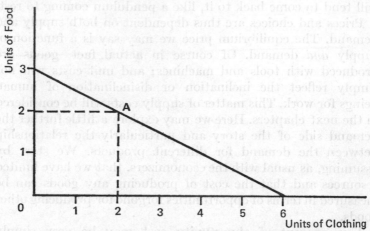

Figure 2.2. Production possibility boundary, or opportunity cost curve

Within Crusoe's production possibilities he has a range of choices illustrated by the diagonal line on the graph. This is called a PRODUCTION POSSIBILITY BOUNDARY or OPPORTUNITY COST CURVE. Anywhere along the line there will be a possible mix of the two goods. In our example Crusoe has chosen two weeks' food and two weeks' clothing (Point A). If his total capacity could be increased, the boundary could be shifted to the right and, if this increase did not involve any change in the relative efficiency of production of the two goods, the second line would be parallel to the first. He could now have, for example, four units of clothing and two of food, (Point B, Fig. 2.3).

So far we have been talking about the resources available to one person and not to a whole people. If we were talking of national resources, then the production possibility boundary is called a TRANSFORMATION CURVE and will probably be in fact a curve as in Fig. 2.4.

In other words, if this corresponds to Crusoe's second situation with the increased resources available, it will be possible to have a mix of four units of clothing and two units of food (Point B) but not four units of food with no clothing or eight

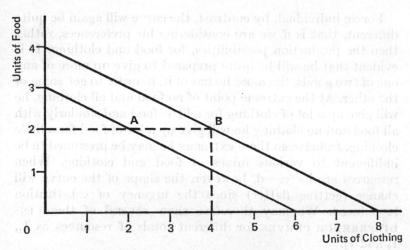

Figure 2.3. Shifting production possibility boundary

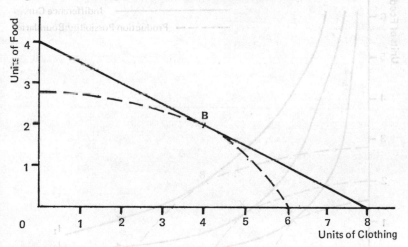

Figure 2.4. More realistic transformation curve or production possibility boundary for national aggregates

units of clothing with no food; the reason being that, as we saw earlier, the more we have of something the greater the cost of getting still more, i.e. the more we have to give up of other things to get the same increase. Even with larger resources the curve will be the same shape but of course shifted up and to the right.

For an individual, by contrast, the curve will again be quite different, that is if we are considering his preferences, rather then the production possibilities, for food and clothing. It is evident that he will be quite prepared to give up more of any one of two goods, the more he has of it, in order to get some of the other. At the extreme point of no food and all clothing, he will give up a lot of clothing for a little food and similarly with all food and no clothing he will give up a lot of food for a little clothing. In between these extremes he may be presumed to be indifferent to various mixes of food and clothing. When resources are increased, however, the shape of the curve will change (getting flatter) since the urgency of substitution is reduced. We may therefore show several of these IN-DIFFERENCE CURVES for different totals of resources as I_1, I_2 and I_3.

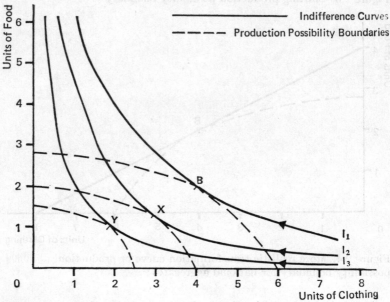

Figure 2.5. Indifference curves and production possibility boundaries

With less resources consumers are forced on to lower in-difference curves I_2 and I_3 from point B to X and X to Y in terms of three production possibilities. The best mix of goods at each level of resources will be where the indifference curve and the possibility curve meet at X, Y and B. These would be the equlibrium points, since a consumer would tend to move to these points from whatever other positions he started on each curve.

The great merit of these curves on a diagram is that they have shown us two different kinds of change in the pattern of our wants – one which we saw as movements *along* the line of the curves according to the urgency of substituting one good for another (this depends on tastes, incomes and relative prices of goods); the other which we saw as shifts of the *whole* curve to the right or left as the total of resources available to us changed (this depends on levels of technology and relative prices of factors). We can now apply these two concepts to a situation which we have not yet considered and that is one where relative changes in production possibilities occur between our two goods. These changes are best thought of as price changes or opportunity cost changes. Suppose the price of clothes doubles while food prices remain constant, then we could simply show this as a change in the production possibility boundary. Thus:

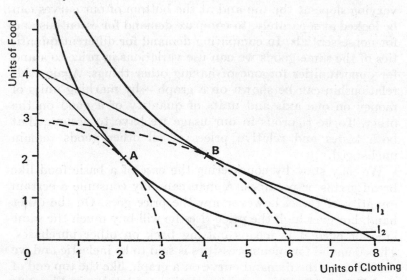

Figure 2.6. Indifference curves and a shifting production possibility boundary

Since a price increase reduces purchasing power, it forces consumers on to a lower indifference curve (I_2). Instead of having
the possibility of two units of food and four of clothing, only
two of food and two of clothing would be possible, so that
equilibrium would be moved back from B to A. We should
now have to take into account the shape of the curves at the
top left and at the bottom right, i.e. the response to a shortage
of clothing and a shortage of food respectively. We have shown
the indifference curves on the diagram as being much steeper
at the top left and gentler lower down. This is because much
more clothing will be given up for food at a low level of food
(low on the curve also) and much less at a high level of food
(high on the curve also). This is not because food is more essential than clothing; it simply means that we are examining in
this case the demand for food in relation to clothing. We could
as easily have looked at clothing in relation to food and found
a similar result. The curves are symmetrical.

In fact food may be more essential than clothing in some
climates; and this leads us to consider the varying urgencies
for human beings of different classes of goods, or the varying
ELASTICITIES OF DEMAND, as the economists call them. The
varying slope at the top and at the bottom of our curves can
be looked at separately, to compare demand for essentials and
for non-essentials. In comparing demand for different quantities of the same goods we can use variations in price to stand
for opportunities forgone of having other things. Again, this
relationship can be shown on a graph – by marking units of
money on one axis and units of quantity of a good on the
other. To be rigorous in our usage we have to assume that
both tastes and relative prices of all other goods remain
unchanged.

We may start by considering the case of a basic food like
bread grains or potatoes. A man can only consume a certain
quantity of these, however low the price goes. On the other
hand, however high the price rises he will buy much the same
amount even if it means cutting back on other purchases.
Thus demand for such necessities is said to be inelastic and we
should show the demand curve on a graph, like the top end of
the curves of food demand in relation to clothing in Fig. 2.6;
we may see this in Fig. 2.7.

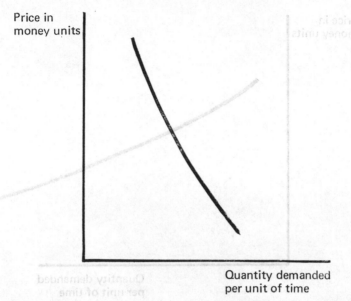

Figure 2.7. Inelastic demand curve (necessities)

It is seen that the quantity demanded does not 'stretch' much for essentials like potatoes even though the price changes greatly. The case of a non-essential like a motor-car will be far different. We may consider peoples' purchases in a whole country rather than individual purchasers this time. At higher prices fewer and fewer people can afford cars, but as prices fall more and more people can afford them. The quantity demanded stretches greatly as prices change; and the demand curve is said to be elastic like the lower part of the curve of food demand in relation to clothing in Fig. 2.6. We may see this in Fig. 2.8.

We have not quite finished with the concept of elasticity. We noted earlier that, as people's resources or incomes rose, they changed the pattern of their spending. They might in fact buy more food and clothing, but the share of food and clothing in their total household budget would probably fall as they used most of their *extra* income to buy cars or personal services at hotels and restaurants. This gives us the concept of INCOME DEMAND ELASTICITY. Suppose a man's income is doubled, that is increased by 100 per cent, he may increase his food

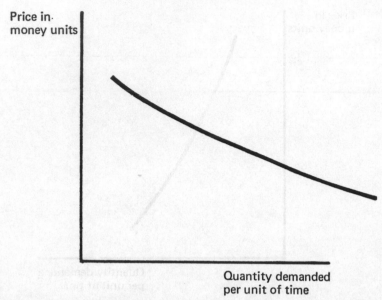

Figure 2.8. Elastic demand curve (luxuries)

consumption by only 20 per cent, his purchases of clothing by 60 per cent, but he may increase his spending on cars and holidays tenfold. It is how he spends his extra money that is so important – his marginal spending – and we shall see later the importance of how much of his extra money he saves – his marginal PROPENSITY to save.

Table II.2 shows the changes in spending patterns in Britain between 1953–4 and 1967 according to Ministry of Labour Surveys, and the income elasticities of demand for each class of goods that these changes imply. The economists will remind us that of course relative prices and tastes have changed over this fifteen-year period. But we have here a quantitative statement of income elasticities over time which appears to validate our assumption that human beings prefer variety (though not apparently that they increase their propensity to save as their incomes rise).

3. STATISTICAL FACTS

So far in this chapter we have stated certain assumptions about

Table II.2

Income-Demand Elasticities in UK Household Budgets 1953–68

Item	Weekly Household Expenditure 1953/4				Weekly Household Expenditure 1968				Increases 1953/4 to 1968 in Value	in Prices	in real terms*	Income-Demand Elasti-city**
	£	s	d	(%)	£	s	d	(%)	%	%	%	
Total Consumption	11	18	11	100	24	18	7	100	108	52	37	0·7
Food	4	1	9	(34)	6	11	9	(26·5)	62	47	10	0·2
Tobacco	0	16	7	(7)	1	5	8	(5)	52	53	0	0
Drink	0	8	3	(3·5)	1	0	6	(4)	150	56	60	1·2
Housing	1	0	9	(8·5)	3	3	2	(12·5)	218	114	148	2·9
Fuel, etc.	0	12	3	(5·0)	1	11	0	(6)	152	80	140	2·7
Clothing, etc.	1	7	2	(11)	2	4	2	(9)	62	23	31	0·6
Durable/Consumer Goods	0	16	7	(7)	1	13	6	(6·5)	100	10	80	1·6
Other Goods	0	16	11	(7)	1	16	3	(7)	112	59	33	0·6
Transport	0	16	5	(7)	3	5	5	(13)	300	69	35	2·7
of which cars	0	6	8	(2·5)	2	11	5	(10·5)	680	20	550	10·8
Services	1	0	8	(8·5)	2	5	7	(9)	120	76	25	0·5
Miscellaneous	0	1	7	(0·5)	0	1	6	(0)	0	—	—	—
Other Payments	2	1	8	—	7	6	3	—	252	(52)	132	2·6
Taxes and National Insurance	0	15	11	—	4	5	7	—	440	(52)	255	5·0
Mortgages	0	5	9	—	1	4	8	—	370	(52)	208	4·1
Savings	0	17	7	—	1	14	0	—	95	(52)	28	0·5
Betting	0	2	5	—	0	2	0	—	0	(52)	—	—
TOTAL Income	14	0	7	—	32	4	10	—	130	(52)	51	1·0

Source: *Family Expenditure Surveys* 1953–4 and 1968. *Statistics on Incomes, Prices, Employment and Production.*

Notes: *Increase in real terms = increase in expenditure divided by increase in prices, i.e. for total consumption $\frac{208}{152} \times 100 = 137$.

**Income Demand Elasticity = Increase in real terms for item divided by increase in real terms for income, i.e. for food $\frac{10}{51} = 0·2$.

human preferences in general and made certain deductions from them in the manner of economists. On the surface these assumptions may have seemed acceptable enough to the student but lying behind them are three further assumptions that we have not explored.

The first is that in the economy we are speaking of there is the possibility of variety and choice. A nomadic shepherding tribe will scarcely be faced by a choice between food and clothing. They come together in fixed proportions as the joint product, as it is called, of the sheep.

The second is that even where variety exists we have to suppose that people are fully informed about what is available and at what prices and are fairly used to bearing such IN-FORMATION in mind and reasoning about it.

The third is that the producers of goods should not have it in their power to alter consumer preferences by ADVERTISING or other influences. It is necessary for the two variables, the schedules of demand and the schedules of supply, to be independent of each other for any meaning to be attached to an equilibrium where the two forces of demand and supply intersect.

These three assumptions suggest to us that we need to look at the way goods are produced and distributed in any economy, before we apply to the real world the simple economizers' principles based on general human behaviour like Robinson Crusoe's that we studied in the last section. We need to begin by remembering once more what as we saw earlier Dudley Seers had emphasized, that even our economy in Britain is not at all typical. There are only about twenty advanced industrial economies like ours comprising less than a third of the world's population. The rest of the world's people are divided amongst at least a hundred other economies at quite different stages of economic development and standards of living.

One of the great advantages for an economist studying an advanced industrial economy is the great mass of statistics (literally and originally numerical facts about the state) which are being collected all the time and which he can work on. Apart from the systems of deductive reasoning we have been looking at, the analysis of these statistics is the economist's main working tool. We noted at the end of the last section how the Ministry of Labour's annual surveys of family expenditure enable us to see the changing patterns of household spending and so to quantify the concept of income elasticities of demand for different classes of goods. As we look at different aspects of the economy we live in, we can note the assortment of statistical measures and techniques of comparison that economists use. In marshalling these statistics we shall also note the dangers and pitfalls that open up for the unwary. We need to understand how the CLASSES into which persons or goods have been assigned are defined and to make sure that, in making comparisons of time and place, we are comparing like with like.[6] We can only pick out here the bare essentials that we need to know about the economy we live in.

We shall start by distinguishing between STOCKS and FLOWS. At any time that seems suitable to the statisticians an INVENTORY can be drawn up for any nation of the land and its uses, of the labour force and its division between different occupations and industries and of the capital or wealth of the nation in its varied forms and LOCATION. This is the STOCK of factors of production as we learnt to call them earlier. Such a stocktaking is often called a census and has to be carried out on a single day if possible, in order to ensure that there has been no double counting through land and capital changing hands or people changing jobs from one day to another. By contrast the actual processes of production, which lead to flows of goods and services and of incomes, are measured over a particular time span – over a year, a quarter, or a month or even in some cases over a week, a day or an hour. Some measurements of both stocks and flows can be made in physical terms, in numbers of people or acres of land or tons of coal and iron. Even here there are difficulties since tons of coal cannot be added to tons of iron to obtain any meaningful result (except in a blast furnace!). Capital stock and flow of income can in any case only be measured in terms of a standard – that is usually of money, and this will generally be the national CURRENCY, although this can be converted to other currencies by applying a RATE OF EXCHANGE.

Measurement in money terms also involves a difficulty in that prices change. Movements in prices can of course be

[6] Students will need to study as much as they can of an introductory book on statistics like Freda Conway's *Descriptive Statistics* or *The Use and Abuse of Statistics* by W. J. Reichmann; and they can get a good laugh by reading *How to Lie with Statistics*, by an American statistician called Darrell Huff. For an introduction to British statistics they will find *The Use of Economic Statistics* by C. A. Blyth a most helpful guide.

measured, however, and these measurements provide an important part of the statistician's work. In the Table of Income Elasticities we recorded the changes in price of the different parts of a household's expenditure between 1953 and 1968. This enabled us to take out the price changes and discover the 'real' increase in spending on different classes of goods and services so as to arrive at the income elasticities of demand. When adjusted for changes in prices, the changes in 'real' terms are sometimes called changes in VOLUME, for example of goods produced or of goods exported. The Americans call these changes in QUANTUM. We cannot add together the output of coal and iron, but we can measure their values at different times and we can then take away the increase in their prices to arrive at changes in volume. In this way many different classes of goods like coal and iron can be combined to show changes in volume over time.

There are many problems of definition and classification when we come to add together different products and different men's work. A textile mill may make cloth from cotton and man-made fibres. Is its output to be included in the cotton or the man-made fibre industry? The usual answer is to put it in the industry appropriate to the largest part of its output. A man may do two jobs; he will be assigned to that one in which he spends most of his time. There are even worse difficulties involved in making comparisons over time. The output of cars may be said to have doubled over the years and we know quite well that this is only a numerical comparison; the cars will be different in many respects. This is a special problem where we want to speak of volumes of motor vehicle output and need to add together cars and lorries and vans. We can find the price of a two-door, 10 h.p. saloon in one year and the price of its successor ten years later and adjust for the price changes the value of total motor-car output in the two years. Then we have the increase in volume; and we can do the same for the prices of all other motor vehicles. But over the ten years new models have come out, the car has changed and you may or may not be getting a better product.

We may still feel uneasy, moreover, that in AGGREGATING different products and adjusting for price changes in this way we have found no 'real' standard of comparison. We are then driven back to questions of value theory and of finding some measurement or at least some DETERMINANT of the ratios in which goods exchange for one another. Prices inevitably reflect both short term movements of supply and demand and longer term inputs of labour, including what we called 'dated' labour to include the labour that went into producing the raw materials and capital equipment necessary to producing the final product. Prices must at the same time reflect what Marx called the SOCIALLY NECESSARY LABOUR, that is the labour that at any given level of technology is necessary to produce certain goods. He called this abstract labour and it may seem a strange abstraction, but it does provide, as we shall see in the last chapter, the basis for building a model of prices *as they should be*, with which to compare the actual prices incorporating concrete labour.

Measurements over time are generally shown as an INDEX. A base year is chosen and the value of output or income in that year is called 100. Our household expenditure figures in Table II.2 showed first the percentage increase in purchases in 1968 over 1953 in current values (i.e. of the goods and services at the actual prices in each year), then the increase in prices and finally the 'real' increase in purchases. Students must note that the way to work out the adjustment for price increases is to divide the percentage increase in money value, plus 100 for the BASE year, by the percentage increase in price, plus 100 for the base year, and then multiply by 100, as we showed in the note to Table II.2. A terrible howler was perpetrated in one widely distributed elementary economics course when the growth in real terms was found by simply subtracting the percentage increase in prices from the percentage increase in values. In our household expenditure example this would have given a real growth in consumption of 56 per cent between 1953 and 1968, i.e. 108 per cent minus 52 per cent, instead of 37 per cent, i.e. $\frac{208}{152} \times 100 = 137$.

Another way of relating the flows in our economy is to show the relations of different sectors at the same time rather than those of the same sector at different times. This is done by building up what is called a MATRIX of relations through INPUT and OUTPUT tables (as in Table II.7 below). The value of the materials and of other INTERMEDIATE PRODUCTS going into each industry from other industries is measured over a period of time, generally a year, and the value of the output of each industry going to other industries is also measured over the same time. This gives us a figure for the VALUE ADDED by those who work in each industry, and this can be divided up into wages and salaries and surplus (going in TAXES, DIVIDENDS, etc.) These tables provide very useful information, as we shall see later, both to government and industry for planning ahead the interchange between SECTORS of the economy. In the same way Tables can be prepared showing the aggregates of National INCOME and expenditure divided between several main groupings like SAVING and CONSUMPTION, both personal and government consumption, private INVESTMENT and government investment, EXPORTS and IMPORTS. These can all be valued at current prices or they can be adjusted to allow for price changes so as to give us the real change over time which economists want to know about, like the change in real growth of national income per year which we hear so much about today. We shall examine many of these Tables in the course of this book as we study the relations between the different flows of economic life in a large and complex economy like our own.

Returning to our search for the facts of the economy we live in, we may pick out those essential points first of all in the stock of labour and land and capital and then in the flow of production which distinguish our industrial economy from the not yet industrialized economies. Dudley Seers provides an excellent list of these essential differences in his article on 'The Limitations of the Special Case', to which reference has already been made and on which we may base our own list.

4. ESSENTIAL FEATURES OF THE BRITISH ECONOMY IN THE 1960S

(a) *Factors of production*

(i) Land: Most land is cultivated, and by private owners (or farmers with secure LEASEHOLDS) in plots of economic size. Only 3½ per cent of the working population are engaged in agriculture, forestry or fishing and 80 per cent of the people live in towns. Density of population is over 850 to the square mile in England, about 570 in the UK as a whole.

(*ii*) Labour: The working population is literate and fairly MOBILE; a half of the men organized in Unions; a third of the women. About $2\frac{1}{2}$ per cent of the men are unemployed at any time; about a half of the women go out to work. Occupations were distributed in 1966 as is shown on the following block graph or HISTOGRAM (Fig. 2.9).

The working population of about sixteen million men and nine million women was distributed in the following main industries in 1966. This time we may give them as percentages of the total, grouped together in what economists call PRIMARY, SECONDARY and tertiary industries. Statisticians now use a STANDARD INDUSTRIAL CLASSIFICATION (SIC) with twenty-four divisions and hundreds of subdivisions.

Table II.3

Working Population by Industry, Great Britain 1966
(Men and Women Percentage of Total Occupied)

Primary Industries	
Agriculture, Forestry and Fishing	3·0
Mining and Quarrying	2·2
Secondary Industries	
Manufacturing	34·5
Construction	7·5
Public Utilities and Transport	8·1
Tertiary Industries	
Distribution	13·0
Professional and Other Services	23·3
Government Administration	4·0
Unemployed	2·7
Armed Services	1·7
TOTAL	100
Total in Numbers	24·9 millions

Source: 1966 Sample Census.

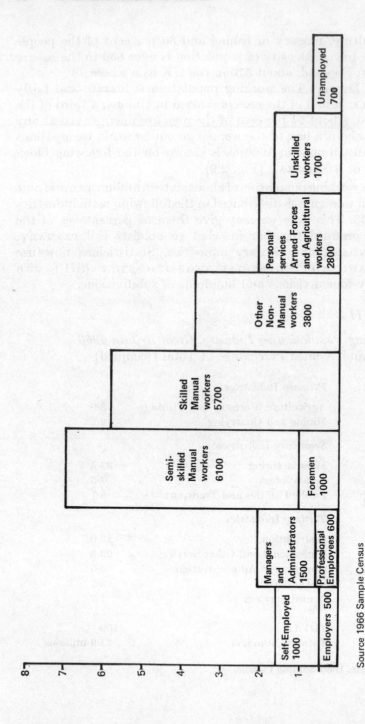

Source 1966 Sample Census

Figure 2.9. Histogram of occupational distribution of active population, Great Britain 1966

(*iii*) Capital. All sectors of the economy are heavily capital-
ized with modern machinery and with some spare CAPACITY;
there are comprehensive and mainly publicly-owned systems
of transport, communication and power generation. State
property was valued in 1966 at about £34,000 millions compared with private property valued at £48,000 millions. The
NATIONAL DEBT, however, of the State to private persons
exceeds £31,000 millions. Private property is very unequally
distributed. The richest 5 per cent of the population owned in
1960 about 75 per cent of the total personal wealth and drew
92 per cent of all PROPERTY INCOME. Only about 12 per
cent of all adults are company SHAREHOLDERS. Company
wealth itself is also highly concentrated. The largest 150 companies owned in 1963 about half the net company assets;
less than fifty companies owned half the assets in manufacturing industry. Foreign companies own about a fifth of the assets
in Britain in manufacturing and smaller proportions in
distribution and finance.

(b) *Markets and market information*
There are national markets for land, labour and capital and
comprehensive information available about prices in each.
Most products are standardized throughout the country with
widespread national advertising by newspaper and television.
Prices (and rents and wages) are somewhat higher in the
London area; but elsewhere the variations are small. Price
COMPETITION is not widespread; competition taking the
form mainly of product DIFFERENTIATION by advertising,
packaging and service. FINANCE and industry are closely
linked.

(c) *Standard of living*
The variety of goods and services – both private and social –
available to all citizens is wide. We might look at this first of
all in terms of the stock of goods and secondly of the flow of
income. But this is not so easy since most people would think
of all their possessions as their stock; and we may note that the
percentage of households owning various goods in 1956 and
1967 was as follows:

Table II.4

Household Ownership of Consumer Durables UK 1956 and 1967
(By Percentage of Households)

	1956	1967
TV Set	40	88
Vacuum Cleaner	51	81
Washing Machine	19	61
Refrigerator	7	51
Car	25	46
Telephone	16	25

Source: *Economist* Diary, 1969.

These (apart from the last) are, however, thought of by economists as DURABLE CONSUMER GOODS, not as capital stock, since they have to be replaced quite frequently and do not make possible further production if they are just used at home. On the other hand, a house is regarded as a part of capital stock, since a large number of people pay rent for their houses and their length of life is considerable. In fact about 50 per cent of householders in Britain in 1967 were owner-occupiers.

We have already noted that not much more than 5 per cent of the adult population own capital from which they can derive a current income. Another 45 per cent own some capital which consists usually of a house and some small savings for the future in an insurance policy or a savings bank. The standard of living for most people therefore is based on their weekly or monthly wage or salary. We may show the national product in 1963 as divided into slices of what is often called a PIE CHART according to incomes from the different factors, as in Fig. 2.10.

Income distribution is less unequal than capital distribution. There is, however, serious poverty among old age pensioners and low wage workers. While the top 10 per cent of incomes account for over a quarter of all personal incomes, the bottom 30 per cent account for only about 10 per cent; and these proportions are little changed whether income is calculated before or after tax. Details can be found in Table IV.2.

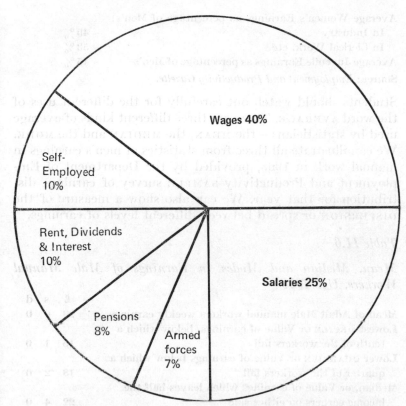

Figure 2.10 Shares in factor incomes: Pie chart for United Kingdom 1963

Average incomes may be estimated in various ways. The following are some figures for pre-tax incomes in 1968.

Table II.5

Average Incomes U.K. 1968

Average Income per head of whole population	– £650 *p.a.*
Average Income per Household	– £1,670 *p.a.*
Average Weekly Earnings of Adult Male Industrial Workers	– £23 0*s* 0*d*
Average Weekly Earnings of Adult Male Administrative, Technical and Clerical Workers	– £29 15*s* 0*d*
Basic weekly Pension for Married Couple	– £6 10*s* 0*d*

Average Women's Earnings as percentage of Men's:

In Industry	– 49%
In Clerical Work, etc.	– 53%
Average Juvenile Earnings as percentage of Men's	– 45%

Source: *Employment and Productivity Gazette.*

Students should watch out carefully for the different uses of the word AVERAGE. There are three different kinds of average used by statisticians – the MEAN, the MEDIAN and the MODE. We can illustrate all three from statistics of men's earnings in manual work in 1968, provided by the Department of Employment and Productivity SAMPLE survey of earnings distribution for that year. We can also show a measure of the DISPERSION or spread between different levels of earnings.

Table II.6

Mean, Median and Modes in Earnings of Male Manual Workers, UK 1968

	£	s	d
Mean of Adult Male manual workers weekly earnings	23	0	0
Lowest DECILE or Value of earnings, below which a tenth of the workers fall	15	1	0
Lower QUARTILE or Value of earnings below which a quarter of the workers fall	18	2	0
Median, or Value of earnings which leaves half the income earners on either side	22	4	0
Upper Quartile (for definition, see lower quartile)	27	4	0
Highest Decile (for definition, see lowest decile)	33	1	0
Mode or Modal Group, or the Mean Income of the most frequent range of income	21	0	0
Upper Quartile as % of Lower Quartile	150%		
Highest Decile as % of Lowest Decile	220%		

Source: *Employment and Productivity Gazette,* June 1969.

The standard of living in Britain has been rising fairly steadily since the war. If this is measured in terms of national income per head, the rise has averaged just over 2 per cent per year. This is the figure which governments have wished to raise to the 3 per cent or 4 per cent per year achieved on the European continent. It must be remembered that such an average is cumulative and compound interest must be used in calculating growth over several years. Thus the standard of living would be doubled in 35 years at an average of 2 per cent per annum or in 23½ years at 3 per cent and 17½ years at 4 per cent.

(d) *Production*

As was made clear when we looked at the distribution of the labour force between different industries, mining and agriculture form quite small sectors of production in our economy, and manufacturing industry by far the largest, accounting for nearly 35 per cent of the DOMESTIC product as well as of the labour force. The manufacturing sector is best summarized by considering inputs of goods and services and total output and then by deducting the one from the other, thus finding the value added by each main industrial group. This provides a very simple input–output table for 1963 as follows:

Table II.7

Input–Output Table, UK 1963

Industry	Goods and Services Input (£m)	Input and Output (£m)	Value Added (£m)	as % of Total
Agriculture	992	1,694	702	2·6
Mining	343	1,095	752	2·75
Food, Drink and Tobacco	1,991	3,069	1,078	3·0
Oil Refining	437	498	61	0·2
Other Chemicals	1,070	1,802	732	2·7
Metal Manufacture	935	1,723	788	2·9
Vehicles (incl. ships and aircraft)	1,645	2,807	1,162	4·25
Other Engineering	2,188	4,852	2,664	9·75
Textiles, etc.	793	1,878	1,085	3·95
Other Manufacturing	1,495	3,164	1,669	6·1
TOTAL Manufacturing	10,554	19,793	9,239	33·75
Construction	1,322	3,150	1,828	6·7
Gas, Electricity and Water	706	1,603	897	3·3
Services	2,648	12,422	9,774	35·6
Public Administration	—	4,172	4,172	15·3
TOTAL	16,565	43,929	27,364	100

Source: *National Income and Expenditure* Blue Book, 1968.

The diversification of output is evident from the table and also significant is the large metal-using industry, producing machinery and vehicles and other engineering products. Note also the great importance in a modern economy of SERVICES which include transport, distribution, communications, education, the social services, etc.

(e) *Foreign trade*

Exports and imports of goods are roughly in balance and the same is true of services, but, as we know to our cost and will study later, government overseas spending and TRANSFERS and flows of capital and PROPERTY INCOME tend to upset the balance. They are excluded in the Table below. Exports and imports (of goods and services) each amount to about one fifth of the national product. The contribution of different industries to the foreign balance may best be summarized as follows for 1968:

Table II.8

Foreign Trade Balance UK 1968

Item	Imports (£m)	Exports (£m)
Total Services (£m)		
excluding Government Transfers and		
Property Income	1,831	2,305
Total Goods (£m)	6,809	6,103
of which as a percentage-Total	100	100
Food, Beverages and Tobacco	24·0	6·5
Basic Materials	15·5	3·0
Mineral Fuels	11·5	2·5
Semi-Manufactures	27·5	21·5
Finished Manufactured Goods and of all	21·5	65·5
Manufactures – Metals	8·0	11·0
– Engineering Products	13·0	41·0
– Chemicals	6·0	9·5
– Textiles	3·0	4·5
– Other	19·0	21·0

Source: *Report on Overseas Trade,* May 1969.

The overwhelming proportion of exports of goods are of manufactures, nearly a half of them engineering goods, while most imports are still of food, fuels, and raw materials, although the proportion of manufactured imports is rapidly rising and thus disturbing the BALANCE OF PAYMENTS.

(f) *The role of the government*
State activity in the economy is widespread and on a large scale. The government (central and local combined) collects about 49 per cent of the national income in TAXES of different kinds and by borrowing, and spends this in the following pro-portions – about 15 per cent of National Income in payments to persons, mostly pensions and debt interest, 20 per cent in purchases of goods and services (6 per cent on arms) and over 10 per cent in capital investment in schools, hospitals, roads, etc. Included in this last figure is the investment in NATIONAL-IZED INDUSTRIES whose output accounts for about one-sixth of the country's net output. Government regulation of the economy, moreover, goes far beyond what has already been indicated and concerns itself with the general level of economic activity, the balance of payments, the location of industry, the modernization of plant, and many other forms of economic planning, which we shall examine later.

5. A COMPARISON WITH OTHER ECONOMIES

We are now in a position to look for the major differences between a developed industrial economy like ours and the undeveloped types of economies. We must say types, because in fact there is much more in common among the developed economies than there is among the undeveloped. We have therefore to consider briefly the different types of undeveloped economy. Putting economies into types is a difficult exercise, which has been carried out in different ways by historians, archaeologists, geographers, anthropologists, technologists and economists:

(*a*) Some have emphasized the difference in the materials from which tools were made by men in the processes of produc-tion throughout history. Thus they speak of a Stone Age, including the use of bone and wood as well as stone for tools, a Bronze Age, Iron Age, then the first INDUSTRIAL REVOLU-TION and the use of steel, leading to the new industrial revolu-tion of so-called 'SCIENCE-BASED' INDUSTRY. Examples of economies based on some of the earlier types of tools can still be found as well as those based on the first and second industrial revolutions.

(*b*) Others have emphasized forms of organization of production, distinguishing:

    (i) Hunting and food gathering;

    (ii) Pastoral and nomadic;

    (iii) Agriculture – based on centrally controlled irrigation;

                       – based on small plots;

                       – based on large estates;

    (iv) Industry   – based on household HANDICRAFTS;

                       – based on small factories;

                       – based on large and complex enterprise groups;

    (v) Industry based on science and automation.[7]

(*c*) Marx made distinctions which connected the techniques of production with the working relations of men in production and particularly the forms of appropriation of the product. By these he meant above all the relations between owners and producers when ownership of the means of production is generally found in the hands of what he called an ECONOMIC CLASS:

    (i) PRIMITIVE COMMUNISM of Stone Age hunters and food gatherers;

    (ii) Asiatic Societies of Bronze Age central irrigation empires;

    (iii) SLAVERY of the Bronze and Iron Age despots;

    (iv) FEUDALISM of many different kinds of Iron Age landowners;

    (v) CAPITALISM of the capital owners during and after the industrial revolution;

    (vi) SOCIALISM in which he hoped the whole people would own and control the modern instruments of production.[8]

Marx thought of these as distinct and successive eras of

[7] The earlier of these are described in Gordon Childe's book, *Man Makes Himself,* and the later ones in S. Lilley's *Men, Machines and History.*

[8] These distinctions can be found in Marx's own words in R. Freedman's book *Marx on Economics.*

history, with their own modes of production, or 'systems' as we described them in Chapter 1.

(*d*) A more recent distinction of successive STAGES has been drawn by Professor Rostow,[9] who distinguishes five stages:

  (i) The traditional society of all undeveloped non-industrialized economies;

  (ii) The Pre-conditions for TAKE-OFF into industrial economies;

  (iii) The Take-off or Industrial Revolution;

  (iv) The Drive to Maturity as modern technology spreads;

  (v) The Age of High Mass-Consumption of industrial products;

He looks forward to a sixth stage 'Beyond Consumption'.

Rostow, like Marx, believes that the stages have 'an inner logic . . . rooted in a dynamic theory of production', although it is not at all clear what Rostow's theory is. Marx's stages are intended to follow quite definitely the major leaps in man's technical control over his environment. The whole concept of 'stages' is a difficult one, which cannot be validated in Popper's sense but is only suggested to us by our model of reality or 'guiding insights' for examining successive periods of history, as we indicated in Chapter 1. There certainly appears to be no inevitability about the successions; and the idea that un-developed economies can develop simply by copying the developed ones is being proved today to be dangerously untrue, as we shall see when we look more deeply at the nature of economic growth in the final chapter.

All that we shall do here is to list briefly the most obvious differences between our own industrial economy and the typical undeveloped economy. As we do so we shall have to bear in mind that these undeveloped economies include all the distinct types that have just been indicated, and many that have been distorted in their development and may be termed 'underdeveloped'. We shall also have to remember from Chapter 1 that economic differences involve not only differences of tools and the organization of production but occur within a related social and political framework. Many students of undeveloped economies regard the hang-over of social

[9] In his book *The Stages of Economic Growth* which he subtitled 'A Non-Communist Manifesto'.

institutions and ideas, which were appropriate to earlier technological forces and relations of production, as the main obstacle to their economic development – and this is what a Marxian analyst would have expected.

If we start with the factors of production in an imaginary typical undeveloped economy and go on to the organization and control of production, we may follow the same headings as we used in describing our own economy:

The land will be mainly cultivated in small, uneconomic plots, some privately owned, some subject to feudal dues, but many subject to heavy debts and insecure tenancies. Mineral resources will not have been fully surveyed. The vast majority of the people – 80 per cent in India – will live on the land or at least outside the towns, although cities are growing fast (see later Table III.4).

Labour will be illiterate, unskilled and rather immobile despite the movement into the cities; it will be almost wholly unorganized. There will be heavy unemployment especially in the cities and much UNDEREMPLOYMENT or seasonal unemployment on the land. Manufacturing will occupy a very small proportion of the work force; mining a somewhat larger proportion.

Capital will be scarce and concentrated in the hands of a few rich families and a number of large foreign companies, especially in those sectors of the economy organized for export.

ENTERPRISE apart from some foreign managements will tend to be in merchanting rather than in manufacturing.

Markets will be local rather than national in respect both of factors of production and products, apart from the international market for special minerals, raw materials and foodstuffs; so that there will be wide variations in prices and incomes in different parts of the economy.

The standard of living will be low – about £30 per head per annum in India – with consequent very limited diet and variety of goods. Durable consumer goods like cars will be confined to a few rich merchants and chiefs or political leaders. Income will be most unequally distributed, and growth of the national income per head generally slow if not stagnant.

Production will be concentrated in agriculture and mining, much of the latter for export to more developed countries. A great part of the economy will be of a SUBSISTENCE type, production being for use and not for sale on the market.

Foreign Trade will dominate the economy, the overwhelming proportion of exports being of food and raw materials and the imports being of manufactured goods, many of them because of the unequal distribution of income consisting of luxuries. Capital flows will consist of foreign investment in mining and similar export-oriented activities with a very high rate of return often exceeding in outflow of income the inflow of capital.

The role of government will be limited and, even where economic plans have been prepared, the government's power to raise taxes and to carry out plans will be severely circumscribed by the power both of local merchants and of foreign companies. Exceptions to these generalizations will be found in the communist countries, where production and distribution have largely been taken into state hands and foreign companies have been expropriated. Where economic plans exist they will tend to require savage enforcement, since growth in these economics will in general be held back by the difficulty of persuading people on the margin of subsistence to give up something of their bread today to make jam available tomorrow.

Such is the nature of the economy of two-thirds of the world's people. This brief list is presented not as an exhaustive study but rather to emphasize by contrast the special nature of the quite different type of economy we live in.[10] Some of the special problems faced by underdeveloped economies will be considered at the end of the next chapter, but a full study of these problems requires a book on its own.

[10] Descriptions of such undeveloped economies can be found in J. de Castro's book *The Geography of Hunger*, 1952, or in L. Dudley Stamp's *Our Developing World*, 1963.

3 Industry and Commerce: Occupations and Their Location

SUMMARY

The mix of occupations and industries varies greatly from country to country and changes have been increasingly rapid since the first INDUSTRIAL REVOLUTION in Britain almost two hundred years ago. Different economists and economic historians explain these differences in terms of

(a) a country's endowment of resources: land, minerals, rivers, access to the sea;

(b) the cumulative effect of the growth of markets;

(c) the DIVISION OF LABOUR and ECONOMIES OF LARGE-SCALE production;

(d) the EXTERNAL ECONOMIES of location and reduced transport costs.

To clarify these principles, the causes and processes of Britain's industrial revolution are examined and comparisons drawn with countries that are not yet industrialized. Once again, what emerges is a picture of the interaction of economic and social relations, but here we meet a fundamental economic principle: that development is cumulative. Economic activity generates more economic activity. The first in the field has huge advantages over those that would follow. Winner takes all and devil take the hindmost!

1. WHY THE FIRST INDUSTRIAL REVOLUTION WAS IN BRITAIN

Britain, as we have just seen, is one of the few advanced industrial economies in the world. Britain was in fact the first country to become industrialized, in what is called the industrial revolution at the end of the eighteenth century. The high proportion of our population in industry, the pattern of our occupations and the location and structure of our industries and our foreign trade all stem from this important fact. Economic historians have spent much time and ingenuity in considering why Britain should have been the site of the first industrial revolution.[1]

We are brought up at school to attribute our industrial pre-eminence to the coal and iron deposits in our soil and the inventiveness of men like Arkwright and Watt and Stephenson. But many other countries had far more extensive and richer mineral deposits. Indeed some historians attribute the pioneering spirit of early British merchant adventurers to the very absence of many essential raw materials in our islands. British inventiveness has to be seen against the fact that most of the crucial inventions of man occurred elsewhere. The Chinese discovered printing, the compass and gunpowder; our alphabet was evolved by the peoples of the Eastern Mediterranean; our numbers were brought by the Arabs from India. Iron was for long wrought in India of a quality that far surpassed anything known in Britain before the industrial revolution. When the Lancashire textile mills first began to manufacture cotton cloth they had to seek from Parliament a 75 per cent tariff to protect them from Indian competition. Even in the seafaring 'discoveries' by Europeans of the lands of the Western world, of Africa and the Far East, the Arabs had often been there first and it was not in any case the British who made the running but the Spanish and Portuguese. Yet in China and India, in Spain and Portugal and in the Arab lands it is only today that the long process of industrialization is beginning – one hundred and fifty years after Britain. Why?[2]

There is indeed no simple answer, but some of the factors to which economic historians have drawn attention may be reviewed here. They help to explain both the way in which the British economy came to be what it is and more generally the nature of the process of economic growth which will engage us later. The economist's division of resources into three or four factors of production provides a starting point – land, including

[1] We may instance the early chapters of G.D.H.Cole and R.Postgate *The Common People* as a good starting point for study because in them the authors so effectively unite economic and social history.

[2] The same question is asked and an answer suggested in my own book, *After Imperialism*, 1963.

raw materials produced from the land; capital, that is an accumulation of means of payments; labour available for work and with the necessary skills; and distinguished by some as a separate factor, enterprise, men with the will and capacity to bring together the other factors. Such distinctions serve to indicate that an industrial revolution, implying by its name an historical moment of rapid industrial change, is likely to follow only after a fairly long period of social, political and economic development. Beneath and on the surface of the land mining and agricultural techniques must have advanced to a stage where a surplus can be produced for the needs of industry and beyond the immediate needs of the PRIMARY PRODUCER. Capital must have been ACCUMULATED to cover the long delays between starting the process of industrial production and selling the finished product. Labour must have been freed from the land for work in industry and new skills must have been acquired; and a class of organizers, or entrepreneurs, must have emerged with an interest in making money by bringing the other factors together in the process of industrial production.

Such a combination of factors is likely to be a rare occurrence. Neither a society of slaves and masters, nor what is called a feudal society, in which men are tied to the land in a hierarchy of rights and duties from king to serf, would be expected to produce this combination of factors. For an industrial revolution to arise out of slave or feudal society some solvent of the old society has always been required, involving a political and social revolution first. Historians of the liberal school have emphasized the power of new ideas about society – the dreams of poets and the concepts of philosophers – to provide the solvent for changing society. Others following Marx have emphasized the cumulative effect of new inventions in man's control over his environment, new technology requiring new relations between human beings in the processes of production and throwing up a new class related in a new way to the productive process.

Marx believed that we can understand the world best if we see the mode of production as primary and ideas as derived from it; but in our model of the world we ourselves are actors. Today, as human beings become increasingly conscious of their natural environment and social relations, so they become conscious of the conflict between new technology and old relations in production. Before our own times social and economic change came almost unconsciously as the result of the efforts of individuals who scarcely knew or cared what the overall results of their actions would be, but acted with the self-confidence of a new class of men, knowing new ways of doing things. Today change can come consciously as the result of great numbers of men (and, Marx insisted, primarily the working class which had nothing to lose from ending the old relations of production) seeing the need for change and acting consciously to achieve it.

If we look back then at the industrial revolution in Britain, we can see that by the middle of the eighteenth century important technical advances had been made in developing and popularizing crop rotation (by Lord 'Turnip' Townsend of Raynham), mechanical seeding (by Jethro Tull, also of Norfolk) and animal husbandry (by Robert Bakewell of Dishley), in the use by the Darbys of Coalbrookdale of coal instead of charcoal for smelting and casting iron and for raising steam in the pumping engines (of Thomas Savory and Thomas Newcomen in Cornwall and Devon), in large-scale mining and in weaving (the 'Flying Shuttle' of John Kay of Bury) and in spinning (the Spinning Jenny of James Hargreaves of Blackburn). A new class of men, Puritan in morals and manners, individualist in their freedom from the ties of land and patronage, were at the centre of this technological revolution, inventing, managing, employing, competing and accumulating capital for new ventures.

Similar changes in technology associated with the emergence of a new class had occurred in Italy and Spain and Portugal at the end of the fifteenth century (the period of Leonardo da Vinci, of Columbus and Vasco da Gama) and in Holland and England in the seventeenth century (the period of the English and Dutch revolutions). Many economic historians[3] see these revolutions in England and Holland as marking the end of landed feudal power and the victory of the town merchants, or the BOURGEOISIE, as they called themselves. Thus the historians explain the delayed industrialization in France and

[3] E.g. Eric Hobsbawm, in his book *The Age of Revolution*, 1962

D

Italy, Spain and Portugal in terms of the perpetuation of
feudal power in such countries until the French Revolution
and the republican movements of nineteenth-century Europe.
The freeing of labour from the land, the spread of a money
economy outwards from the towns, the emergence of a merchant capitalist class in the towns to rival the landed feudal
aristocracy all required the political defeat of feudal power.

Economic historians have still to explain why in England
and Holland the industrial revolution did not follow sooner
after the political revolution, why in Holland indeed the delay
was far longer than in Britain. Some have pointed to the exhaustion following the civil wars, others to the very success (particularly for Holland) of the overseas trade that developed so
rapidly in the seventeenth century. This trade provided the
growing points in English and Dutch ports of the skills and
techniques of manufacturing that were important precursors
of an industrial revolution. The profit accumulated from this
trade both raised the demand for new goods and made capital
available for an agricultural and an industrial revolution, yet
the very profitability of the trade led to capital being ploughed
back into it rather than into home industry. Thanks to the fact
that British traders followed only where Spanish, Portuguese,
Dutch and French had gone before, they had to buy their way
into the trade with a range of manufactured goods for export
which gave them a claim with which to challenge existing
monopolies.

Overseas markets rather than overseas plunder are thus
regarded by some historians as the key to Britain's industrial
primacy. And when the exchange of British manufactures for
American cotton became the major feature of this trade in the
middle of the eighteenth century, the industrial revolution in
Britain was assured.

This emphasis on the development of markets fits in well
with the views of KEYNESIANS on economic history. For them
it is the expansion of the market, the growth of demand, rather
than an improvement in capacity to supply that is all important. The end of feudalism is thus crucial because it freed
the market from feudal restrictions and led to growth in the
size of towns and the interconnection of urban markets. The
eighteenth-century growth in the population of the ports of

Table III.1
Capital Cities' Shares of Total Population 1650–1950

Date	Country	Population of Country	Population of Capital City	Population of Capital City as percentage of Country Population
1650	France	18,000,000	450,000	2½
	Holland	1,900,000	150,000 (Amsterdam)	8
	Britain	5,700,000	400,000	7
1750	France	21,000,000	520,000	2½
	Holland	2,500,000	200,000	8
	Britain	6,100,000	675,000	11
1850	France	36,000,000	1,050,000	3
	Holland	3,100,000	224,000	7
	Britain	21,000,000	2,700,000	13
1950	France	42,000,000	2,800,000	6½
	Holland	10,000,000	800,000	8
	Britain	49,000,000	8,300,000	17
	USA	152,000,000	7,800,000 (New York)	5
	Germany (1940)	80,000,000	4,300,000 (Berlin)	5½
	USSR	195,000,000	4,500,000	2¼
	China (1940)	465,000,000	3,700,000 (Shanghai)	¾
	Japan	83,000,000	4,700,000	5½
	India	385,000,000	2,500,000 (Calcutta)	¾
	Argentina	17,000,000	2,600,000	15
	Egypt	20,000,000	2,200,000	11
	Australia	8,000,000	1,500,000 (Sydney)	18

Source: W. S. and E. S. Woytinsky, *World Population and Production.*

Britain and above all of London play in this theory the central
role in explaining Britain's industrial revolution. Not only was
more food required from the land to feed the new town populations but the use of coal became more important than ever to
replace the dwindling supplies of timber; and from these
urgent demands followed in rapid succession the improvements
in agriculture and in mining and the associated developments
in iron working and steam power. In no other country in

Europe or in the world of the eighteenth century was so large
a part of the population concentrated in the capital as was the
case in London. It is interesting to list the population figures for
the country as a whole and for the capital cities at different dates
in the case of France, Holland and Britain, as in Table III.1.

London and Paris were the largest European cities in the
seventeenth century but London was not only far larger in
relation to Britain as a whole than Paris was to France, but
actually overtook Paris in absolute size by the end of the
century. London is almost alone of the national capitals in
combining seat of government, major port and commercial
and financial centre.

The implications of the rapid growth in the eighteenth
century of a single homogeneous market of over half a million
people in London as 'an engine' of industrial revolution have
recently been examined by E.A.Wrigley[4], who lists ten inter-
connected economic, DEMOGRAPHIC and sociological changes
associating the growth of London with the industrial revolution.

Economic		
	1.	Increased agricultural productivity, re-leasing men and food for secondary industry;
	2.	the creation of a single national market involving
	3.	improved transport by land and water;
	4.	changes in raw material supply especially of coal for timber;
	5.	better commercial and credit facilities – including a National Bank;
	6.	higher real incomes partly made possible by
Demographic	7.	a rough balance of births and deaths in the country as a whole;
Sociological	8.	new consumption patterns providing an incentive to increased output;
	9.	replacement of 'traditional' by 'rational' modes of behaviour;
	10.	new forms of social mobility leading to the emergence of new groups and classes.

[4] See his article on 'London's Importance 1650–1750' in *Past and Present*, No.
37.

It is not possible here to do more than list these inter-connected changes but it is important to notice the emphasis given to the sociological factors associated with the economic changes.

It would be a mistake to imagine that industrial development took place mainly in London itself in the eighteenth and early nineteenth centuries. The industrial development of London was to come later and would account for the continuing rise in London's share of Britain's total population. The early importance of London as an 'engine of economic growth' lay in its markets, its centralizing and unifying force and its role in the process of capital accumulation. The new industries of metal and textile manufacture grew up, as we shall see, around the ports and coal mines of the Midlands, Lancashire, Yorkshire, Durham and Scotland. London's share of the total population actually dropped for a time between 1750 and 1800, but London has always had a population about equal to that of the next largest twenty cities added together as we can see in Table III.2.

Table III.2
The Growth of Towns in Britain 1750–1950

	1800	1850	1900	1950
Population of UK	12m	27·5m	38m	50m
Birmingham (Bir)	70,000	260,000	760,000	1,100,000
Manchester (M)	75,000	330,000	640,000	700,000
Glasgow (G)	77,000	375,000	900,000	1,100,000
Liverpool (L)	82,000	376,000	685,000	790,000
Edinburgh (E)	83,000	202,000	395,000	467,000
Bristol (Br)	61,000	137,000	329,000	443,000
Belfast (Be)	(30,000)	103,000	350,000	444,000
Leeds (Le)	53,000	172,000	429,000	505,000
Sheffield (Sh)	46,000	135,000	381,000	513,000
Plymouth (Pl)	40,000	90,000	178,000	208,000
Norwich (Nor)	36,000	68,000	112,000	212,000
Newcastle (New)	33,000	88,000	247,000	292,000
Portsmouth (Po)	33,000	73,000	188,000	234,000
Hull (H)	30,000	85,000	240,000	299,000
Nottingham (Not)	29,000	57,000	240,000	306,000
Bath (Ba)	33,000	54,000	50,000	79,000

Population of UK	1800 12m	1850 27·5m	1900 38m	1950 50m
Leicester (Lei)	17,000	61,000	212,000	285,000
Coventry (Co)	16,000	36,000	70,000	258,000
Bradford (Bra)	13,000	104,000	280,000	292,000
Cardiff (Ca)	2,000	18,000	164,000	244,000
Stoke on Trent (St)	(28,000)	66,000	215,000	275,000
TOTAL 20 Cities				
(excl. London)	888,000	2,800,000	7,064,000	9,655,000
as % of UK TOTAL	7·5	10	18·5	18
London	1,100,000	1,700,000	6,600,000	8,300,000
as % of UK TOTAL	9·0	10·0	17·0	16·5

Notes:

1. Stoke-on-Trent population figure for 1,800 is from the 1811 Census.
2. All towns are included which had either 30,000 population in 1801 or 240,000 in 1951.
3. Abbreviations are those used on the map, Fig. 3.1.

Source: B. Mitchell and P. Deane, *Abstract of British Historical Statistics*.

To explain London's primacy we referred to its combination of port, seat of government and commercial centre. This may seem in part an historical accident but it is also an inevitable result of London's geographical position at the head of a long estuary near the centre of the southern half of England, but only just across the water from the Continent and connected by the Channel to the Atlantic Ocean and the sea lanes of the world. The result of this combination of roles provides us with an example of an important economic principle suggested by a Swedish economist, Gunnar Myrdal.[5] This is the principle of CUMULATIVE CAUSATION. The larger the accumulation of wealth or population in one place the larger it is likely to become. The largest market attracts labour and production to it, and these make it still larger. Wealth has attracted capital, labour and enterprise to London from Dick Whittington to Charles Clore. Poverty has repelled them, as we may see on the reverse side of the coin in the DEPRESSION and depopulation of Scotland and Ireland and the North of England. In 1750 Scotland and Ireland together had 40 per cent of the population of the British Isles. Today the proportion is less than 20

[5] See his book *Economic Theory and Underdeveloped Regions*, 1957.

per cent. We can see this principle even more drastically at work today in the impoverishment of two-thirds of the world, while the industrial third advances towards greater and greater affluence.

2. THE PROCESS OF INDUSTRIALIZATION IN BRITAIN

The industrial map of Britain dates back to the industrial revolution. Today's declining areas of the distribution of industry that occurred then present for us a problem of social and economic policy. The structures of industrial enterprise and finance date back to the foundations of modern industry and banking 150 years ago. To discover the principles by which that distribution and those structures were determined it is necessary for students to read about the process of industrialization in Britain.[6] What follows provides no more than a few indicators of the process, but these may serve as an introduction to the principles that will be examined in the next sections. In describing the process we shall distinguish (a) the development of the Coal and Iron industries; (b) the FACTORY system in textile manufacture; (c) the transport system – roads, canals, railways and communication; (d) banking and finance at home and overseas.

Given the attraction of London as a market and centre of commerce and production, it is evident that there must have been strong forces at work to engender the development of industry outside London. The main centres of population and economic activity outside London before 1750 were the ports – particularly Bristol, the second city of the land, Glasgow, Edinburgh, Plymouth and latterly Liverpool – and the traditional areas of cloth manufacture, East Anglia and Somerset with the West Riding of Yorkshire becoming increasingly active. The iron industry based on charcoal from the forests of the Weald and the Forest of Dean was already moving by the beginning of the eighteenth century to the combined iron and coalfields of Shropshire, Staffordshire and South Yorkshire, thanks to Abraham Darby's discovery of a practical method of using coal for iron smelting. The shifts that followed may be traced in the figures in Table III.3.

[6] E.g. Phyllis Deane's *The First Industrial Revolution*, 1967.

Table III.3
Location of Population and Industry U.K. 1750s–1960s
(All figures are percentage of totals for UK except in the last three lines)

REGION OR CONURBATION	POPULATION OR INDUSTRY	1750[1]	1800[1]	1821	1850	1871	1900	1920	1950	1965[5]	Est. 1980
SCOTLAND	Population	15	13·5	13·5	13	12	12	11	10	10	(9)
	Coal	—	(10)	—	11	14	15	15	11	9	(10)
	Iron (pig)	(10)	(8)	6	25	16	13	11	7	10	(10)
WALES	Population	—	5	5	5	5	5	6	5	5	(5)
	Coal	—	(10)	13	13	11	17	21	12	10	(10)
	Iron (pig)	(15)	(29)	40	24	11	10	9	14	25	(30)
N.E. ENGLAND Tyneside	Population	—	—	—	1·3	1·3	1·8	1·9	1·6	1·5	(1·5)
	Coal	—	(30)	—	24	24	20	18	20	18	(10)
	Iron (pig)	(4)	(10)	3	9	31	33	33	25	15	(15)
S.E. LANCS.	Population	—	—	—	3	3	5·5	5·5	5	4·5	(4·5)
	Coal	—	(10)	15	15	16	13	8	7·5	6	(3)
	Iron (pig)[2]	(35)	(24)	4	5	11	9	9	3	9	(5)

W. MIDLANDS Population	—	7·5	7·7	7·5	7·7	7·8	8·5	8·7	9·0	(9·5)
Coal[3]	—	(20)	—	11	11	7·5	6	9	7·5	(7)
Iron (pig)[3]	(10)	(20)	31	27	10	7	9	5	3·5	(2·5)
W. YORKSHIRE Population	—	—	—	4	4	4	3·5	3·5	3·4	(8·3)
Coal	—	(10)	—	11	12	12·5	18·5	21	22	(30)
Iron (pig)	(5)	(6)	3	2	5	3	4[6]	3[6]	1·5[6]	(1)
E. MIDLANDS Population	—	5·7	5·6	5·3	5·3	5·3	5·5	5·7	6	(6·5)
Coal	(5)	(10)	—	11	12	12·5	18·5	21	22	(25)
Iron (pig)[4]	—	(4)	3	2	8	13	19	36	24	(33)
GREATER LONDON Population	10	9	10	12	14	17	17	16·5	16	(17)
IRELAND Population[7]	10	7	9	5	4	3·5	3	2·5	2·5	(2·3)
TOTALS Population in millions	9	12	15·5	22	27·4	38	44	50	53	(60)
Coal output in million tons	(6)	(8)	(20)	60	133	225	243	202	180	(100)
Iron output in million tons	(·06)	(·24)	·68	3·0	6·4	9·0	8·0	9·6	20	(30)

Notes: 1. Figures in brackets are estimates only; 2. including Shropshire; 3. including Staffordshire; 4. including Lincolnshire; 5. iron figures for 1965 = capacity in the 1960s; 6. in steel production Sheffield was nearer 10% using pig from other areas; 7. Northern Ireland as after 1920.

(a) *The development of the coal and iron industries*
It was the expanding demand for coal as a house fuel and for
metal working and then for the development of cotton textile
manufacture that changed the industrial map of Britain. Fig.
3.1 shows that a rough parallelogram bounded by the Welsh

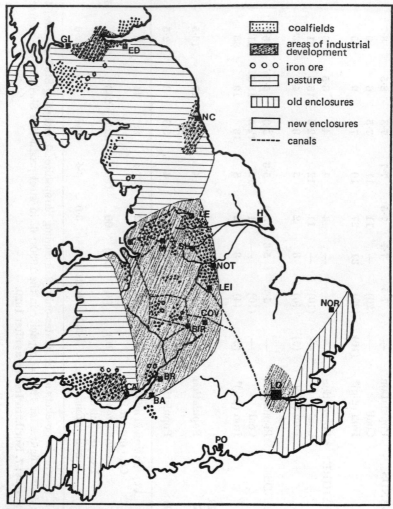

Source: I.Richards & J.R. Morris,
Junior Sketch Map Economic History of Britain,
Harrap, 1961.

Figure 3.1. Map of industrial Britain, 1800

border to the west, the Ribble and Aire rivers to the north, the Trent and Soar to the east and the Avon to the south contained the heart of industrial England. It embraced the coalfields of Lancashire, Cheshire, Yorkshire, Derbyshire, Nottinghamshire, Leicestershire, Staffordshire and Warwick. The extension of coal mining, which was not itself mechanized for almost two centuries, but continued to depend upon the most exhausting labour of men, women and children in the most appalling conditions underground, nevertheless encouraged mechanical inventions all around it. Newcomen's steam pump, Watt's steam engine and Trevethick's steam locomotive were all designed to solve mining problems of pumping water and transporting men and coal. Iron refining and casting developed rapidly with the use of coal.

Outside the parallelogram, as we have described it, coal mining developed also in Scotland, South Wales and in the North East. Most of London's coal came from the Tyne and Tees and ironworks were soon established in all these areas (Table III.3), but that the heart of industrial England remained inside the parallelogram provides another example of cumulative causation. The canal building of the last quarter of the eighteenth century connected the Mersey, the Humber, the Severn and the Thames estuaries, with Birmingham at the centre of the system. The towns that grew fastest during the industrial revolution were inside the parallelogram. Lancashire's population doubled between 1800 and 1830 while the population of Britain as a whole rose by 50 per cent. Labour was drawn in from what had been the most populous counties of England south-east of the line from the Humber to the Severn. It was in these counties that ENCLOSURES of common fields took place in the eighteenth and nineteenth centuries; thereby permitting the new agricultural techniques to be applied and releasing manpower from the land. The process was continued after the Napoleonic Wars when the price of grain fell and many smallholders were ruined and forced into the poor house, into the new towns or into crime and transportation to Australia. We may read of all this in the novels of Thomas Hardy like *Far From the Madding Crowd*.

By the end of the eighteenth century and the beginning of the nineteenth, except in the war years, wheat was being imported into Britain to the extent of a million tons a year, much of it from Ireland. Total imports to Britain, mainly of food and raw materials, trebled in value between the 1770s and the first decade of the nineteenth century and exports mainly of coal, metal goods and textiles rose in line with them. Britain was already an industrial nation and foreign trade amounted to one-eighth of the national income. Whereas half the occupied population had been engaged in agriculture in the middle of the eighteenth century, by the time of the Census of 1821 the proportion in agriculture was only one-third – already fewer than in many developing countries even today, as we can see in Table III.4. – and nearly a half were engaged in trade, manufactures and handicrafts.

Table III.4
Occupational Distribution of the Labour Force (per cent) for Different Countries in Different years

Country	Year	Agri-culture	Mining	Mfg. and Constr.	Trade	Transport and Communica-tions	Other Services and Professions (incl. Government)
Thailand	1937	88	0·3	2	4	1	4
Bulgaria Turkey Yugoslavia Rumania	} 1930	78–80	0·2	8–10	3	2	7
Egypt Philippines Columbia	} 1937–8	70–75	1–2	10–11	5–7	2–3	8–9
India Poland Brazil Mexico	1930–1 } 1939–40	65–70	1–2	10–15	5–10	1–2	12–15
Britain Italy Eire Spain Venezuela Japan	1700 1930 1940 1941 1947	50–60	1–2	15–25	7–9	3–5	13–18

Country	Year	Agri-culture	Mining	Mfg. and Constr.	Trade	Transport and Communica-tions	Other Services and Professions (incl. Government)
Britain	1750						
USA	1880–90						
Hungary	1940–1	40–50	1–2	20–30	6–10	3–6	15–25
Cuba	1943						
Austria	1939						
Britain	1800						
USA	1900						
Norway	1930	30–40	2–3	25–35	8–12	4–7	18–25
France	1946						
Canada	1931						
Britain	1850						
USA	1930						
Germany	1939						
France		20–30	1–3	30–40	10–12	5–10	20–28
Japan	1960						
Italy							
Britain	1870						
USA	1940						
Belgium	1930						
Holland		10–20	2–5	30–40	15–20	5–10	25–30
Australia	1947						
W. Germany	1961						
USA	1930	22	2	29	12	8	27
Britain	1931	6	6	40	16	7	25
USA	1961	9	2	31	24	5	30
Britain	1961	3	2·5	46	16	7	25·5
Est. Britain	1975	2·5	1	42·5	15	6	33

Note: Construction makes up 6 per cent–7 per cent of the latest Manufacturing and Construction figures for Britain.

Sources: Woytinsky and Woytinsky, *World Population and Production*. United Nations *Statistical Yearbooks*. Department of Employment and Productivity *Manpower Projections*.

(b) *The factory system in textile manufacture*
The main element in this revolutionary change was the development of cotton textile manufacture in large mills. Cotton

could be grown easily, quickly and cheaply (compared with sheep) and was more susceptible than wool to mechanical processing. Plantations in the West Indies and later in the southern states of North America were developed to supply the growing demand of the English mills. Cotton textile exports from Britain surpassed the exports of woollen manufactures in 1802 and were double their value by 1807. The markets of the world were opened up to British manufacturers – not only in North and South America but in India and China too. The handicraft weavers and spinners and metal workers of these great lands, which had once supplied not only their own vast populations but the trade of the whole world, were destroyed by the factory products of Manchester and Birmingham. The division of the world into European manufacturers on the one hand, and producers of primary products elsewhere had been established. Cotton was king. By 1810 cotton goods were providing a third of Britain's exports.

Nearly all the cotton mills were in Lancashire, although Richard Arkwright of Preston, and Jedediah Strutt and others built factories on the river Derwent in Derbyshire, These were connected with the river Goyt and the Mersey by one of the first major railway lines, the Peak Forest – Cromford horse-drawn line. At first the mills were driven by water-power – hence their location on the rivers of the Pennines – but soon steam replaced water, and power weaving was added to power spinning, particularly in the Midlands where water power was short. One by one the hand spinning and the hand looms of traditional DOMESTIC INDUSTRY, which had for so long supplemented agricultural work in the villages along either side of the Pennines, were replaced by the factory system, first in cottons and then in wool and silk and hosiery.

The cotton mills were the first large-scale factories. The division of labour, to which Adam Smith ascribed the great advance of productivity, had occurred much earlier in nail manufacture in the Midlands,[7] but each part of the process of manufacture was still carried on by one or two men in small workshops set close to each other. Cotton spinning was established by contrast in mills employing hundreds of people at serried lines of machines. The output per man, or rather per

[7] Described by W.H.B.Court, *The Rise of the Midland Industries*, 1938.

woman and child, rose enormously. Unit costs of production fell sharply; for it proved possible for fifty years or more to pay the same or lower wages per day, while output per day steadily rose. Prices fell, ruining the old craft industries, and profits rose which could be ploughed back in new machines. The change to the factory system did not come without fierce resistance, especially from the hand-loom weavers; for the factories meant long hours, up to 18 a day, and harsh discipline in terrible conditions for women and children and the end of independence for the superseded craftsman. The men who broke frames in the name of King Ludd added a word to the English language and a stirring chapter to the history of English labour.[8]

(c) *The transport system: road, canals and railways – and communications*
By the opening years of the nineteenth century Britain had a road and canal system, ports and harbour installations and a navy and merchant shipping far in advance of any other country in the world. Nelson's victory at Trafalgar in 1805 gave notice of the fact. But the revolution in transport had hardly begun. If cotton manufacture had provided the growth point of the first stages of the industrial revolution, railway building carried the process several stages further. The potential market in Britain was already well established. The railways completed its unification; they ended the MONOPOLISTIC position of isolated producers and ushered in the age of COMPETITION; they provided MOBILITY of labour and in the process of their construction drew in thousands of Irish migrants as navvies – the original 'navigators' whose monuments of earth and stone far surpassed the Pyramids and other wonders of the ancient world.

By the mid-1840s a Victorian economist, Thomas Tooke, estimated that one million people – men and their families – were living and working on the railways.[9] But the railways did much more than this; they required for their operation and maintenance not only great quantities of high quality iron and steel for rails and bridges and a great development of precision

[8] See Edward Thompson's *Making of the English Working Class*, 1963.
[9] Their story is told in the *Railway Navvies* by Terry Coleman, 1965.

engineering; they required new forms of organization, communication and finance. It is not by chance that the railway 'servants' have always been dressed in uniforms; the only experience available to be drawn upon for such a large-scale organization as a railway system required was in fact the army, and it was from commissioned and non-commissioned officers of the Army that most of the early railway staff was drawn.

The invention of the telegraph and the telephone and the investigation into the properties and use of electricity all derived directly from the communication requirements of the railways. The implications for the development of national consciousness, for the breakdown of local loyalties and above all in the long run for the centralization of government were obvious. A single glance at a map of Britain's railway network, confirmed by experience of attempting to travel from coast to coast, east to west or vice versa, at any point between Scotland and London, reveals that the whole system is a radial one, radiating from the ten main line stations in London. The railways were invented and developed in the north of England, but London created the railway system and in so doing confirmed its social, economic and political primacy. London created the system because the system required, and in turn generated, a vast accumulation of capital, which only centralized finance and BANKING could provide.

(d) *Banking and finance – at home and overseas*

The finance of industrial development in Britain in the last half of the eighteenth century had been effected primarily, and often with great difficulty, by the manufacturing inventors themselves and one or two partners ploughing back year by year the profits of their enterprise. Loans from a country banker, and more rarely from a London bank, were anxiously sought to cover major investments. The difficulties of even such an inveterate commercial traveller as Matthew Boulton, James Watt's partner in the famous Soho steam engine works, in raising capital were considerable. The typical form of industrial enterprise up to the railway boom was nevertheless the PARTNERSHIP.

The wide extension of the JOINT-STOCK COMPANY as a

corporate person in law with the LIMITED LIABILITY of stock holders was among the most important economic inventions of the Victorian era. The public joint-stock company under Royal, and later under Parliamentary, charter had for long existed as a privileged form of enterprise in finance and commerce. The great monopolies of the seventeenth and eighteenth centuries, like the East India Company, were joint-stock companies. Railway finance required the joint stock of thousands of small capital owners all over the country. To obtain the privilege of corporateness from Parliament was, however, costly and time-consuming, and the liability of stock-holders was not always limited to the stock they put up but might extend to debts incurred. The Company Laws of 1844 and 1856 were designed to meet the needs of the railway boom, although they became the basis of all commercial and manufacturing enterprise. In effect they opened the privilege of corporateness to all for a nominal registration fee and provided limited liability to any registered public company.

Henceforth the functions of inventor, manager and owner which had once been combined in one man were split up. A RENTIER class of SHAREHOLDERS, many of them women, widows and sisters of business and professional men, emerged, inhabiting the villas in seaside watering places, as the railways reached to Eastbourne and Bournemouth, and in the London suburbs, like Sydenham and Mill Hill, far removed from any of the processes of production. With the emergence of a rentier class, and symbiotic with it, came the growth of the role of the STOCK EXCHANGE and of the private and then of the joint-stock banks.

Joint-stock enterprise and banking had a long history in Britain, to be traced back to the companies of merchant overseas adventurers in the sixteenth century. The private or MERCHANT BANKERS, who play the leading role in the City of London's finance of industry today, rose to eminence as financiers of overseas trade. The London Stock Exchange from its early beginnings in the coffee houses of Lombard Street dealt mainly in the stock of overseas ventures and continued to do so right down to the First World War, despite additions of government stock from the beginning of the eighteenth century and of railway stock from the middle of the nineteenth. Investment in competitive manufacturing industry at home remained a risky business. Huge sums were in fact lost in the railway building boom. The British rentier preferred to put his, or more likely her, money into loans to governments and public utilities both at home and abroad. Only with the rise of giant monopolistic companies – the so-called 'BLUE CHIPS' of the Stock Market – did home investment attract the rentier. Private industry at home continued to rely and still relies today, primarily on its own INTERNALLY GENERATED FINANCE.

The importance of the City of London has always lain in its international financial connections – the finance of foreign trade and of OVERSEAS INVESTMENT. The balance of foreign payments that plagues Britain's economy today was assured from the 1850s onwards, and for a hundred years, not by a surplus of exports of goods and service over imports but by the accumulation of earnings on overseas investment. The mopping up of markets overseas established the factory system in Britain for textiles and light manufactures; overseas investment sustained the growth of heavy industry and particularly of railway building and shipbuilding in the heyday of Britain's world economic supremacy; the return on earlier investments cushioned British capitalists in the decline of their industry and trade.[10] The implications of this original overseas orientation of British capital are with us with a vengeance today.

3. THE DIVISION AND PRODUCTIVITY OF LABOUR

We have now to analyse precisely wherein lie the economic advantages of industrialization, and of factory production for the market. We shall leave until the next chapter detailed examination of the working of the markets for goods and services, for land, labour and capital, in determining their prices and in allocating total resources. Here we shall confine ourselves to studying the firm and industry. But we must not forget the emphasis that was laid at the beginning of this chapter on the London market, the unifying of a national

[10] The story may be read in Eric Hobsbawm's *Industry and Empire*, 1968.

market and the opening up of overseas markets in the process of industrialization in Britain. For it is production for the market which lies at the centre of the economic system that emerged in the industrial revolution and which made possible the productive processes that we shall be analysing.

The inventions of the industrial revolution consisted mainly of the replacement of human hands and arms and legs by mechanical ones. These could move faster and bear greater weights and they were driven by fuel energy that added more and more horse power to human energy. A century later, in 1939, a United States worker had about 5 h.p. at his disposal, a British or German worker about a half of that and a worker in a poor East European country like Bulgaria about half again, or $1\frac{1}{4}$ h.p. Of course these figures varied greatly from industry to industry – in the USA from 10 h.p. in iron and steel, chemicals and paper to a third of 1 h.p. in clothing, and 1–2 h.p. in agriculture. With this motive power the average United States worker was using the energy equivalent of 20 tons of coal a year; his British counterpart about 10 tons. From 1820 to 1938 in fact the world's supply of energy had been multiplied a hundredfold. By 1958 the 1938 figure had been doubled and by 1968 almost doubled again, with two thirds then coming from oil and natural gas and a third only from coal. The sheer addition of mechanical to human energy provides the first advantage of industrialization.

If that were all, however, the full advantages of mechanization would not have been exploited. Each man would still be working at his old craft but with powered tools, hoists and transport to help him. The factory system we saw earlier implied the introduction of large machines and large numbers of machines in one place. The advantages of this are explained by economists in terms of two connected principles, that of the division of labour and that of the economies of scale. Combined together they can result in a very great increase in output per man per hour, what we now call labour productivity. In 1776 Adam Smith[11] had already identified these two as the 'causes of improvement in the productive powers of labour'. The reasons are not hard to seek.

[11] In his *Inquiry into the Nature and Causes of the Wealth of Nations.*

The division of labour implies SPECIALIZATION, not only indeed of labour but of the land and machinery and enterprise applied with the labour. Industry is divided up into separate industries and firms; production into separate processes and tasks; general labour into special trades and skills, for which men and women can be trained and special aptitudes and abilities exploited. By breaking down a production process into its component parts, specialized machines can be designed which can be kept working almost continuously. The pieces produced can then be assembled and put together. At first this was done by establishing the plants which were involved in different stages of the process next door to each other, as in the forging, stamping, grinding, plating, polishing, hafting of the Sheffield cutlery trades and in the Manchester cotton textile processes of bleaching, dyeing, spinning, doubling and weaving. Later, all the processes came to be housed under one roof and ASSEMBLY took place on a continuously moving conveyor system with mechanized processing and transfer operations. In today's industry both the processes themselves and the transfer of operations are becoming automatically PROGRAMMED and controlled. We have to note that as a result the traditional division of labour and specialization of trades and skills is being superseded not only by new technical specialization but by the requirement of a more flexible work force with a higher and more generalized education.

The advantage to be derived from foreign trade has always been regarded as an important example of the division of labour. Each country produces what it is best suited to produce. Moreover, even a country like the USA that can perhaps produce everything cheaper than any other country may still benefit from foreign trade, because there will be some products in which its advantage is relatively less than in others. This was described by Ricardo as the law of comparative advantage. There is no doubt much truth in it and all countries can benefit from some specialization. We noticed earlier, however, that the head start of Britain and other European, and European-settled, countries in the advance of industrialization created an artificial world division of labour between primary producers and manufacturers. In this the manufacturing countries gain more than the primary producers for several reasons:

(*a*) primary produce is often perishable and cannot be held off the market;

(*b*) a country may have only one or two primary products for sale and this puts it in a vulnerable position compared with the wide range of products of the manufacturers, particularly since many primary products have substitutes;

(*c*) the large numbers of primary producers are much less able to co-ordinate and manage their marketing than the much smaller number of manufacturers;

(*d*) primary producers have become dependent on manufacturers for their own industrialization;

(*e*) all this would be much less important if it were not that with very few exceptions output per man in industry has tended for all these reasons to be valued more highly than output in agriculture. One of the reasons for this we have already seen in the higher level of mechanical energy that has been applied to industry than to agriculture, but price ratios between industrial and agricultural products have been determined more by such bargaining positions in the division of labour as have just been listed than by any comparative labour and 'dated labour' inputs.

Shifting resources from agriculture into industry has certainly been the main way in which productivity has been raised by men in the past. We may compare the occupational distribution of the labour force in different countries at different times as in Table III.4; and we can see at a glance that the richer countries are those with the lowest proportion of their populations engaged in agriculture. It has been estimated recently by the Brookings Institution that between one-third and one-fifth of the superiority in post-war economic growth rates for Germany, France and Italy, compared with those for Britain, has been due to the shift of their workforce out of agriculture. The Table shows us, however, that when about 40 per cent of the occupied population comes to be engaged in manufacturing and construction the growth of this sector levels off and the proportion engaged in the provision of services including government increases, while the proportion in agriculture declines. Estimates made for Britain in 1975 continue the trend. This is what we should expect from the income elasticities of demand for goods and services which we saw in Chapter II (Table 2). We shall have to leave aside consideration of the problems of resource allocation facing those countries whose industrial development has been held back in the artificial world division of labour between primary production and manufacturing industry, and which are for this reason best thought of as underdeveloped and not just undeveloped.

4. THE ECONOMIES OF SCALE

What has been said above about the advantages of the division of labour implied the possibility of a large scale of production with long runs of output of standardized parts. Large-scale production – MASS-PRODUCTION as Henry Ford called it – has great economic advantages besides making possible the division of labour. These result mainly from the reduction in UNIT COSTS, that is costs per unit of output, where total OVERHEAD costs can be spread over the large number of units. Overhead, or FIXED COSTS are those which continue whether or not production is taking place. They can thus be distinguished from VARIABLE OR PRIME COSTS which vary with output as more or less labour, fuel and materials are required (see later Table III.8). Overhead costs include the capital cost of the plant and its maintenance and the costs of management, research and sales staff, all of which will vary little with variations in output. There may also be considerable savings to be gained from other aspects of large-scale production – from BULK TRANSACTIONS (one driver and one signalman will be needed for one or for fifty wagons) from pooled reserves of spares (a small garage must keep the same stock of spares as a large one); from the INDIVISIBILITY of men and machines (one storeman is needed for a large or small stock of spares); from common services of heat and energy (steam made in heating iron ore may be re-used); from the use of BY-PRODUCTS which might otherwise be wasted. As a result of all these considerations iron and steel making plants, for example, have become a vast complex of INTEGRATED activities.

The results of the economies of scale may be seen in the

rapid increase of recent years in the size of manufacturing establishments. Whereas in 1935 only a fifth of all those employed in manufacturing in Britain were in plants with over 1,000 workers, about a third are so today and in coal mining and the iron and steel industry the proportion is two-thirds (Table III.5). Economists always used to suppose that DIS-ECONOMIES are encountered when plants expand beyond a

Table III.5
Size of Manufacturing Establishments in Great Britain 1930 and 1961

Number of Workers per Plant	All Manufacturing Industry				Coal % of Workers		Iron and Steel		
	% of Plants		% of Workers		E.		% of Workers		% of Plants
	1935	1961	1935	1961	Yorks 1967	Mids 1967	1935	1961	1961
1–10	73	72	9	8			—	—	—
11–99	21	20·3	23	18	7	2	4	3	60
100–499	5·1	6·8	33	29			21	17	28
500–999	0·6	0·9	12·5	13	21	26	20	11	6·5
1,000–1,999	0·3	0·4	19·5	12	53	66	55	69	3
2,000 plus		0·2		20	19	6			2·5
TOTAL	100	100	100	100	100	100	100	100	100
in Numbers (000s)	181	195	5,694	8,667	115	90	136	220	2

Sources: *Annual Abstract of Statistics*. National Coal Board. British Steel Corporations *Iron and Steel Annual Statistics*.

certain optimum size, but the use of computers in solving problems of process control and information retrieval for management has greatly extended the optimum size. Outside Britain the size of plants has been growing even faster than inside. Tables III.6 and III.7 show that considerable economies are still being obtained in both capital and production costs when output from a steel plant is raised to 4m. tons a year and oil refinery throughput 10m. tons a year. There are plants of this size in the USA, USSR and Italy but not yet in Britain.

Table III.6
Economies of Scale in Steel-Making Plants

Capital and Current	Relative Costs at Different Annual Outputs (100 = Cost at 250,000 tons)					
Items of Costs	100,000	250,000	500,000	1m	2m	4m
Open Hearth Furnaces						
Capital	124	100	81	74	—	—
Operating Costs	106	100	79	74	—	—
Bessemer Converters (Basic)						
Capital Costs	167	100	68	54	—	—
Rolling Mills						
Labour Costs	191	100	51	36	—	—
Overheads and Power	200	100	100	100	—	—
Capital Costs	127	100	93	90	—	—
Total	172	100	73	64	—	—
Production Costs						
Blast Furnaces	120	100	94	89	85	82
Steel Furnaces	125	100	90	82	78	82
Finishing	137	100	82	68	56	47
Total	128	100	89	79	72	67

Table III.7
Economies of Scale in Oil Refining

Items of Cost	Relative costs of Annual Tonnage Outputs in million tons (100 = cost at 500,000 tons)				
	0.5	1.5	3.0	5.0	10.0
Investment Costs					
Process Equipment	100	66	52	45	45
Utilities, Offsites, Tankage and Docks	100	63	53	48	43
0·6 Factor	100	63	48	38	29
Operating Costs	100	57	46	40	36

Source: C. Pratten and R. M. Dean, *The Economies of Large Scale Production in British Industry*, CUP, 1965, who provide the following note:

Note: The 0·6 rule states that if the capacity of a plant is doubled then the capital cost is increased to $2^{0 \cdot 6}$, i.e. by 52 per cent. The rule was based on the cost and capacity of individual units of plant, such as distillation units. Empirical work (1) based on the prices of plant has shown that an approximate relationship of this kind exists, though the calculated factor for different kinds of plant varies between 0·5 and 0·9. The estimates relate to the range of plant sizes in production and cannot be assumed to extend beyond it. Economies tend to be greater than those implied at the lower end, and less towards the upper end, of the range of sizes made.

The 0·6 rule is attributable to the economies of large dimensions. The volume of pipes, tanks and pressure vessels determines their capacity, and the surface area determines steel requirements. If the gauge of steel is not affected, then volume and surface area are related in a similar way to the 0·6 rule. Also the number of separate parts, which is an important determinant of the cost of fabrication, does not increase in proportion to scale for many items of process equipment such as tanks and pumps.

The economies of scale of which we have been talking are only obtained if plants are working at, or near, full capacity. The larger the investment, and with it the proportion of overhead costs in TOTAL COSTS, the more important it is for the plant to be working at full capacity, if unit costs are to be reduced. We may study this in the case of the coal industry in Table III.8. The concept of full capacity is likely to be a

Table III.8
Total and Average Costs per Ton of Coal, National Coal Board Collieries, 1967–8

Items of Cost	Average Unit Cost Per Ton £ s d			Total Cost (Per 170m tons) (£m)
Fixed Costs (TOTAL)	1	16	1	300
Interest Charges	0	4	1	34
Non-Colliery Administrative and General Expenses	0	8	6	71
Colliery Depreciation, Salaries and General Expenses	1	3	6	195
Variable Costs (TOTAL)	3	12	5	600
Wages, etc.	2	9	3	408
Materials, Power, etc.	1	3	2	193
All Costs (TOTAL)	5	8	5	900

Source: National Coal Board, *Report and Accounts, 1967–8.*

flexible one for an industry, and may even be so for a firm, but economists have always supposed that costs fall as output increases up to a certain point, when either full capacity is reached or costs begin to rise again. This rise takes place because old and more inefficient plant has to be brought into use, or in mining poorer and more difficult seams must be worked; breakdowns become more frequent, overtime payments have to be made and so on. These are the explanations for the economists' habitual graphical use of a 'U' shaped cost curve, sloping down from the left, as economies of scale are reaped but then rising again on the right. When we looked at supply curves in Chapter II we concentrated on the second half of the U, since it was supposed that eliciting extra supply would encounter just such difficulties leading to rising costs. Obviously we are talking here of the short run; in the long run new capacity can be built which may be more efficient than the old.

An important distinction has to be made here between the average and the marginal in relation to both costs and output. In a quite unmechanized operation these will not be far different. The average output per man in unmechanized coal mining will be what the average man can produce with a pick and shovel. If an extra (marginal) man is taken on, his output is likely to be near the average. In mechanized production, by contrast, average output per man will depend on the machine's degree of utilization. Taking on another man will make little difference to output, unless he is needed to maintain full capacity working. For this reason employers tend today to keep on labour with special skills even in times of undercapacity working, but to dismiss general labourers. There is a widening gap between the hourly earnings of the two. We shall see later what problems this gap may cause in the future as mechanization and automation spread. We need to consider here why for a firm, and also for a single firm industry like the Coal Board and the Steel Corporation, the distinction between marginal and average costs is an important one.

The variable costs per ton of pits and areas operated by the Coal Board in 1967 fluctuated greatly: from about £2 10*s* 0*d* a ton to over £6 a ton. The pits or areas could be placed in an order from least cost to highest cost; and then we could say

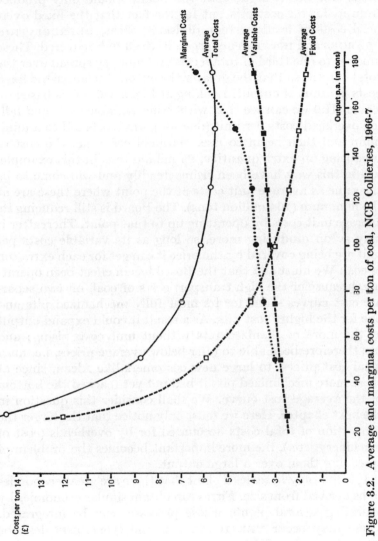

Figure 3.2. Average and marginal costs per ton of coal, NCB Collieries, 1966-7

that the Board was operating with rising average variable
costs. One might argue that the Board should only produce
from its lowest cost pits but for the fact that the fixed overhead costs of headquarters, divisions, areas, DEPRECIATION
CHARGES and INTEREST charges, have all to be covered. These
amount to one third of total costs and must be spread over the
total output, so that the greater the output the lower the fixed
costs per unit of output. Looking at Fig. 3.2 which is based on
Table III.9 we can see that with rising variable costs and falling overhead costs per unit (one ton), unit costs fall to a minimum and then begin to rise. Marginal costs, i.e. the cost of
producing an extra quantity, 25 million tons in this example,
will in this way have been rising steadily and will come to be
the same as average unit costs at the point where these are at
the minimum (164 million tons). The Board is still reducing its
average unit costs by operating up to that point. Thereafter it
may go on producing more, so long as its variable costs per
unit are being covered by the price it can get for each extra ton
of coal. We must add that the Board has in effect been operating, because of the high transport costs of coal, on two separate cost curves – one for its most fully mechanized pits and
one for the higher cost pits. As a result it could expand output
at the more mechanized pits without unit costs rising; and
has therefore been able to offer below average prices, i.e. marginal cost prices, to large new customers like Alcan, since at
these more mechanized pits it had not yet reached the bottom
of the average cost curve. We shall consider this question in
the next chapter. Here we must only notice that the larger the
proportion of total costs accounted for by overheads (cost of
machinery, etc.), the more important becomes the problem of
spreading them over a large output.

It is not only in scale of plant that there are great economies
to be derived from size. Firms can obtain similar economies by
operating several plants whose processes can be integrated.
These may occur VERTICALLY, as the economists describe
integration when for example a steel-making company owns
and operates all the processes from raw material to finished
product – iron ore mines, coal mines, iron making, steel making, special steel and chemical plants, engineering factories
and constructional enterprises. HORIZONTAL integration, by

Table III.9
Average and Marginal Costs per Ton of Coal,
National Coal Board Collieries 1966–7

Overall output in m. tons	Average Costs per Ton (£.s.d.)			per unit of 25m. tons		Marginal Costs per ton (£.s.d.)
	Fixed	Variable	Total	Units	Cost	
25	12 0 0	2 10 0	14 10 0	1	14 10 0	—
50	6 0 0	2 15 0	8 15 0	2	17 10 0	3 0 0
75	4 0 0	3 0 0	7 0 0	3	21 0 0	3 10 0
100	3 0 0	3 4 0	6 4 0	4	24 16 0	3 16 0
125	2 8 0	3 7 0	5 15 0	5	28 15 0	3 19 0
150	2 0 0	3 11 6	5 11 6	6	33 9 0	4 14 0
175	1 14 3	3 19 6	5 13 9	7	39 16 3	6 7 0

Note: The last line assumes the continuation of the trend from 150–165m. tons.
Source: NCB *Report and Accounts* 1966–7.

contrast, describes the ownership by one firm of many similar plants in different parts of the country or in different countries. The giant INTERNATIONAL FIRM is becoming increasingly the typical unit of capital control, as we shall see in Chapter V. Great advantages accrue to such firms in savings on overheads from sharing common research and development and marketing services, but above all in their control over sources of capital and over market prices.

5. THE LOCATION OF INDUSTRY

Scale of output is associated with the size of market. The limitations of the market for any firm's products will be set by the competition of rival producers and by the rise in transport costs as the distance increases from the point of production. Competition which was once local, and at most regional in the late eighteenth century, is today international. The number of producers of any product has steadily declined as scale of output has increased and transport costs have come down. The roads and canals of the eighteenth century and the railways and steamships of the nineteenth century greatly reduced transport costs. The great speed of air transport, the huge expansion of road haulage and the increased size of shipping –

giant tankers and ore containers – and the speeding up of port handling in our own time have continued the process. The world is one market; but the location of industrial plant has a historical as well as an economic explanation.[12]

As we have seen before, economists consider the location of industry in terms of the four factors of production, available land and raw materials, available labour and skills, available capital, available enterprise; but this time they must add the crucial factor of available markets. What importance each of these factors has will depend first on the particular industry and the mix of factors involved in its processes. Obviously mining can only occur where mineral deposits exist. Agricultural production is tied to suitable soils and climate, although glass, heat, ultra-violet light and soil-less culture can simulate these conditions at a cost. Forestry and fishing are similarly tied, although the possibilities of fish husbandry in place of fish hunting are now being explored. Industries, moreover, which use great quantities of raw material – coal, iron ore, bauxite, timber, limestone – or need great quantities of water or electricity will tend to be placed near where these are to be found. Such considerations certainly explain the original siting we described earlier of British industry on the coalfields and associated iron ore deposits of the Midlands, Yorkshire, Lancashire, South Wales, Durham and Scotland. More modern examples are the coal-fired power stations built all along the River Trent, on account of their need for water and the proximity of the Trent to Britain's most productive coalfields, or the aluminium plant using cheap hydro-electric power and the paper mill using local timber, both at Fort William in Scotland.

As transport costs are reduced, and in Britain's case as high quality and easily accessible minerals – coal, iron, copper, tin – are used up, it is the relative transport costs of the different factors and of delivering the product to the market that become important. The key economic principle here is that of the value-to-bulk or value-to-weight ratio. The value of iron ore per ton is very much less than the value of steel per ton; so it is likely that transport costs will be least if the material is

[12] A good American study of industrial location will be found in E.M.Hoover, *The Location of Economic Activity*, 1963.

refined as much as possible near to where the mineral is found. Giant bulk ore carriers have tended, however, in recent years to reduce sea transport costs so much that steel plants sited on deep water coastlines anywhere in the world may be little more costly in operation than plants sited by the ore mines. Available labour with the appropriate skills, available capital and local markets thus became the governing considerations. There may be other reasons why transport costs should suggest the siting of plants near to the market. Many modern products are themselves very bulky, being in fact rather large and complicated metal boxes – washing machines, refrigerators, dishwashers – where the bulk-to-value ratio may be higher than the components that they are made up of.

When speaking earlier of the growth of London's population in relation to the rest of Britain, we met the economic principle of cumulative causation – the more it grows, the more it goes on growing. This has led in Britain to a steady drift of industry to the south-east where the most concentrated and most affluent market lies. There were 2½ million more people employed in Britain in 1966 than in 1951; 1½ million extra in the south-east, no more men employed in Scotland, Wales and the north, and only 20,000 more each in Yorkshire and the north-west. The same process is taking place inside the European COMMON MARKET in the concentration of industry on the lower reaches of the Rhine. Other areas have been left with higher than average rates of unemployment, as industries based on coal or local materials have declined. Government measures to encourage industry to these declining areas have been designed, firstly, to make use of unemployed reserves of labour, which have proved their unwillingness to move, and secondly, to ease the congestion and excess pressure on resources in the growth areas.

Apart from such artificial stimulation that governments may provide, there are forces at work to reverse the recent trends. Nuclear power stations, steel mills, oil refineries all need today to be sited on the coast near to deep water. Modern science-based industries involve, as we have seen, a whole complex of processes in which by-products of chemicals, heat, steam and energy are integrated together. The emphasis of the 1969 Hunt Committee Report on *The Intermediate*

Areas, concerning the need to encourage zones of economic growth, points in the same direction. One of the limits to the regional integration of processes has been the pricing policy adopted in Britain and elsewhere by the steel, coal and electricity generating industries, whereby their products are sold at the same price both next door to the producing plant and three or four hundred miles away. In this way the north of England, where such heavy industry is mainly situated, has in effect been SUBSIDIZING the transport costs of the south.

Artificial pricing policies and government subsidies are only some of the many restrictions on that free movement of goods and capital and labour which economists have always regarded as a main requirement for their most efficient use. National markets for example are surrounded by TARIFFS and other PROTECTIONIST devices. Under the General Agreement on Tariffs and Trade most countries have agreed not to raise these and to try to lower them; but no underdeveloped country can export to establish its INFANT INDUSTRIES without some protection. The movement of goods is almost wholly free today inside the European Common Market, but the Market itself is surrounded by an external tariff on industrial goods and a system of LEVIES on agricultural imports.

Mobility of labour is restricted by housing problems inside national frontiers and by differences of language and custom outside. Enterprise is perhaps even more restricted in its movement by the preference of entrepreneurs and managers, and in particular of their wives and families, for places where they may enjoy the cultural life to which they are accustomed. Capital is undoubtedly the most mobile factor. United States exports and imports of capital are to be measured in four to five thousands of millions of dollars a year; those into and out of Britain are of the order of four to five hundreds of millions of pounds, almost a quarter of the total industrial investment inside Britain. Capital movements are none the less restricted both by government EXCHANGE CONTROLS and by fears of investors for the security of their capital. International movements of capital today consist increasingly of cross-investments between the advanced industrial nations, and are concentrated in the hands of a few giant firms whose operations we shall examine in Chapter 5. The flow of capital from the developed into the underdeveloped lands is small and partly offset by the large return flow of debt payments on past investments.

We are brought back again to that central concept of economics, the principle of cumulative causation. Wealth attracts and poverty repels, 'To him that hath shall be given; from him that hath not shall be taken away even that which he hath'. One aspect of this principle is referred to by economists as EXTERNAL ECONOMIES, that is to say those which occur as the result of changes in scale or location of operation *outside* a particular firm. The examples drawn from the Manchester textile processes, the Sheffield cutlery trades and the future zones of growth in Britain all illustrate the possibility of such external economies. Their achievement provides an important reason for government planning, as we shall see later. For governments can take into account diseconomies *and* economies for the whole of society – social costs and benefits as they are now called – in a way that no individual firm can do in its own accounting. We shall return to this question in the last chapter.[13]

[13] A popular introductory book which students could read at this stage is J. L. Sampedro's *Decisive Forces in World Economics*, 1967.

E

4 The Market Economy – I
Wants and Incomes

SUMMARY

In this chapter and the next the economists' model of a market economy is critically examined. According to this model it is the result of movements of prices in the various markets for the factors of production and for goods and services that existing resources are used in the most efficient way to meet consumers' wants. Such a model is based on certain assumptions about income distribution and free competition which are criticized. In this chapter attention is concentrated on the influences affecting demand in the market – information and advertising, money and CREDIT and the distribution of income between persons and between factors of production – rent, profits, salaries, wages. Illustrations are taken from recent movements of incomes in Britain. The conclusion is drawn that the market not only fails to anticipate future demands but inevitably responds to the pull of those with most money. Income distribution cannot then merely be seen as determined by labour demand and supply in the market but must be seen as emerging from a bargain between owners of the means of work and workers. The inequalities which arise from this bargain, although corrected by state taxation and full employment, are always being recreated by the pull of money in the market. It is further suggested that they may perhaps be worsened in future by increasing automation.

It is in order to understand, and so learn how to influence, economic events, that economists construct models. As we saw in Chapter 2 this means that they isolate certain relationships that seem to them important. Then by assuming that certain factors are given (in the same way we often use the Latin word for 'given' which is 'data'), they study the relations of the several variables and particularly those of price and quantity. Thus, the market is regarded by the economizing type of economists as the essential model of economic activity.

Consumers' wants are given and with them the distribution of income which makes these wants effective. Given also are the total of available resources and the current state of technological progress. The market model is, therefore, a static model in the sense that it is concerned with the way that resources are allocated as things are. Such a model is also stable in the sense of tending to a position of balance or equilibrium. Attention is concentrated on the behaviour of consumers (persons and organizations) and producers (firms and industries) in the market. This kind of model is often referred to as the subject of MICRO-ECONOMICS – economics in the small. Models of the way whole economies change, as resources grow and the state of technology advances, are referred to as the subject of MACRO-ECONOMICS – economics in the large. We shall deal with this in Chapter 6. We must now consider what economists mean by a market.[1]

1. WHAT THE MARKET DOES

A market is first of all a place – an open or covered space – where men and women come to buy and sell. To produce for the market, however, is the way we speak whenever goods are produced for exchange either by BARTER or sale, as opposed to producing them for oneself or to order. Where families produce largely for their own needs economists speak of a subsistence economy. Today, a few goods are still made to order – bespoke tailoring, specialized machinery, what is sometimes called ONE-OFF production. The overwhelming majority of goods in an advanced market economy are produced 'on spec', as we might say, in the hope of a sale. In planned economies once again a wide range of goods are produced to order, although the role of the market is being reintroduced in Russia and elsewhere in Eastern Europe.

Producing for the market is inevitably an uncertain business. No one may want to buy some of the things that have been brought to market at a price which covers the cost of production. At the end of the day in a market place it is often possible to find perishable goods at give-away prices. Similarly

---

[1] Students can start from any economics textbook, but the first part of R. G. Lipsey's book *An Introduction to Positive Economics* is recommended.

shops closing down may have grand clearance sales. By contrast other goods will sell like hot cakes and a late shopper
may find that the price of a successful new line has actually
gone up. All this is simply to say what is a common experience,
and the basis of much economic analysis, as we saw earlier,
that prices in a market economy are determined by supply and
demand in the market. We can find the same principle at work
not only in markets for goods, but in auctions for land and
houses, in the stock market for capital and in the labour
market.

Producers of goods for the market have to work on past
experience in deciding what goods to bring to the market, how
much and at what price to sell. They will set their prices to
cover their costs plus what they think the market will bear. Of
course, most will sell through shop-keepers who will add their
own percentage MARK-UP. Their success or failure in disposing
of particular lines at profitable or unprofitable prices will
determine their future actions. They will switch their efforts
as far as they can out of the unprofitable and into the profitable lines of production. In this way, as the market economists claim, the market not only fixes prices but also allocates
resources to meet people's wants. The price indicators in the
market are all the time flashing their warning and 'go' signs
which reflect consumer demand. These assure what the
'economizers' claim to be the most efficient use of resources;
since there are not only markets for goods but also for each of
the factors of production – land, labour and capital.

Shoppers will make their purchases with an eye to the price
of alternative products, substituting this for that, so that they
feel they are getting equal satisfaction from the last shilling
spent on each group of products; and they could not do
better with any alternative mix at ruling prices. Similarly,
producers combine the factors of production according to the
price of each, so that they couldn't do better with a different
combination. If wages rise relative to interest rates, they will
try to substitute new capital equipment for labour and vice
versa. We noted in Chapter 2 that different time scales are
important here. Alfred Marshall distinguished three time
scales (a) the MARKET PERIOD; (b) the short run and (c) the
long run. In the market period goods have been produced and

the quantities available for sale are fixed, although stocks may be called upon or built up if the goods are not perishable; in the short run existing plant can be worked up to full capacity; and finally in the long run new plant with new combinations of production factors may be introduced. Thus the market not only sets today's prices but indicates the line of future investment and in theory ensures thereby that what is produced is what people want.

When we looked at the economists' concept of economizing in Chapter 2, we had to reveal certain assumptions about human behaviour that were being made. Now that we are looking at the market we have to reveal certain assumptions about economic relations that are being made, before we can conclude that the market ensures that people's wants are being met in the most efficient way. This may best be done by spelling out the several assumed steps that exist between the starting point of people's WANTS and the production of FINISHED GOODS and services to meet them. The assumptions are as follows, first from the side of demand and then from the side of supply:

(1) *On the demand side*

(*a*) People's wants are given and they are aware of their preferences in case of a scarcity of resources;

(*b*) people are informed on market availabilities and prices;

(*c*) they have money to turn their wants into EFFECTIVE DEMAND;

(*d*) incomes are distributed according to the contribution different people make in production of goods and services and to the market price put on this contribution;

(2) *On the supply side*

(*e*) No barriers exist to competition between suppliers or producers and there are many of them, so that prices move freely to relate supply and demand;

(*f*) suppliers' profits move directly in relation to prices: high prices compared with costs creating high unit profits; low prices creating low profits or losses;

(*g*) capital moves to where profits are highest;

(*h*) labour follows capital;

(*i*) enterprises combine the labour and capital to produce the most profitable goods and services, which by definition are the ones people want.

We can take each of these steps in turn and examine the assumptions lying behind the working of the market economy both at earlier periods of time and today. In this way we shall see both how the market worked and how far the assumptions still apply. In this chapter we shall deal with wants and incomes from the demand side; in the next with prices and profits on the supply side.

2. WANTS AND PREFERENCES

Economists are bound to assume that people know what they want and can express their preferences rationally. But we all know that we often behave irrationally and that no housewife carries around a carefully constructed SCALE OF PREFERENCES in her handbag. The problem of consumer preference is not so difficult when wants are fairly simple and related to the basic necessities of food, clothing and shelter. It becomes much more difficult when the economizers' assumption of scarcity is removed. Then the urgency of wants is reduced and consumers find that they have what is called DISCRETIONARY INCOME, to be spent on a whole variety of different goods and services.

The concept of 'given' wants is made much more dubious by the development of advertising. The claim of advertisers is that they reveal to us what we really wanted all along. The 1968 Ford Capri is the car 'you always promised yourself'. The economic impact of advertising is not primarily that choices are presented between rival brands of similar products – of toothpaste, cigarettes, detergent, chocolates. It lies in the attempt to attract discretionary income to a whole area of consumption – 'Beer is Best', 'Go to work on an egg', 'Join the Tea Set', 'Are you under-insured?', 'Own your own house', 'Invest in a second car', are all examples of such appeals.

It is evident that wants are being created by this kind of advertising. Producers have already decided what to produce and are setting out to persuade consumers to buy. As the American economist J. K. Galbraith has pointed out,[2] the

[2] In his book *The New Industrial State*, 1967.

production of a new model of a motor-car today requires many years of planning, including design, research into new techniques, purchases of raw materials, setting up of new plant and a huge investment of capital before the final product appears in the showrooms. If the whole operation is to be profitable, tens of thousands and even millions of each model must be sold to spread the high fixed costs over many units. So you have to be persuaded that it is indeed the car you always promised yourself.

The title of this book refers to four categories in economics. One of these is the consumer, and consumer sovereignty is the most cherished belief of many economists. The market assures it, they claim, through the working of supply and demand, but if the demand curves of the consumer are themselves influenced by the supply curves of the producer, it is meaningless to begin with 'given' wants. We can still concede that the urgency of 'keeping up with the Joneses' may be felt just as strongly as physical hunger and thirst and cold. What critics of the market economy claim is that the whole growth path of the economy comes to be determined by the largest producers, but more of that in a moment. We shall have to return later also to the whole question of individual and social welfare in economics.

3. INFORMATION AND KNOWLEDGE

Consumers in the market are assumed by economists to have full information about availabilities and prices. Many municipal markets in big towns have very large numbers of competing suppliers of different products under one roof. Shops selling the same product, moreover, congregate in one street or part of a town. A new supplier will tend to set up shop next to an existing one because shoppers are accustomed to going there for a particular product. Wholesale markets and complex markets like the Stock Exchange and Lloyds have a whole battery of notice boards and signs and other systems for revealing the prices of different QUOTATIONS at any time. Advertisers claim that their main contribution to social welfare is the information they provide about what is available. Consumers have nevertheless found it necessary to establish associations for testing and reporting on the efficiency, safety and value for money of the many products in the market. Governments have increasingly been expected to lay down standards of safety, of measurement, and accuracy of description and even of profit margins. With all this information the discerning consumer is increasingly well protected against misinformation and deception.

Consumers can therefore get to know, if they wish, what is available in the market and at what prices. What they cannot know is what is not available but might be available and at what cost. The hoary examples of the long-life lamp bulb and the everlasting razor blade will spring to mind, although in both cases recent government investigation have gone a long way towards making these available. What is much more important is the future range of available goods and the possibilities of public provision. Governments from time to time reveal the estimated costs of an expansion of the public services in various directions. A clear picture of an alternative mix of goods and services, public and private, which would be technically feasible at different levels of national income has not, however, been presented by any government, not even by those which have largely replaced the market by a planned economy. Until the advent of computers, this would have been an impossible picture to present. Today it would be difficult but not impossible, and new systems of consumer choice and democratic control of the economy may be opening up.

Freedom of choice for consumers has recently been put forward by one group of economists belonging to The Institute of Economic Affairs[3] as requiring primarily that public spending on behalf of individuals, e.g. on housing, education and medical services, should be reduced and people should be left with the money to spend as they wish. Critics of this view like Richard Titmuss[4] are concerned with the special needs of the poor and with protecting children from the vagaries of their parents. We shall consider the problem of increasing inequalities in a moment. Others like E. J. Mishan[5] have concentrated on the

[3] See A. Seldon, 'Which Way to Welfare?', *Lloyds Bank Review*, October 1966.
[4] See *Choice and the Welfare State*, Fabian Society Tract No. 370.
[5] In *The Costs of Economic Growth*, 1967.

'indivisibility' of many public services like roads and parks (only the very rich can own their own, others must share) and on the external diseconomies of such a form of free choice (congestion, noise and stench on the roads for example). We shall return to this problem at the end of the chapter. What must be stated here is that freedom of choice involves knowledge not only of what is available on the market at what price but what could be made available.[6]

4. MONEY AND EFFECTIVE DEMAND

We need money in a market economy to make our wants effective. We reckon value in money terms. Of course we all speak of certain things that money could not buy, but most goods and services may be bought for money in the market. Shakespeare was only one in a long line of those who have inveighed against the cash nexus, the corruption by money of natural human relationships:

> That daily break vow; he that wins of all. . . .
> That smooth faced gentleman, tickling commodity,
> Commodity, the bias of the world. *(King John,* Act II.)

Although we now say that everything has its price, we also draw a distinction in our minds between money value and real value. 'It's really worth much more,' we say of a handmade product which we know to have been a labour of love but may not appear as much superior to the machine job. In speaking like this we confirm Marx's distinction between USE VALUE and EXCHANGE VALUE. Use value he thought of as satisfying a want but determined by the actual labour incorporated in production, and exchange value as the market value and therefore the abstract proportion of all a society's labour that need goes into production at the reigning level of technology – what he called 'socially necessary labour time'. We shall come back to this point in the last chapter but what we must notice now is that in the last resort a commodity must have use value in order to have exchange value. It must seem to be to what we call 'worth it'.

[6] An extremely lucid introduction to this subject may be found in G. B. Richardson's *Information and Investment*, 1960.

The role of money is always said by economists[7] to be threefold:

(*a*) Money is a measure of value, that is, we can now say, a measure of relative exchange values or prices. For this purpose it needs to be simply understood and easily divisible. Hence Britain's transition to decimal coinage.

(*b*) Money is a medium of exchange, whether in the form of coins, paper notes, cheques or BILLS OF EXCHANGE. For this purpose it needs to be both available and reliable. Obviously these are conflicting requirements. We shall consider later, especially in relation to the various countries' currencies, which make up the world's money, how the more of a currency is available the less people may rely on its preserving its current value. If every time it rained it rained pennies from heaven their value would soon DEPRECIATE.

(*c*) Money provides a store of value in the sense of a store of purchasing power. For this purpose money has either to consist of a very durable material like gold and other metals or take the form of a paper claim that can be relied on. For it to be what the economists call LIQUID MONEY, it must be in the form of easily realizable financial claims that can be turned into money.

Money as a store of value is important, first, because such a store makes possible the payment of wages, required in the process of production, in advance of receipts from the sale of any products. Secondly, the aim of making money provides a crucial incentive in a market economy. As Marx put it, while most of us sell our COMMODITIES including our labour power for money to buy other commodities with – this he called Commodity-Money-Commodity (C-M-C) – capitalists, on the other hand, who are the owners of a store of money, buy commodities including our labour power for the express purposes of making more money (M-C-M). We shall come back to examining this notion as the driving force of capitalist economic growth. Here we need to notice only that people may come to the market with small sums of money for immediate purchases or with a store of money for long-term purchases.

In addition, we must remember that it is possible to borrow from other people's long-term store for our own current

[7] A good first book on money is Alan Day's *Economics of Money*, 1959.

purchases. The money supply today consists as much of credit as
of cash. About £3,000 million of notes and coin are circulating
with the British public. Bank loans to persons total about
£2,000 million and HIRE PURCHASE, credit another £1,000
million. This figure of £6,000 millions of cash and credit may
be compared with annual private consumers' expenditure of
about £26,000 millions. Although Hire Purchase credit outstanding has gone up and down in recent years, it has been
fluctuating around the £1,000 million mark while the banks'
personal loans by contrast have more than doubled in ten
years. Bank loans to the PUBLIC SECTOR and to companies
in fact trebled between 1958 and 1968, while currency in
circulation rose by only 50 per cent. It is this increase in
credit that has led governments to attempt to bring money
supply under control, a problem which we shall consider in a
later chapter; but for the moment its importance lies in the
effect it has on the pull of demand in the market. Thus we have
people coming to the market with money for current purchases, with a long-term store of money behind them and also
with borrowed money or credit. There are also major
inequalities in the incomes people have.

We saw in Chapter 2 (Fig. 2.10) the factor distribution of
incomes – that is, wages and salaries from employment, pensions and social security payments, incomes from self-employment and incomes from rent, dividends and interest. The
money gets into hands that spend it in very different ways. We
also saw something of the resulting distribution of incomes between different persons. It would be interesting to know how
these two combine to give us a picture of income groups and
income distribution such as is attempted in Table IV.1. This
can only be a very broad estimate for two reasons connected
with the way the statistics are collected for tax purposes:

(a) The INLAND REVENUE does not show how the income is
made up of those who have income from several sources – from
salaries or self-employment, and rent, dividend and interest;

(b) the Inland Revenue divides people into INCOME UNITS
and counts as one unit equally a man and wife, a widow, or a
child with a private income.[8]

---

[8] A detailed study of the difficulties resulting from these practices may be
found in R. M. Titmuss, *Income Distribution and Social Change*, 1962.

Table IV.1

Estimated Income Groups and Income Distribution UK 1963

Group	Numbers (Millions)	Percentage of Income Receivers	Percentage of Pre-Tax Incomes Received	Approx. Average Incomes p.a. £s
Self Employed	1	3	10	2,000
Employers	0·5	1·5	10 as RDI (²)	3,000
Managers	1·5	4·5		
Tech. and Admin.	1·5	4·5	28 as	1,500
Clerical	2	6·0	Salaries	1,000
Non Wage Earners	6·5	19·5	48	1,750
Wage Earners in				
Manufacturing	6	17		850
Other Industry	2·5	7		600
Mining and Agriculture	1·5	4·5	45	500
Distribution, etc.	9·5	27	—	500
Armed Forces	0·5	1		700
All Wage Earners	20	56·5	45	600
Pensioners and Unemployed	8·5	24	7	250
TOTAL of Above (¹)	35	100	100	750

Notes:

1. Dependents, both children and women not at work or of pension-able age, make up the total to 52 millions.

2. RDI = Rent, Dividend and Interest.

Sources: MBB, Estimates from many sources.

Although it seems absurd to speak of scarcity in our affluent society, we nearly all have wants beyond what we can afford. Moreover, a large minority of the population even of Britain lives in poverty. This may be regarded as relative poverty compared, say, with that in India; but it means that perhaps

8 million people and their children in Britain live at or below the SOCIAL SECURITY STANDARD. This standard is the equivalent of about 45 per cent of the national average wage in industry; the pre-war public assistance standard was 60 per cent of the average wage then. This bottom fifth of the population share perhaps 7 per cent of all pre-tax incomes. At the other extreme the top fifth of the people – employers, managers and professional men and their children – share something over 40 per cent of the pre-tax income. That leaves about half the income for the remaining 70 per cent in the middle. Such an unequal distribution of income has an important influence on effective demand. It is money that exercises pull in the market not people. Even after taking taxation into account and remembering that these figures are for income units and exclude CAPITAL GAINS, we can see from Table IV.2 that the top third of income-receivers probably have as much pull on the market as the bottom two thirds. What is the effect of this?

Table IV.2

Shares of Personal Income Before and After Tax UK 1938–66

Percentile Groups	1938		1949		1957		1966	
	Before	After	Before	After	Before	After	Before	After
Top 1 per cent (including Benefits)	16·2	11·7	11·2	6·5	8·0	4·9	7·6	5·1
	19·5	15·2	18·5	10·5	15·0	9·1	—	—
Next 9 per cent	21·8	21·9	21·8	20·4	20·0	18·6	20·6	19·7
Top 10 per cent	38·0	33·6	33·0	26·9	28·0	23·5	28·2	24·8
2nd 10 per cent	12·0	12·8	14·5	15·4	13·5	14·5	14·5	14·8
Top 20 per cent	50·0	46·4	47·5	42·3	41·5	38·0	42·7	39·6
Lower 80 per cent	50·0	53·6	52·5	57·7	58·5	62·0	59·3	60·4
Bottom 30 per cent	—	—	12·7	14·6	11·3	13·4	1·04	11·9

Note: The figures 'including Benefits' derive from an attempt to take account of capital gains, insurance, superannuation, etc., but do not take account of expenses. See H. F. Lydall, *Royal Statistical Society Journal*, Part I, 1959.

Sources: H. F. Lydall as above for 1938–57; *National Income Expenditure* Blue Book for 1966, and R. J. Nicolson *Lloyds Bank Review*, January 1967, for the last line.

When we looked at income demand elasticities in Chapter 2, we saw that as income rose some items took a smaller and smaller share of the household budget – bread and many other basic foods, for example, and fuel and light. When an item takes such a small part of the total budget a large change in price will have little effect on the quantity sold. Thus where this is true for an important part of the population it may be possible for suppliers to push up the price of such items if they have a MONOPOLISTIC POSITION, which is something we shall examine in the next chapter. For the items where demand is more elastic, by contrast, prices will have to be kept down. We can show that this is in fact what has happened in the last ten years or so. The prices of those goods which make up the larger proportion of low income household budgets – food, housing, fuel and light – have risen faster than the prices of those goods making up the larger proportion of high income household budgets – cars and clothes and household goods. The result is to exaggerate inequalities: the cost of an average pensioner's weekly budget has risen much faster than that of a household with £40 a week or more to spend. We can see from Table IV.3 that the percentage increase over the years 1956–67 was 50 per cent for the lower income groups, only 30 per cent for the higher.

Some students will notice in Table IV.3 that the items on which prices have risen fastest are those provided mainly by public authorities or nationalized industries. In fairness to the public sector it has to be pointed out that private house rents were decontrolled during this period; that the pit-head price of coal rose by only 27 per cent, while wholesale coal prices rose by 50 per cent and retail coal prices by 80 per cent; and that INTEREST RATES, which affected especially the public services requiring large sums of borrowed capital, rose during the period from 4 per cent to 7 per cent. The effect on the market of both public and private monopolies will be examined further in the next chapter, but we must now consider how through the different elasticities of demand the proportion of income spent on different commodities itself influences prices, wherever these can be fixed by the producer.

We all know of different shops in a town in the same line of business but selling in rather different price ranges; one may

Table IV.3
Prices and Incomes of U.K. Households 1956–67

	A. Distribution of Expenditure in 1967 for Household Budgets by Income (%)			Price Increases 1956–67
	Low Income Under £10	Medium Income £20–25	High Income Over £40	1956 = 100
1. Low Income: Larger Proportion of Expenditure				
Food	38	30	16	134
of which				
Bread and Cereals	6	5	2	148
Housing	18	10·5	7	188
Fuel and Light	14	6	3	164
Public Transport	3	2·5	4	180
2. Middle Income: Larger Proportion of Expenditure				
Alcohol	2·5	3·5	3·5	135
Tobacco	5	6·5	5	150
Recreational Goods ('Other')	0·5	7	6·5	145
3. High Income: Larger Proportion of Expenditure				
Clothing and Footwear	7	8	10	120
Durable Household Goods (excl. cars)	3	5·5	6·5	111
Cars and Vehicle Running Costs	1	9	13·5	120
Services	7	8	12	165
4. Other Payments				
Taxes (on Income and N.I.)	1·5	11·5	20·5	(165)
Saving	2·5	4·5	6·5	(190)
B. Incidence of Price Increases by Household Income 1956–67	150	142	130	140

Note: Price increase figures in brackets for Taxes and Savings are real increases over the period.

Source: *Family Expenditure Survey 1967* and *Statistics on Incomes, Prices and Employment.*

operate in the poor east end of the town on a smaller MARGIN
OF PROFIT and high TURNOVER, while another selling in the
rich west end of the town works on a higher margin and smaller
turnover. The difference can be illustrated by the two graphs
we used earlier to show the different elasticities of demand
where goods form a large or small, essential or inessential, part
of household budgets.

From the graphs in Fig 4.1 we can see that in the case of Commodity 'A', where demand is inelastic, the total receipts from
sales at £5 a unit (5 × 2 = 10) are greater than at £1 a unit
(1 × 4 = 4); by contrast, in the case of Commodity 'B', where
demand is elastic, total receipts are greater at £1 a unit (1 × 9)
than at £5 a unit (5 × 1). This does not prove that it will be
more profitable to sell 'A' at £5 rather than at £1 and 'B' at
£1 rather than at £5, but it suggests the possibility.

This effect of income distribution on market demand and on
the variety of goods produced can be seen in another way. If
we imagine a community with roughly equal household incomes, we should expect to find that the cars produced, for
example, would be in the same price range with small variations in design for size of family and for age and interest of the
owner. The more unequal the incomes, the wider the price
range and the variations in design. The pull of the richer end
of the market will tend to encourage the differentiation of
models at the expense of a cheaper more standardized car.
With a moderately unequal distribution of incomes, manufacturers have to decide whether they will sell a large number
of cars at a low price or a smaller number at a high price. One
can distinguish further the short runs of expensive models for
a specialized market (as for sports cars) and the long runs of
cheaper models for the general market (as for minis.).

5. INCOME DISTRIBUTION

The influences of income distribution on effective demand have
just been shown to be considerable. We have now to examine
what determines that incomes should be distributed in a particular way. The economizing economists argue that, since
incomes are in effect the price of labour, income distribution
is only a special case of price theory – that is of the forces of

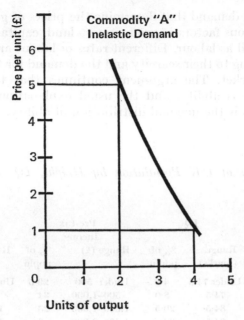

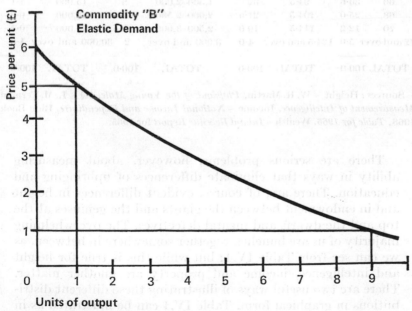

Figure 4.1. Elasticities of demand and total receipts

supply and demand that determine the prices of goods and of all the various factors of production – land, capital and enterprise as well as labour. Different rates of labour are then paid for according to their scarcity and the demand for them on the labour market. The argument continues that the scarcest commodity is ability, and the usual explanation of income inequalities is the unequal distribution of ability.

Table IV.4

Distribution of UK Population by Height, IQ, Income and Wealth

Height of Persons		IQ		Pre-tax Income		Wealth (Net Worth)	
Range (inches)	% of popln	Range (marks)	% of popln	Range (£)	% of popln	Range (£)	% of popln
Under 62	1·6	Under 74·5	4·0	Under 500	29·5	Under 5,000	85·6
62	6·4	74·5	8·0	500–1,000	34	5,000	8·2
64	19·2	84·5	20·5	1,000–1,500	23	10.000	2·5
66	30·6	94·5	32	1,500–2,000	8	15,000	1·1
68	25·0	104·5	21·5	2,000–2,500	2	20,000	0·6
70	12·2	114·5	10·0	2,500–3,000	1·5	25,000	0·4
72 and over	5·0	124·5 and over	4·0	3,000 and over	2	30,000 and over	1·6
TOTAL	100·0	TOTAL	100·0	TOTAL	100·0	TOTAL	100·0

Sources: Height – W. R. Martin, *Physique of the Young Male.* IQ – L. M. Terman, *Measurement of Intelligence.* Income – *National Income and Expenditure,* Blue Book, 1968, *Table for 1966.* Wealth – *Inland Revenue Report* for 1965.

There are serious problems, however, about measuring ability in ways that eliminate differences of upbringing and education. There are, of course, evident differences in height and in endowment between the giants and the geniuses at the top and the dwarfs and mental defectives. The overwhelming majority of us are bunched together somewhere in between, as we can see from Table IV.4; but while this is true for height and intelligence, income and property are another matter. There are two useful ways of illustrating these different distributions in graphical form. Table IV.4 can be illustrated as in Fig. 4.2 by marking off the frequency of different ranges of

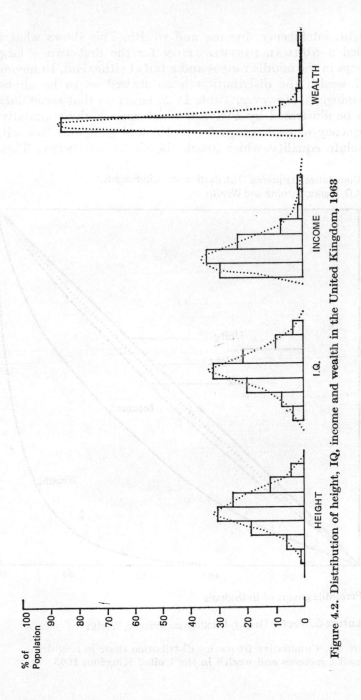

Figure 4.2. Distribution of height, IQ, income and wealth in the United Kingdom, 1963

height, intelligence, income and wealth. This shows what is called a NORMAL DISTRIBUTION for the first two – large groups in the middle ranges and a tail at either end. In income and wealth the distribution is so skewed as to be almost meaningless. However, Table IV.5, based on that same data, can be illustrated by Fig. 4.3, which records the cumulative frequency of each range by tenths and compares this with absolute equality which would be shown as UNITY. These

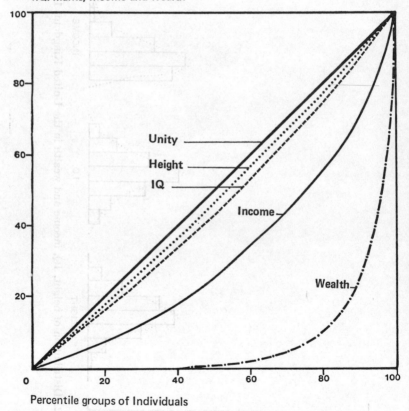

Cumulative Frequence Distribution share in Heights,
I.Q. marks, Income and Wealth

Percentile groups of Individuals

Lorenz Curves for Height, Intelligence, Income, Wealth

Figure 4.3. Cumulative frequency distribution share in heights, IQ marks, incomes and wealth in the United Kingdom 1965

curves are called LORENZ CURVES; the flatter they are, the more equal the distribution.

Table IV.5

Distribution of UK Population in Percentile Groups to show shares in Height, IQ, Income and Wealth

Tenth Groups for each Separate Characteristic	Height Share		IQ Share		Income Share		Wealth (Net Worth) Share	
	%	Cum.	%	Cum.	%	Cum.	%	Cum.
Top 10%	10·7	100	12.2	100	30	100	75	100
Second Tenth	10·5	89·3	11·4	87·8	12	70	15·6	25
Third	10·3	78·8	10·9	76·4	11	58	5·7	9·4
Fourth	10·1	68·5	10·5	65·5	11	47	2·4	3·7
Fifth	10	58·4	10·3	55	10	36	1·0	1·3
Sixth	10	48·4	10	44·7	8	26	0·3	0·3
Seventh	9·9	38·4	9·9	34·7	6	18	0	0
Eighth	9·7	28·5	9·2	24·8	5	12	0	0
Ninth	9·5	18·8	8·3	15·6	4	7	0	0
Bottom Tenth	9·3	9·3	7·3	7·3	3	3	0	0
TOTAL AND MEDIAN	100	48·4	100	44·7	100	26	100	0·3
MEAN (in inches, IQ marks and £s)	67½"		100		£685		£1,100	
Range	48"–81"		55–145		£50–£20,000+		£1–£5,000+	

Notes: Wealth = Positive Net Worth = Difference between assets and liabilities but excluding household and general goods and insurance policies.

Negative net worth is not shown but affected 13 per cent of population while another 21 per cent had no net worth.

Cum. = Cumulative frequency.

There would seem to be little ground here for attributing to innate ability the great differences in income, still less in property ownership. There is at the same time much evidence to suggest that differences in upbringing and environment are curcial in determining educational attainments. Despite the great increase in the size of universities it is as true today as it was in the pre-war years that only a quarter of undergraduates come from the homes of manual workers. Yet manual workers make up three-quarters of the population.[9] Inequalities in educational opportunity probably remain the main cause of unequal earnings, but the failure of professional and clerical workers' earnings to rise as fast in the last thirty years as manual workers, earnings have, suggests that the narrow spread in advantages of educational opportunity are being widened. Table IV.6 provides evidence of this, but shows also how greatly the managers and administrators have advanced their position.

Table IV.6

Occupational Distribution of Men UK 1911–60 and Relative Earnings and Growth of Earnings

Group	Occupational Class	Nos. % of Total 1911	Income % of Av. 1913–4	Nos. % of Total 1931	Income % of Av. 1935–6	Nos. % of Total 1951	Income % of Av. 1960	Nos. % of Total 1959	Growth 1911 to 1959 (1911 = 100) Nos.	Income
1	Employers and Proprietors	6·7	—	6·7	—	5·0	—	—	—	—
	(without employees)	(2·5)	—	(3·0)	—	(2·9)	—	—	—	—
	Managers and Admin.	3·4	218	3·7	236	5·5	228	—	925	—
	Sub-Total 1	10·14	—	10·36	—	10·5	—	10·06	131	—
2	Professional –									
	Higher	1·0	365	1·1	344	1·9	250	2·26	297	620
	Lower	3·0	172	3·5	166	4·7	105	5·5	238	546
	Sub-Total 2	4·0	—	4·6	—	6·6	—	7·8	252	—
3	Clerical	4·8	110	7·0	103	10·7	84	12·0	327	689
4	Foremen/Supervisors	1·3	126	1·5	145	2·6	125	2·5	272	898
5	Skilled Manual	30·6	110	26·7	105	24·9	99	24·6	106	804
6	Semi-skilled Manual	39·5	76	35·0	72	32·6	72	31·3	104	842
7	Unskilled Manual	9·6	70	14·8	69	12·0	66	11·6	159	849
	Sub-Total 4–7	80·97	—	78·07	—	72·19	—	70·16	—	—
	TOTAL	100	100	100	100	100	100	100	132	874
	in million persons or £s average income	18·35	92	21·03	185	22·5	808	24·2	—	—

Sources: Guy Routh, *Occupation and Pay in Great Britain* Tables 1, 2 and 47, 48,.

[9] The evidence is summarized by Mrs Lerner in *The UK Economy: A Manual of Applied Economics*, edited by A. R. Prest, 1968.

Given the differences in educational opportunity we shall
need to bear in mind the social effects that follow from different
types of education. It has been shown by Anthony Sampson[10]
that a high proportion of Britain's bankers and top civil servants were educated at a handful of public schools and then
at Oxford and Cambridge. Barbara Wootton[11] has questioned
many of the assumptions of the economists' theory of wages.
Custom and convention seem to count for far more than considerations of economic return in the relative rates paid in
different occupations. The very distinctions that are drawn
between wages and salaries, for example, or between manual
and non-manual work, are distinctions of status with little or
no economic or operational justification. Status differentials in
earnings have always been more important criteria in wage
bargaining than economic return. The resulting wage structure
roughly illustrated in Fig. 4.4 could hardly be explained on any
economic grounds.

Now that we are duly warned by Lady Wootton, we can proceed to examine how the economizing economists do explain
wage determination. The demand for labour is determined,
according to those who use the economists' concept of the margin, by the relationship between the cost of taking on an extra
worker or group of workers (marginal labour cost) and the
value of extra output that the extra worker or workers will
provide (marginal net product of labour). A firm will only
take on extra workers if their extra product at least pays for
taking them on. Demand for labour is said to be derived from
demand for the product. An earlier analysis of demand curves
(in Chapter 2) helps us to see that a worker thus faces a
demand curve which is first of all in a certain position according to the demand for his product and secondly of a certain
shape according to the relative costs of labour and of substituting capital (machinery) for other factors of production. Thus we
may describe coal miners in the 1950s and 1960s as facing a
shifting demand for their product and within that a falling
demand for their labour (see Fig. 4.5).

Miners like other workers will also have their supply price.

[10] See *Anatomy of Britain*, 1962.
[11] In *Social Foundations of Wage Policy*, 1955.

Fig. 4.4.

The Wages and Salary Tree in Great Britain in the 1960s

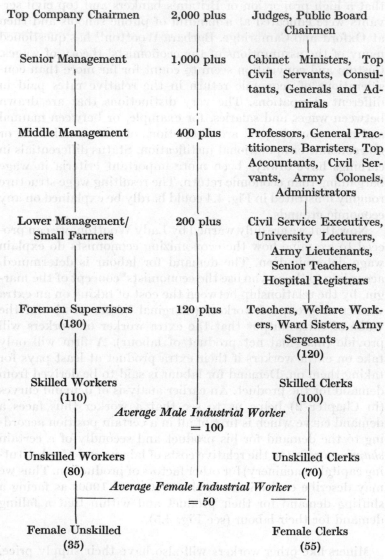

Top Company Chairmen	2,000 plus	Judges, Public Board Chairmen
Senior Management	1,000 plus	Cabinet Ministers, Top Civil Servants, Consultants, Generals and Admirals
Middle Management	400 plus	Professors, General Practitioners, Barristers, Top Accountants, Civil Servants, Army Colonels, Administrators
Lower Management/ Small Farmers	200 plus	Civil Service Executives, University Lecturers, Army Lieutenants, Senior Teachers, Hospital Registrars
Foremen Supervisors (130)	120 plus	Teachers, Welfare Workers, Ward Sisters, Army Sergeants (120)
Skilled Workers (110)		Skilled Clerks (100)
	Average Male Industrial Worker = 100	
Unskilled Workers (80)		Unskilled Clerks (70)
	Average Female Industrial Worker = 50	
Female Unskilled (35)		Female Clerks (55)

Source: D. J. Robertson, *Economies of Wages*, p. 82. Note: The figures are not £s but relatives to the average male industrial worker.

Below a certain wage they will simply move into other industries as they have indeed been doing. The market for labour thus in theory ensures that labour moves where it is most needed, a step in our market assumptions that we shall defer for later consideration. The concepts we have been examining so far, however, provide us at best only with a picture of wage determination within the labour market. Political economists

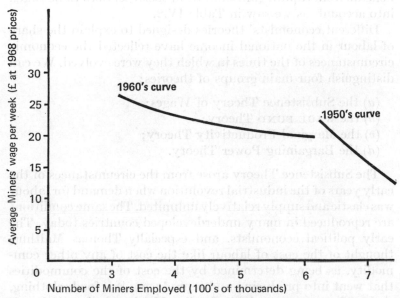

Figure 4.5. Apparent demand for coal miners, United Kingdom, 1950s and 1960s

have always been interested in examining further the relation between the return to the different factors of production and particularly the relation between wages and profits.

6. WAGES IN THE NATIONAL INCOME

It is often pointed out by economists that the share of wages in the national income has remained extraordinarily stable at about 40 per cent. In Britain over the last century wages rose from about 38 per cent of all incomes in 1880 to 42 per cent in 1925, fell off to about 39 per cent in the 1930s and recovered

during and just after the Second World War to about 42 per
cent. This is, however, a very misleading way of speaking
because the proportion of wage earners fell during this period
while the salariat increased (see Table IV.6) and the share of
salaries rose from about 16 per cent to 23 per cent of the total.
Personal incomes are in any case only a part of the benefits
accruing to persons from the national product. There are also
benefits from capital gains and from social services to be taken
into account, as we saw in Table IV.2.

Different economists' theories designed to explain the share
of labour in the national income have reflected the economic
circumstances of the times in which they were evolved. We can
distinguish four main groups of theories:

(a) the Subsistence Theory of Wages;
(b) the WAGE FUND Theory;
(c) the Marginal Productivity Theory;
(d) the Bargaining Power Theory.

The Subsistence Theory arose from the circumstances of the
early years of the industrial revolution when demand for labour
was elastic and supply relatively unlimited. The same conditions
are reproduced in many underdeveloped countries today. The
early political economists, and especially Thomas Malthus,
thought of the cost of labour like the cost of any other commodity, as being determined by the cost of the commodities
that went into producing and reproducing it – food, clothing,
shelter for a man and his family. Malthus believed that if
wages rose above such subsistence then over-population would
in time force them down again. Marx replaced Malthus' views
on population with his own theory of the RESERVE ARMY OF
UNEMPLOYED that was always being created by capital
accumulation and was bound to keep wages down to subsistence level. Marx ran into trouble because he allowed for a
subjective element, a 'historical element' as he called it, over
and above subsistence, that had to include things a man felt
he had a right to at any period of history. Such a subjective
element makes it impossible to regard the supply cost of labour
as a determinant of wages, except in the sense of a basic
minimum below which they cannot go.

What economists would argue today about underdeveloped

countries,[12] is that cheap labour is all that these countries have
to offer on the world market. Any attempt to raise wages will
only lead to the introduction of more machinery. This is not
the same as the Wages Fund Theory which followed the Subsistence Theory, although it is sometimes confused with it.
Early capitalists soon saw that any increase in wages reduced
their funds available for reinvestment and in conditions of
primitive accumulation this led to the Wages Fund Theory.
There was only so much money available for the total wage
bill, they argued. If more was paid out to each worker, fewer
workers could be hired. This argument was easily shown to be
fallacious: (a) output per man could be increased and with it
an increase in wages *and* in capital accumulation could follow,
(b) higher wages and shorter hours were actually found to
increase output per man, (c) the expansion of the market with
higher wages increased the demand for products. In all these
ways total labour costs might be raised but unit labour costs
could be reduced.

The increases in productivity during the nineteenth century
and the elaboration of improved costing systems led to the
development of the Marginal Theory, which we have already
considered. Its weakness we saw was that it left the general
question of the share of capital and labour indeterminate, since
it accounted only for the varying demands of firms for extra
labour and left out of account the supply price of labour itself.
Marx had always insisted that the whole way of speaking of
capital and labour was to confuse the person and the thing –
the labourer and the labour, the capitalist and the capital.
What a man sold on the labour market was his LABOUR
POWER. The actual value of his labour will depend on the
machinery he works with, the hours he works and the skill and
intensity of his work. This distinction was of course central to
Marx's belief that it was out of the actual system of labour
relations that profit emerged; what was denied to the worker
was available for the capitalist. How much went to each was a
matter of bargaining in which Marx believed that the scales
were heavily weighted against the worker.

Trade unions have historically been concerned to keep up

<hr/>

[12] As James Meade does in his *Efficiency, Equality and the Ownership of
Property*, 1964.

the supply price of labour. If they have not raised the share of
wages in the national income, they have perhaps prevented it
from falling. To this end they have used three main means:

(*a*) restricting the supply through imposed limitations on
entry to apprenticeships, the CLOSED SHOP, etc.;

(*b*) bargaining collectively so that bargains forced upon
individual workers do not spoil the market;

(*c*) taking political action to obtain full employment so that
a queue at the gate does not reduce their bargaining power.

It should be noticed here that the introduction of trade
union bargaining into wages theory led to some adaptation of
the theory; but anyone with the least familiarity with trade
unions will know that the status differentials, which Lady
Wootton emphasized, are firmly built into trade union thinking whether it is in the form of craft premia or seniority
ladders, neither of which have much to do with marginal net
product.

In the bargain between trade unions, acting on behalf of
owners of labour power, and managers, acting on behalf of
owners of capital, it has always been argued by the unions that
they start from a weaker position than the capitalists on
several grounds:

(*a*) the worker, even with the aid of trade unions, has only
his labour power to offer on the market; the owner of capital
has labour power and capital;

(*b*) the worker again, even with the aid of trade unions,
cannot hold out for so long as the owner of capital in a strike
or lock-out, because the workers' savings will be used up
sooner;

(*c*) the worker cannot move himself and his family or change
his trade so easily as the owner of capital can move his capital
to another place or industry;

(*d*) the worker cannot, even with the help of trade unions,
know so well as the owners of capital what the exact value is of
his net product or what price his labour power might command
elsewhere.

Aubrey Jones, as Chairman of the Prices and Income Board
has spoken of 'supreme power no longer at the top but at the

bottom' where today 'workers could hold society to ransom'[13] The Donovan Commission, on Trade Unions and Employers Associations, reporting in 1968, took a very grave view of the effect of unofficial strikes, whose growing number it attributed to what it called the 'chaotic' system of collective bargaining procedures at company and plant level. Nevertheless, it made the following statement on the relative power of employer and employee in a contract of employment. 'In practice there is usually no comparison between the consequences for an employer if an employee terminates the contract of employment and those which will ensue for an employee if he is dismissed.'

Much of the bargaining power of labour depends upon the general level of employment and it is the relatively full employment since the war that has evidently improved labour's position. The prospects in the future are however regarded by some economists as less encouraging for labour. On the one hand, much of the advantage of full employment has been offset by INFLATIONARY price increases which have eaten into money wage advances. Some governments, the British among them, have been driven into adopting economic policies which deliberately increase unemployment, with the purpose of checking inflation. On the other hand, the relative contributions of capital and labour are being altered as a result of changes in production processes. With increasing mechanization and automation, large and complex processes can be operated with little or no labour. It is reported, for example, that an oil refinery in the United States today is being run by the owner and his family.

The implications of automation for the distribution of income have been explored by James Meade[14] who starts from the economist's view, which we have already seen, that wages are determined by the marginal net product of labour. An employer will take on an extra worker just so long as the value of the extra production the worker accounts for exceeds the cost of employing him. With increased mechanization, as we saw in Chapter 3, the machine more and more determines the average output per man. Taking on an extra man will make

---

[13] Sidney Ball Memorial Lecture, Oxford, November 1965.
[14] See his book *Efficiency, Equality and the Ownership of Property.*

little difference to total output; so that the value of the marginal net product will be small compared with the value of average output per man. This, as we saw, may be contrasted with pre-mechanized production where each man was equipped with his own tools, in mining for example with a pick and shovel, and an additional man produced much the same as the average.

Now, if the economist's view is accepted that wages are determined by the value of the net product of the last man taken on, and if this really is becoming much less than the value of average output per man, then, Professor Meade argues, the bargaining power of labour is greatly weakened. Two things may happen. Firstly, the wages of labour will be driven down and the return to capital will be correspondingly increased. Secondly, employers in automated factories will tend to pay high wages to a small labour force for the sake of its stability and experience. At the same time an increasingly large part of the population in the less CAPITAL-INTENSIVE and service industries will find their wages falling steadily behind those in the automated capital-intensive sector. There is already clear evidence of this in the USA. Professor Meade calls this prospect the 'Brave New Capitalists' Paradise':

> There would be a limited number of exceedingly wealthy property owners; the proportion of the working population required to man the extremely profitable automated industries would be small; wage rates would thus be depressed; there would have to be a large expansion of the LABOUR-INTENSIVE goods and services which were in high demand by the few multi-multi-multi-millionaires; we would be back in a super-world of an IMMISERIZED proletariat and butlers, footmen, kitchen maids, and other hangers on.

Once again there appears to be a strong element of cumulative causation in income distribution. 'Unto him that hath shall be given . . .' This is obviously true in relation to property ownership, but in recent years there is some evidence in Britain as well as in the USA of a widening gap between the better paid and the less well paid. Table IV.7 shows that property income was rising faster than any other income between 1960 and 1968, except for transfer incomes, that is mainly pensions. The rise in the numbers of pensioners must here be taken into

Table IV.7

*Movements in Weekly Earnings and Hours of Adults
and in the Factor Incomes in the UK 1949, 1960 and 1968*

A. *Groups of Workers*	Numbers June 1969 (000s)	Average Earnings April 1960 £ s.		Average Hours April 1960	Earnings Index (1960 = 100) 1949	1968	Hours Index (1960 = 100) 1968
Men							
Salaried Total	1,033	18	18	—	—	156	—
Manual Total							
Manufacturing							
Vehicles	700	17	10	49	44	148	94
Metal Mfg.	511	15	16	47	54	147	96
Chemicals	372	14	7	43·5	45	163	97
Food, Drink and Tobacco	466	13	1	49	—	163	96
Manufacturing Total	5,919	14	16	47·5	49	154	96
Coal Mining	390	15	19	—	56	151	—
Other Construction	1,409	13	14	50·5	—	167	97
Public Admin.	950	10	16	46	—	161	96
Other Industries and Services Total	4,015	13	2	49	50	158	96
Salaried Clerical	281	13	2	—	—	146	—
Agriculture	372	10	1	50	53	154	95
Women							
Salaried Clerical	399	9	17	—	—	142	—
Manual Manufacturing	2,819	7	5	—	—	151	96
Pensioner							
Man and Wife	2,250	4	0	—	52	178	—
		4	5	—	53	176	—
B. *Factor Incomes*							
Property Income	—	—		—	50	180	—
Self Employment Income	—	—		—	68	135	—
All Employment Income	—	—		—	48	167	—
Transfer Incomes (Pensioners, etc.)	—	—		—	45	230	—
TOTAL Personal Income	—	—		—	50	169	—

Source: Ministry of Labour *Gazette*. *National Income and Expenditure* Blue Book.

account, but nevertheless pensions were catching up with other incomes after 1960. The Table shows further that clerical workers' earnings were falling behind those of other salaried workers and that women's wages were falling behind men's in clerical work and in manufacturing. Among the industries grouped together under Manufacturing and 'Others' some have fared better, some worse; and it has not necessarily been those with high average wages that advanced their average most after 1960, although there were some signs of this widening gap before 1960.

Table IV.8
Low Earnings for Men and Women by Industry UK 1968

		Men			Women	
		% of Men earning less than £15			% of Women earning less than £12	
Industry	% in		Non-	% of		Non-
All Industries and	sample	Manual	Manual	sample	Manual	Manual
Services	100	9·4	4·6	100	64·3	31·6
Non-Manufacturing						
Total	57	13·4	5·8	66	74·0	29·2
Agriculture, etc.	1·3	36·6	—	—	—	—
Professional and Scientific Services	6·2	30·4	7·0	20·4	72·5	25·6
Nat. Government	3·2	25·4	5·5	4·6	—	13·3
Misc. Services	4·6	25·0	6·3	9·2	78·1	37·5
of which catering	0·9	47·5	—	2·3	81·6	—
Local Government	5·7	20·1	4·2	5·1	53·7	15·6
Distribution	7·3	19·4	6·2	14·3	83·6	49·5
Coal Mining	3	11·0	5·1	—	—	—
Road and Rail	3·4	6·0	2·8	1·6	22·4	21·7
Manufacturing						
Total	43	4·6	2·6	34	54·6	40·3
Food, etc.	3·6	5·9	3·8	3·6	65·1	40·0
Engineering, etc.	11·5	4·8	2·1	8·5	45	40·5
Chemicals	2·8	3·5	2·1	2·0	63·0	26·4
Paper and Print	3·0	3·3	1·3	2·9	55·3	30·9
Metal Mfg.	2·9	2·6	2·2	2·0	63·6	49·1
Vehicles	4·5	1·7	1·9	0·1	—	42·3
Textiles, etc.	3·3	8·5	3·5	8·1	56·5	48·9

Source: *Employment and Productivity Gazette*, June 1969.

We do have evidence, however, from the 1968 Department of Employment and Productivity Sample Survey, from which Table IV.8 is taken, that the proportion of low paid workers is very much higher in the non-manufacturing, mainly service, industries than in manufacturing. We can also compare the 1968 survey figures and those for 1960. There is evidence here of an increase in inequality, as may be seen in Table IV.9 which shows the changes in income distribution around the median which we recorded in Chapter 2. The industry averages

Table IV.9

Distribution of Weekly Earnings for Manual Workers, Men and Women in UK 1960 and 1968

Men/Women Industry	Year	As % of Median		Median		As % of Median		Top Decile as % of Bottom
		Bottom Decile	Lower Quartile	£	s	Upper Quartile	Top Decile	
Men	1960	70	82	14	8	120	144	206
	1968	67	81	22	4	122	148	221
Women	1960	72	84	7	6	117	138	192
	1968	71	83	10	8	121	148	208
All Mfg Men	1960	71	83	14	17	121	145	205
	1968	70	83	24	0	120	143	204
Coal Miners Men	1960	63	73	16	5	115	135	215
	1968	64	78	23	3	113	136	212
Iron and Steel Men	1960	69	85	16	10	119	140	204
	1968	72	85	24	9	117	135	187
Motors Men	1960	66	82	17	17	119	136	206
	1968	73	85	26	4	116	136	186
Chemicals Men	1960	69	85	15	0	119	140	203
	1968	69	83	24	1	119	141	204

Sources: *Ministry of Labour Gazette*, April 1961. *Employment and Productivity Gazette*, June 1969.

themselves, of course, are made up of a wide range of earnings, and increasing inequalities inside industries may be more important than increasing inequalities between industries. There is evidence, however, that in the case both of men and women the gap between the average earnings of those at the top tenth (top decile) and those at the bottom tenth (bottom decile)

F

widened considerably between 1960 and 1968. This might indeed be the result of the widening gap between earnings in advanced plant and earnings outside, in accordance with Professor Meade's theory. But we also know that in some industries, such as coal mining where mechanization was introduced very fast in these years, the differentials in earnings narrowed; in others they stayed much the same. The evidence is still inconclusive.

We need now to conclude our discussion of the economist's argument that income distribution is a special case of price theory. A person may get an income from possessing land, capital, enterprise or labour power. It makes a great difference to his income whether he is born with only the power to labour or with property in land or capital as well. Ownership of property is extremely unequally distributed. We saw earlier that about 10 per cent of adults in Britain own all the property that brings in an income and that they receive nearly a third of the income (pre-tax) of all different kinds. Now, according to figures given by Professor James Meade,[15] we know that although property income may not account for more than 10 per cent of all personal incomes it accounts for a much larger proportion (up to 80 per cent) of the top incomes. Income distribution is evidently not itself determined simply by the supply and demand for factors of production according to the wants of consumers in the market. It is itself a determinant of effective demand as the result of the distribution of the factors themselves amongst different persons. The problem has arisen through confusing labour and capital as factors of production with their ownership. We have now to consider the results of competition, and its absence, among different owners of capital. If competition is effective amongst them it could reduce the return that any one might expect from his possession of capital. But we now know enough to suggest that the ownership of capital in itself carries a certain bargaining strength that the possession of the power to labour does not.

[15] In *Efficiency, Equality and the Ownership of Property.*

5 The Market Economy – II Prices and Profits

SUMMARY

In this chapter the basic assumption of free competition in the economists' market model of the economy is criticized. The implications of different degrees of imperfect competition are examined, both in their effect on the price mechanism and on the allocation of resources in the economy. This involves studying under these conditions the return to capital, the management of companies' capital and the movements of capital between companies. It is shown that profitability remains a useful test of efficiency. On the other hand, the monopoly of capital in large companies and groups of companies, while making it possible for them to counter the anarchy of the market, leads to their dictating the growth path of the whole economy. What provides the most profitable return to an individual firm's capital may not provide the greatest long-run balance of social benefits over social costs.

In the last chapter we were looking at the demand side of the model of a market economy as economists have constructed it. When we turn now to examine the supply side, we have first to examine the essential step in those assumptions that we saw economists make in order to relate consumer's wants through the market to what is actually produced. This is the assumption of free competition, and it conditions the whole working of a market economy. By free competition it is assumed that no individual firm or group of producers acting together can control the market and similarly, although less improbably, that no individual consumer or group of consumers can do so. The first may seem an extraordinary assumption to make today, but it corresponded to the facts when it was first made 150 years ago, and it still provides economists with a base line from which their analysis may proceed. The competition that continues between the giant companies, moreover, still provides the driving force for their accumulation of capital.

1. FREE COMPETITION

We have already begun to speak of the sales and pricing policies of shops and firms, which can take advantage of inelastic
demand curves to sell a small quantity at a high price instead
of a large quantity at a low price. Such policies imply that
these sellers are able to influence the market and set their own
prices. For the efficient working of the market this kind of
influence has obviously to be kept to a minimum. Competition
in the market and freedom of entry to the market are both
required in a market economy for three main reasons:

(i) to ensure that all available products are brought to the
market and none withheld;

(ii) to ensure that prices are not fixed by the suppliers but
indeed reflect the preferences of buyers;

(iii) to ensure that inefficient suppliers, or those whose goods
or services are inferior, more costly, or not wanted, are driven
out of business by those who are efficient, whose goods
and services are superior, cheaper and are what the buyers
want.

PERFECT COMPETITION would be a theoretical condition in
which there were enough suppliers and all of them so small that
none could influence the market or the price by bringing their
product to the market or withholding it. At the same time,
suppliers would have to be so well-informed that they knew
all the prices at which others were selling similar products to
theirs in the market and which products were selling profitably
and which unprofitably. Something approaching this condition
exists in agriculture (except where farmers have organized
themselves under marketing boards). The result is often a
situation of violent fluctuations from year to year, resulting
both from weather conditions creating gluts and famines and
also from the tendency of farmers to overcompensate. That is
to say that high prices from a short crop of potatoes, for
example, one year lead all farmers to set more land to potatoes
the next year. A GLUT follows and after that perhaps another
famine.

The very responsiveness of the market to relative movements of supply and demand may exaggerate such fluctuations even for imperishable products. The world prices, for

example, of rubber or wool or cocoa have shown rises and falls over the last twenty years of as much as two to three times the five-year average level. In 1950 rubber prices rose four-fold and fell back again by that much early in 1952. Wool prices doubled between 1949 and 1953 and dropped back again by 1955. Cocoa prices rose $2\frac{1}{2}$ times between 1952 and 1954 and were down again to a third of the 1954 level by 1956. They were halved again in 1964 and recovered the next year. Where such crops are the major cash crops of an economy these up and down movements create the most serious problems for the policies of governments as well as for farmers. International COMMODITY AGREEMENTS and other forms of producers' associations have, therefore, been established for some crops in the attempt to regulate supply and demand through the management of BUFFER STOCKS.[1]

Agriculture, however, is now the exception; elsewhere the application of machinery and the economies of scale have enormously reduced the number of producers not only in local and national markets but in the international market also. In many lines of production – oil, steel, motor-cars, tobacco, heavy chemicals and detergents are outstanding examples – a handful of giant international companies (called OLIGOPOLIES) dominate the world market. Between them there may be an open battle of the giants or there may be agreements to keep the battle within the bounds of a CARTEL. National Trade Associations and international cartels all have the aim of regulating competition rather than eliminating it. National and regional markets are shared out between rival producers, QUOTAS are fixed, minimum prices agreed upon – all however subject to revision at a later meeting. This does not mean that competition stops – the advertising campaigns of the oil companies tell us that – but in the words of the leading American authorities on cartels, 'cartels provide a relatively stable framework within which conflicting interests may be reconciled by manœuvre, bargain and compromise'.[2]

In the last few years in Britain the average size of firms has increased rapidly. This is firstly because of the economies of scale, both in plant size which we saw earlier and in all the

[1] See J. W. F. Rowe, *Primary Commodities in International Trade, 1965.*
[2] G. W. Stocking and M.W.Watkins, *Cartels in Action, 1947.*

overheads of sales and research expenditure. Secondly, however, the increase in size is undoubtedly connected with control over the firm's general financial situation – its source of funds and the marketing of its products. A large proportion of the MERGERS and TAKE-OVERS of the 1960s in Britain have

Table V.1

Importance of Large Companies and Public Corporations in the British Economy 1967

Size and Type of Company	Net Capital £000m	%	Net Income £000m	%	Turnover £000m	%	Exports £000m	%	Employees No. 000s	%
Top 10	9,2	18	1,1	17	11	15	0,9	15	1,2	6
Top 50	15,0	30	1,85	31	—	—	—	—	—	—
41 of Top 50	12,8	25·5	1,5	25	18	23	1,45	24	2,3	12
Top 100	18,5	37	2,3	39	—	—	—	—	—	—
81 of Top 100	15,9	32	1,9	32	22	29	1,95	32	3,2	17
Quoted 2660	28,5	57·5	3,4	58	—	—	—	—	—	—
All Companies	(50)	100	5,9	100	(75)	100	6,0	100	19	100
Self-Employed (and non-incorporated)	(8)	—	2,3	—	(5)	—	0,75	—	1,7	—
Public Corporation	12	—	0,45	—	8	—	0,25	—	1,9	—
Government	23	—	—	—	6	—	—	—	1,6	—
Grand TOTAL	(93)	—	8,65	—	(94)	—	7,0	—	24,2	—

Notes:
1. Only the 81 Companies of the Top 100, and the 41 of the Top 50, give turnover and employment figures.
2. Figures in brackets are estimates.
3. Total turnover is found by taking total output less imports and taxes on expenditure (= £90,000m) deducting government, public sector and self-employed (= £20,000m) and adding £5,000m for overseas sales.

Sources:
1. Net capital for all companies and self-employed are based on J. S. Revell, *The Wealth of Britain, 1967*.
2. Top 100 from *The Times* list of 500 Leading Companies.
3. Quoted 2,660 from *Financial Times* 21.1.1969.
4. Totals of net income from *National Income and Expenditure* Blue Book.

been among the largest companies themselves: Unilever–
Allied Breweries; GEC–AEI–English Electric; British
Motor Holdings and Leyland; not to mention the bringing
together of the twelve large steel-making companies in the
British Steel Corporation. Just ten companies now dominate
the UK markets for mineral and vegetable oils, chemicals,
tobacco, motors, electrical engineering, textiles and non-
ferrous metals. These ten firms alone account for nearly one-
sixth of the whole turnover of all UK companies, as we may
see in Table V.1. Below these there are another forty or so,
including the leading firms in distilling, brewing, paper, aircraft, rubber, shipping, stores, cement, entertainment, milling
and baking, chocolate, glass and metal boxes. These make up a
top fifty providing roughly one-third of all company turnover.
Some companies still do not give their turnover figures,
especially for their operations overseas, and there is no generally agreed figure for the sales of all incorporated businesses
as distinct from those of single owner firms and partnerships.
But within the companies QUOTED on the Stock Exchange we
can see the dominant position of the two or three giants in
each industry in Table V.2

Table V.2

The Giant Firms in British Industry 1968

	All Quoted Companies		*Companies with over £100m. Capital*		
	Net Capital Employed		Number of	% of all Quoted	Names of
	Number	£m	Companies	Capital	Companies
A. *All Industry and Materials*	2,200	23,500	52	66	
Oil	16	3,980	4	95	Shell, BP Esso Burmah
Electricals	86	980	3	75	GEC BICC Plessey
Chemicals	66	2,160	1	63	ICI

	All Quoted Companies		Companies with over £100m. Capital		
	Net Capital Employed Number	£m	Number of Companies	% of all Quoted Capital	Names of Companies
Motors	37	850	3	80	BLMC Ford Vauxhall
Drink	49	1,500	7	80	Distillers Bass,etc. Allied Whitbread Watney Scottish and Newcastle Courage
Food	81	1,360	5	75	Unilever Tate & Lyle Cadbury Rank Hovis AB Foods
Tobacco	6	1,200	3	87	BAT Imps Gallahers
Textiles	108	650	2	84	Courtaulds Coates-Paton
Stores	160	1,200	3	40	GUS Woolworths Marks
Shipping	31	750	3	60	P & O Ocean Brit. & Commonwealth
Aircraft	7	500	2	80	Hawker Siddeley Rolls

	All Quoted Companies		Companies with over £100m. Capital		
	Net Capital Employed		Number of	% of all Quoted	Names of
	Number	£m	Companies	Capital	Companies
Minerals	173	800	3	80	RTZ Selection Trust Charter Consolidated
Paper & Packaging	35	725	3	52	Reed Wiggins Teape Dickinson Robinson
Engineering, etc.	1,355	6,775	10	37	GKN Vickers Dunlop Rank Metal Box Pilkington Tubes, Sears British Oxygen Turner & Newall
B. *Property*	129	1,865	3	22	Land Securities City Centre CLRP
C. *Finance*	231	(6,700)	6	?	The Big Four Barclays DCO and Standard

Source: *The Times, 500 Leading Companies, 1968.*

Not only do the top 100 or so firms in Britain dominate the market for goods and services, they also dominate the capital market. One hundred and sixteen firms in 1963 had more than half of all the capital quoted on the Stock Exchange, but

what is more they had obtained 90 per cent of all the new
capital issued through the Stock Exchange between 1957 and
1963 (see Table V.4 later). More and more share capital is now
controlled by INSTITUTIONS like insurance companies. We can
see from Table V.3 that by 1965 this amounted to about one
quarter of all ordinary shares and half of other shares. Institutions want a safe home for their clients' money with growth

Table V.3

Quoted Company Capital, UK 1966

			Share of Capital held by Institutions	
		Issued or		
	TOTAL	Added	of Total	of New
	Issued	in 1966	Issued	Issued 1966
Type of Capital	£m	£m	%	%
Ordinary Shares	5,570	256	39	40
Preference Shares	813	78	53	2
Loans	3,487	545	50	42
Capital and Revenue				
Reserves	7,248	615	—	—

Source: *Financial Statistics* and *Board of Trade Journal.*

prospects; and this leads them to look to the largest companies,
the so-called 'blue chips'. In a period when there is little or no
growth in demand in the economy, as was the case between
mid-1965 and mid-1968, the funds that industrial companies
accumulate would not be invested in new plant as there would
be no demand for it; the only way they could grow therefore
was by merging with or taking over other companies. In 1968
nearly £3,500 millions was spent in this way – three times the
1967 figure and ten times that in 1965 – and the 1968 figure
had already been exceeded by the end of the first half of 1969.

The tendency towards MONOPOLY has been both encouraged
and discouraged by British governments in recent years. On
the one hand, the Monopolies Commission has examined cases
referred to it of mergers and take-overs that appeared likely to
lead to positions of excessive power. Thus the further expansion of Courtaulds in the textile industry has been discouraged,

Imperial Tobacco was required to sell its majority holding in Gallahers and the proposed Barclays–Lloyds–Martins bank merger was prevented. On the other hand, the state-financed Industrial Reorganization Corporation has assisted mergers where it believed that a large British company was needed to face international competition. The Corporation supported the GEC–AEI take-over and provided a loan for the British Motors–Leyland merger and the Chrysler–Rootes take-over. The effects of these great concentrations of capital in producing a system of administered prices in the place of the free working of the market must now be examined.

2. THE PRICE MECHANISM

In a perfectly competitive market by definition there are so many sellers that no one seller can influence the price by entering or not entering the market. The consumer is sovereign. The individual seller must reconcile himself to the going price. If he raises his price he won't sell at all; if he lowers it he may increase his sales, but the price is assumed to have been driven down already to the level of industry costs and unless he has a way of reducing his unit costs in the not so long run he will lose money and be driven out of business. Where competition is imperfect, however, each seller can manage both his price and sales to optimise profits. Because of the IMPERFECT COMPETITION, ruling prices will be above average costs; there is therefore an element of monopoly profit. According to the elasticity of demand for their product, its HOMOGENEITY, and the number of other sellers, firms will be in a position to take different types of action about their prices.

Economists distinguish the different kinds of market situation with different terms which are indicated in Fig. 5.1.

Perfect competition is a rare phenomenon. Almost any seller has some element of monopoly either in his location ('the shop next door') or in his brand ('your favourite'). The most usual situation, where there are many firms competing but each having some influence on the market, is described by economists as MONOPOLISTIC COMPETITION. We may take as an example the RETAIL trade where price-cutting will have only a limited effect on sales because of the convenience or goodwill

Fig. 5.1
Degrees of Competition and Monopoly

Degree of Competition	Perfect Competition	Monopolistic Competition	Imperfect Competition		Monopoly
			Perfect Oligopoly or (Duopoly)	Imperfect Oligopoly or (Duopoly)	
Number of Sellers	Very many	Many or fear of many	Few (or Two)	Few (or Two)	One
Influence of Sellers on Market	Nil	Excess Capacity	'Do as you would be done by'	Cartel or cut throat competition	Total Control
Influence of Sellers on Price	Nil	Small (RPM)	Price Leadership	Administered prices	Fixed prices
Nature of Demand	Very elastic	Fairly elastic	Inelastic	Inelastic	Very inelastic
Homogeneity of Product	Homogeneous but substitutes	Differentiated Service or Location	Homogeneous	Differentiated Brands by Advertising	Single product
Examples	Agriculture	Retail Trade/ Motor Cars	Sugar Cement Steel	Oil Detergents Tobacco	Salt Distilling

Source: Derived from J. L. Hanson, *Textbook of Economics,* p.246.

of the shop 'round the corner'. Retailers' freedom to cut prices in Britain has also been strictly limited in the past because of the system of RETAIL PRICE MAINTENANCE (RPM) operated by most producers of branded goods up to the Retail Prices Act of 1964. Since then RPM has been outlawed on a number of commodities, and the effect has been to reduce the profit margin of retailers. This has been to the advantage of the supermarkets and large stores, whose turnover is higher, and costs lower, therefore, than those of the small shopkeeper.

Where there are only a few producers, because of the scale of production that is necessary, and where demand is fairly elastic, as in the manufacture of motor-cars, dishwashers or refrigerators, there will also be monopolistic competition. This time the monopoly lies in the control of the necessary reserves of capital. The elasticity of demand and the returns to scale, however, encourage firms to cut prices and expand sales. Competition, international if not national, remains. Both BMC's and Rootes' accounts showed losses in 1967–8. As a result, the one merged with Leyland and the other was taken over by Chrysler. Where demand is elastic and a firm or group of firms attempt to make monopoly profits, there is generally a John Bloom waiting to find the capital and enter the market at cut prices. Even if he fails in the end prices are likely to be brought down either because of competition or for fear of encouraging new competitors. John Bloom was an entrepreneur who brought the prices of refrigerators down very sharply in the early 1960s by undercutting the big three suppliers. The fact that he was beaten in the end was due largely to his lack of capital to embark upon manufacturing the whole range of electrical equipment that he would have had to sell once he moved over from door to door salesmanship to retail distribution. The importance of the story is to remind us that it is the threat of free entry that distinguishes monopolistic competition from monopoly or other forms of imperfect competition.

Where demand is inelastic, monopolistic profit can more easily be maintained by managed prices. It is easy to distinguish monopoly (one seller), DUOPOLY (two sellers) and oligopoly (a few sellers), but the most important distinction that economists make follows from the DIFFERENTIATION or homogeneity of the product. With one seller in the market the product is likely to be a single one with no substitutes, like salt or spirits, where demand is very inelastic. Consumers must have their whisky at whatever price! Where the product is homogeneous and demand is inelastic there may, however, be two or more firms in the business, as in steel making, sugar refining or cement production. The economists call this perfect OLIGOPOLY. Consumers have little or no preference for one firm's product rather than another's. If the sales director of one firm cuts prices the others will follow and he knows it; so he works on the old principle of 'do as you would be done by'. In effect the largest firm becomes the PRICE LEADER and the others follow. Sometimes, where there are many shapes and sizes of the product as in steel, firms reach price agreements for their various products.

Governments have recently attempted to prohibit these agreements if they seemed to be against the public interest and have even set maximum prices, as was the case with steel. When the maximum price always became *the* price, as a result of agreement among firms in a Trade Association, such agreements have sometimes been brought, in Britain, before the RESTRICTIVE PRACTICES Court[3]. In certain cases the Association has been told to cease its practice. It remains almost impossible to stop producers from meeting for breakfast once a year at the Station Hotel in York or elsewhere or simply 'doing as they would be done by'. Monopoly and oligopoly are frequently protected by tariffs and other barriers to imports from foreign countries. Lowering these protective devices is an effective way of increasing competition; but if international companies are determined on collusion there is little that governments can do about it, short of nationalizing them. The problems faced by governments in trying to control prices will be considered in a moment, after we have completed our study of imperfect competition.

Where the product can be differentiated, oligopoly is not perfect and firms put great efforts into attaching consumers to their particular brand by advertising. The differences are often only in the packaging and the 'image'. Such firms can, of course, expand their sales by price cutting, and a cut-throat price war may follow. More often the firms realize that this is self-defeating and reach agreements through cartels and other trade associations not to compete in price and/or to divide up the market by regions or by quotas. We referred in the last section to commodity agreements, but cartels of a formal or informal (York Station breakfast) type exist over a wide range of manufactured products. Some part of the monopoly profit is then absorbed by advertising, coupons, free gifts and other additions to selling costs.

Economists sometimes describe the reaction of oligopolists to the market in terms of a 'KINKED' DEMAND curve. (Fig. 5.2.)

[3] For a review of these cases see T. Wilson 'Restrictive Practices' in J.P. Miller, *Competition, Cartels and their Regulation*, 1962.

The first point to note is that the firm's marginal revenue drops faster than the average revenue or demand curve for the industry as a whole in any situation of imperfect competition, since the firm must lower its prices to increase its share of the market. It has in fact to drop twice as fast, for mathematical reasons which students can study in a textbook. Hence the marginal revenue curve must end up half as far along the output axis on the demand curve since they both start at zero.

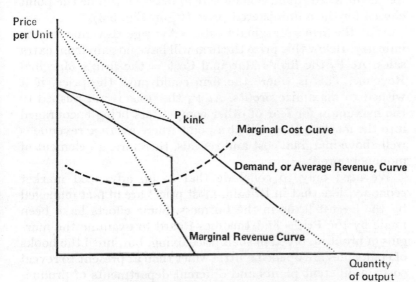

Figure 5.2. Demand for oligopolistic firms' product, or oligopolists' 'kinked' demand curve

Beyond the ruling price (at P on the graph above), in a situation of oligopoly the demand curve drops even more sharply because, if one firm cuts its prices, the other firms will drop theirs in retaliation, and the marginal revenue curve must follow suit – at a very much lower level. It will, therefore, pay all the firms concerned for prices to be managed at as high a level as possible. We must notice here two restraining considerations. The first is that, while firms know very well what the extra costs per unit of output will be (marginal cost) and what their average costs per unit are, the demand curve and extra revenue per unit (marginal revenue) must always be based on estimates from past experience. The second is that pushing the price to the maximum possible level may not pay.

Remembering the story of John Bloom, we can illustrate on a graph where oligopolistic firms are likely to fix their prices. They will raise them above the equilibrium price, at which point marginal cost for the firm equals average revenue for the industry, but they will not necessarily push them to the maximum where marginal cost for the firm and marginal revenue for the firm are equal. Somewhere in between will be the point chosen for the administered price (P_3 on Fig. 5.3).

At P_1 the firm's Marginal Costs = Average Revenue for the industry. Below this price the firm will have no gain from extra sales. At P_2 the firm's Marginal Cost = the firm's Marginal Revenue. This is where the firm could push the price, if it wished to maximize profits. At P_3 the price is not pushed to the maximum for fear of other competitors being encouraged into the market. It is still at a point where average revenue is well above marginal cost and reveals, therefore, an element of monopoly profit.

We need only to conclude that in an advanced market economy, like that in Britain, most prices are in fact managed by the largest firms in the business. Some efforts have been made by the Prices and Incomes Board to examine the margins of profit involved in such price fixing, but, until the books of companies are opened a little wider than at present to reveal costs in different plants and different departments of production, it is hard for an outsider to tell how near prices may be to average unit costs of production in the case of any particular product. What we do know is that it is only necessary to have information on pricing and costings for a quite small number of firms, including nationalized undertakings, to obtain the information we need.

Since the price mechanism is so essential to the market economy and so seriously distorted by monopolistic actions, governments have been increasingly involved, not only in creating the conditions for more competition, as we saw earlier, but in attempts to control prices directly. These involve even more serious problems. Firstly, unless extra production can be encouraged, the attempt to hold down prices with limited supplies may be difficult. In war-time, RATIONING is introduced

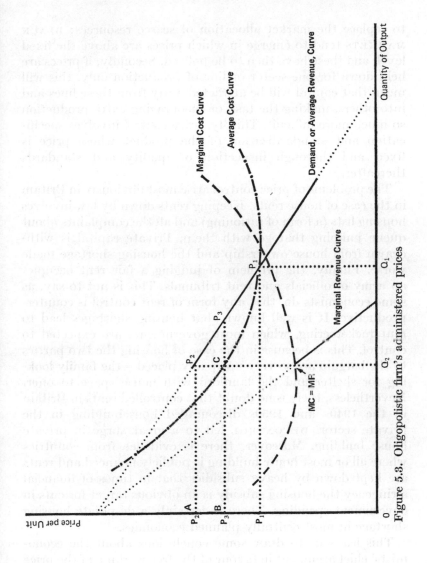

Figure 5.3. Oligopolistic firm's administered prices

to replace the market allocation of scarce resources; BLACK MARKETS tend to emerge in which prices are above the fixed level, and these have then to be policed. Secondly, if prices are held down for one sector or line of production only, this will mean that capital will be attracted away from these lines and into others, making the task of encouraging extra production so much more difficult. Thirdly, price control involves specification and standardization of the product whose price is fixed and thorough inspection of quality and standards thereafter.

The problems of price control arise most obviously in Britain in the case of house rents. Keeping rents down by law involves housing lists (a form of rationing) and all the complaints about queue jumping that go with them. Private capital is withdrawn from house ownership and the housing shortage made worse. Finally, the problem of judging a fair rent occupies an army of officials and rent tribunals. This is not to say, as some economists do, that any form of rent control is counterproductive. It is well known that housing shortages lead to rent racketeering, which most governments are expected to control. This is because in the case of housing the two parties to the bargain are so very unequally placed – the family looking for shelter and the landlord with house space to offer. Nevertheless, there is no doubt that controlled rents in Britain in the 1940s and 1950s discouraged housebuilding in the private sector. DECONTROL led to a great surge in private house building. Moreover, there is evidence from countries where all or most house building is publicly financed and rents are kept down by heavy subsidies that in times of financial stringency the housing subsidy is an obvious target for cuts in government spending. There is certainly a desperate housing shortage in most centrally planned economies.

This leads us to draw some conclusions about the economists' chief argument in favour of the free working of the price mechanism. This is that there is no better way of judging the real value that buyers put upon a thing – whether it is goods or services or factors of production – than the price they are prepared to pay for it; and those who will pay most evidently value it most highly. If there are shortages of any commodity, then the price will allocate resources to those who set the

highest value upon it. A recent example of this argument has
been the case put forward for taxing road vehicles which are
used in congested towns according to the mileage they are
driven there or length of time they are parked. The argument
assumes that the price will test how much of other commodities road users in towns are prepared to forgo for the sake of
their town journeys. Those with the most urgent requirements,
it is said, will use the roads; others will not.

The problem remains that the unequal distribution of incomes, and the prevalence of expense accounts, makes the
importance of the sum forgone a very different matter for
different people. Rationing by the purse favours the rich.
Egalitarian demands in war-time therefore require rationing by
coupon or by licence. In peace-time, however, priorities are
less than universally acknowledged and the allocation of
priority categories leads to bureaucracy, nepotism and corruption. One possible solution will be considered in Chapter 8 –
to provide for direct democracy in agreeing upon local priorities while overall allocations are controlled by indirect democracy at the centre. Experiments in decentralization might
encourage the idea. New institutional forms within which consumers may exercise their voting power are certainly required
to meet the new phenomenon of oligopoly in the giant international company. In the meantime the price mechanism
remains in its distorted form.

3. PROFITABILITY AND THE RETURN TO CAPITAL

If the price mechanism is to do its job of indicating consumer
votes in the market then it must evidently make it more
profitable for firms to respond effectively to these indications.
In the last section it was suggested that monopolistic positions
were widespread throughout industry and that these gave
monopoly profits. If this is so, profitability may be more a
question of monopolistic positions than of effective responses
to the market. We must not exaggerate, however; recent
experience in countries with totally planned economies indicates that the economists are probably right in emphasizing
the importance of overall profitability as a criterion for the
efficient operation of an enterprise. We are not concerned here

with profit as a reward to owners of capital, but with the
return to capital as an objective of a firm's activities. Of
course, the question of who gets the return to capital is not
just a matter of value judgment but may have an important
effect on incentives to work in the firm and on the
firm's investment decisions. These are considered in the next
section.

We must remember that the economist's theory of production and distribution implies that monopolistic positions in any
factor of production – land, labour and capital – can be treated
alike. Shortages of any one should lead at once to higher prices
and these should encourage sooner or later an alleviation of the
shortage. More land is brought into use, saving for capital
investment becomes more attractive, labour switches to new
employment. We shall deal in a moment with the mobility of
capital and labour. What has to be said here is that there is
an element of monopoly in the ownership of land and capital,
and of above average personal ability also, to whatever use these
factors are applied. While labour power is possessed by the
great majority of people, with only small differences of ability,
land and capital and high ability are possessed by few. In most
economies only a few can afford to save much of their income;
in Britain capital and land ownership are highly concentrated,
as we have seen.

In Chapter 1 we quoted Adam Smith's aphorism that
'wealth is power' and land ownership carries with it the right
'to demand a rent even for its [the land's] natural products'.
David Ricardo, who lived in a period when the wealth of manufacturers was challenging that of the landowners, emphasized
that rent could arise simply from ownership and not from
improvements made to the land, since the supply of land is
fixed. Economists have therefore spoken of QUASI-RENTS
where, even in the long run, supply cannot readily be increased. That there is an element of quasi-rent in the return to
all capital is thus very evident, since ownership of capital is
itself a monopoly. Economists in an economy based on social
ownership with decentralization to individual enterprises, as
in Yugoslavia, still use the Ricardian concept of rent in arguing
for the taxation of certain enterprises which enjoy monopolistic positions. The return to capital remains for them

crucial criterion of efficiency, that is to say return to capital including that laid out on wages as well as on capital equipment.

While there is today wide acknowledgment of the importance of return to capital as a criterion of efficiency there are two major lines of criticism of it as the *only* criterion of efficiency: the first arises from the social effects of decisions based entirely on consideration of a firm's profitability,[4] and the second from the effects of such decisions on income distribution.[5] The social costs and benefits of a firm's decision do not enter into its accounts. Since, however, these decisions are based upon profitability, they are assumed to be socially beneficial because profitability depends upon response to the market. But there are a number of benefits which we saw earlier cannot be voted for in the market – goods which are not on offer and public services which have to be voted for in another way – and there are still more costs which cannot be voted against. The loss of AMENITY caused by the burning of coal and oil and by the widespread use of road vehicles provides an obvious example. Another is the cost in new housing, roads, drains, water supply, schools and so on of the decision of a firm to move for example from Scotland to south-east England. This cost does not enter the firm's accounts, but is none the less a social cost if the move leaves behind unused or underutilized housing, roads, drains, water supply, schools and so on in Scotland.

One further problem here is that it is rather easier to buy goods in the shops than to persuade others to vote with you for a park or pedestrian precinct or public transport system. This difficulty enters into the calculations of firms which naturally orient their production towards a market which they can control through advertising, by their influence on personal choice, than towards one where the public is less easily controlled. For plans may be upset by local and national government elections or economic crises. The one public sector market which most firms regard as one to be relied upon is the market for armaments. Very high profits are made here; some

---

[4] This is dealt with at length in E. J. Mishan's *The Costs of Economic Growth.*
[5] This is examined by J.E.Meade in his *Efficiency, Equality and the Ownership of Property.*

of them have recently received notoriety as in the case of
Ferranti's Blue Streak rocket and Bristol Siddeley's aero-
engines. The reason for these high profits is probably the sheer
difficulty of estimating what a rocket, for example, should
cost when there are no comparable household goods to compare it with. Another objection that firms may have to public
contracts except for arms is that goods like schools and hospital equipment last for a long time. The great thing about cars
from this point of view is that they soon wear out and have to
be replaced. Once more this advantage of rapid OBSOLES-
CENCE is shared by armaments.

James Meade's criticism of profitability as the main criterion
of efficiency rests, as we have seen, upon the effect he believes
automation will have upon employment policies. Firms with
high CAPITAL-INTENSITY as a result of automation will maintain a small labour force at high levels of pay but will have no
incentive to increase their numbers. In the LABOUR-INTEN-
SIVE service industries outside the automated sector much
lower levels of pay will obtain, even if full employment policies
are pursued. This possibility is increased by the system of
taxation which has recently emerged in Britain. On the one
hand, tax concessions and direct grants are made to firms for
capital investment; on the other hand, increased national
insurance contributions, payments to the Industrial Training
and REDUNDANCY Funds and, in addition for service industries the new SELECTIVE EMPLOYMENT TAX, are all designed
to discourage the employment of labour. We can add to these
the FRINGE BENEFITS now being demanded from employers,
all of which serve to raise unit labour costs. We may instance
educational schemes, superannuation payments, subsidized
canteens, washroom, locker and car parking space as well as
the overheads of wage calculation and payment, supervision
and labour management. The result is that return to capital as
a test of efficiency will probably indicate that the benefits of
automation should be obtained by reducing the labour force
rather than by reducing the hours of work. Individual unions
will be tempted to go for high wages for a small membership on
the American pattern. It will become increasingly difficult for
governments to maintain full employment and to control the
inflationary pressure of a high-wage, automated sector

of the economy but these are points we must return to in the
next chapter.

4. THE MANAGERIAL REVOLUTION

The view that firms will aim at maximizing profits in the way
we have just indicated, and at the expense of social costs, has
been challenged by those who argue that the motivation of
modern management differs entirely from that of the old-
fashioned employer. Return to capital was inevitably the
owner's only consideration. Management, it is said, is now
divorced from ownership and the managers can take account
of other considerations than profitability. The argument was
originated by James Burnham,[6] who forecast that the new
ruling class to follow the capitalists would be that of the
managers, and not only in capitalist countries but in the communist countries too. The argument is supported by four
assertions of fact, some at least of which can be challenged:[7]

(*a*) Capital holdings are said now to be spread amongst such
a large number of shareholders in the giant companies that no
one group can control the company. The study of Professor
Sargent Florence[8] showed that only a third of the top 100
companies he looked at in Britain were owner-controlled, but
he excluded steel, shipping, shipbuilding, brewing, all PRIVATE
COMPANIES and all those like the oil companies, which operate
mainly overseas; and these groups have been found to be very
largely owner-controlled. Since 1951 the mergers and take-
overs of the 1960s have shown the power of the owners of
capital to be much greater than appeared then.

(*b*) On the Boards of the top companies the majority of
members are said now to be managers and not owners or their
nominees. Managers in this context are assumed to be managers of processes rather than managers of money since they
are expected to have other motivations than that of the return
to capital. In fact my own studies in this field[9] have suggested

---

[6] In a famous book called *The Managerial Revolution*, 1941.
[7] See C. A. R. Crosland, *The Conservative Enemy*, p. 69 ff. and a reply by
M. Barratt Brown in *New Left Review* No. 19, March/April 1963.
[8] See *Ownership and Control of Large Companies*, 1951.
[9] See M. Barratt Brown, 'Who Controls the Economy?' in K. Coates (ed.).
Can the Workers Run Industry? p. 24.

that amongst the top 120 companies about a third had boards consisting mainly of the owner and his family or nominees, a third had boards consisting mainly of what I called CONTROL-LERS, who sit across a wide range of boards in finance, commerce and industry, and only a third had boards which consisted mainly of departmental or group managers.

(c) The largest industrial companies are said to raise most of their funds today from their own internally generated profits; they do not need therefore, to go to the Stock Exchange for capital and thus expose themselves to the requirement that they show a high return on their capital. Compared with the pre-war situation, it is true that today British firms raise most of their capital internally; but my own studies showed that the fastest growing companies of the top 116 between 1957 and 1963 raised as much as 42 per cent of their new funds from outside capital, that is from the Stock Exchange. This can be seen in Table V.4. Once again the latest wave of take-overs has shown that a company that fails to show good profits soon sees the value of its shares fall on the Stock Exchange and then opens itself to a take-over bid from a rival.

(d) The managers of industrial firms are said now to have different motivations from those of the owners and not to be interested primarily in the return to capital. Directors and managers, however, are amongst the most highly paid persons in our economy and, apart from OPTIONS to buy stock at PREMIUM prices and required holdings of shares in their own company, they are likely to be substantial shareholders in many other companies. They will thus tend to share the general views of property owners about the return to capital. One particular argument has been put forward here that carries weight.[10] This is that company size and growth may be more important for managers than profit maximization. The reason for this is partly prestige and partly that managers are paid according to the number of steps up the pyramid to the top; the bigger the company, the larger the number of steps and the higher the pay at the top. None the less, it is to be noted that the managerial controlled firms in the top 120 in Britain did not show a faster growth rate than the other groups of firms between 1957 and 1963. It was the firms owned and

[10] R. Marris, *The Economic Theory of Managerial Capitalism*, 1964.

Table V.4

Assets, Incomes and Finance of 1916 Quoted Companies and of 116 Large Companies UK 1957–1963

	All Companies Total	Smaller Companies Total	116 Largest Companies			
			Total	42 Fast Growers	37 Moderate Growers	37 Slow Growers
Net Assets 1957 (£m)	10,219	4,479	5,740	1,147	2,365	2,228
1960 (£m)	13,495	5,939	7,556	2,100	3,055	2,301
1963 (£m)	15,640	5,916	9,725	2,961	3,895	2,869
Growth for Groups 1957–63 (1957 = 100)	153	132	170	258	164	128
Growth Average for Companies in Group (1957 = 100)	—	—	205	310	167	129
Average Income 1958–63 (£m)	2,386	1,061	1,325	412	558	355
As % of Average Net Assets 1960 and 1963	16·4	18	15·3	16·3	16·0	13·7
Proportion of 1958–63 Income for Groups as a Whole:						
Put to Reserves (%)	21·5	23	20	20·5	20·5	19·2
Provision for Depreciation (%)	24·5	25	24	18·5	25·3	26·0
Raised by New Capital (%)	13·0	2·6	21·5	42	18	8·5
New Capital raised Annual Average 1958–63 (£m)	313	28	285	150	100	35
as % of Total for 1916 Companies	100	10	90	48	32	11

Notes:

(*a*) 1,916 Companies are included in 1963, that is the 2,026 surveyed excluding 110 Property Companies.

(*b*) 2,618 Companies are included in 1960, excluding Property Companies. 1,882 Companies are included in 1957, excluding Property Companies, *but* for the proportions of income going to Reserves and Depreciation and for New Capital raised in 1958–63 Property Companies are included in 'All Companies' and 'Smaller Companies' totals but not in the 116.

(c) New Capital raised by the '1916' and '1800' includes an annual average figure of £47m used for acquiring the shares of other quoted companies.

(d) New Capital raised by the 116 companies is a gross figure. £9·7m on average was disposed of annually over the period but whether to quoted or unquoted companies is not stated.

Sources: *Economic Trends*, February 1966. Board of Trade, *Surveys of Company Assets, Income and Finance* in 1957, 1960 and 1963.

controlled by an individual owner or family that grew fastest.[11]

What can be said is that the return to capital of the largest companies in Britain is at a lower rate than the return to capital of the smaller companies among those with Stock Exchange quotations. In our Table V.4 it is 15·3 per cent compared with 18 per cent. In the recent wave of take-overs it has been noticed how often a large company with slow growth and low return to capital has taken over a smaller fast-growing company with a high return to capital.[12] This would appear to be the very opposite of what should be happening according to economic theory. Only the large American companies in Britain show a consistently high return on their capital and rely little if at all on the Stock Exchange for new funds. The point that was missed in the theory of the managerial revolution was that it is not only a large capital but also a high return to capital that enables a firm to accumulate funds for its own growth without resort to the capital market. Firms which show a poor return to their capital must expand or decline, take over or be taken over. As was shown in 1968 this goes for the giants as well as the tiddlers, but the giants have access to the Stock Exchange which the others are in practice denied. Competition is still the driving force behind capital accumulation, and in the long run, among the giants, return to capital will be the test of survival.

We come back to a point that was made earlier that the institutions like the insurance companies, which hold an increasingly large share of company capital require for their clients' money a good return and some capital growth, but above all investment in a large company which can dominate the market and avoid risks. The reason for the American

[11] M.Barratt Brown, *Can the Workers Run Industry?* Table 8, p. 46.
[12] See *Trade Union Register*, Diary No. 2 for 12 October 1968.

companies' success lies not only in their advanced technology but
in the dominating international position that they have
established. Competition is now world-wide; research and
development on a scale that only the giants can support; the
advertisements in American magazines enter the households
of every land. The market economy has now to be understood
in terms of the international company. The wealth of the
dominating companies enables them to survive even with low
rates of return on capital, by gobbling up their lesser rivals;
but in the long run they will be hard put to it to compete with
the giants unless they do show a high return. In other words,
the American companies will reign supreme unless the technology and operating efficiency of the British companies can
catch up with them. The outstanding feature of American
compared with European companies is not just the size of their
capital assets but the high income/assets and/or sales/assets
ratios as we may see in Table V.5. In their own home markets
the giants can dominate by their sheer size but in the world
stakes profitability is evidently largely a matter of technology
in which Britain and Europe fall far behind the USA.

Table V.5

The World's Top Companies, 1967

		Capital	Sales		Profit	
				% of		% of
		£m	£m	Capital	£m	Capital
Motors						
US	General Motors	4,340	8,046	185	681	15·5
US	Ford	2,184	4,441	202	35	1·6
US	Chrysler	943	2,600	275	84	9
Germany	Volkswagen	590	—	—	29	5
Italy	Fiat	352	—	—	21	6
UK	BMLC	343	772	225	19	5·5
Oil						
US	Standard Oil	5,035	6,030	120	516	10·5
US	Texaco	2,525	2,143	85	316	12·5
US	Gulf	2,084	2,138	102	237	11·5
US	Standard	1,926	1,586	83	176	9
US	Mobil Oil	1,921	2,656	138	161	8·5

		Capital £m	Sales £m	Sales % of Capital	Profit £m	Profit % of Capital
Dutch	Royal Dutch	2,404	—	—	160	6·5
UK	Shell	1,602	1,749	109	231	14·5
UK	BP	1,445	1,667	115	264	18
Chemicals						
US	Union Carbide	1,125	1,065	95	71	6·5
US	Du Pont de Nemours	1,059	1,288	122	131	12·5
UK	ICI	1,399	978	70	126	9
Italian	Montecatini	961	—	—	26	3
Germany	Hoechst	518	—	—	25	5
Germany	Bayer	490	—	—	29	6
Electrical						
US	IBM	1,836	2,236	122	273	15
US	GEC	1,143	3,604	314	142	12·5
US	Westinghouse	684	1,213	178	51	7·5
Dutch	Philips	1,011	—	—	41	4
UK	GEC/AEI/EEC	653	856	131	60	9
Germany	Siemens	514	—	—	17	3
Food and Tobacco						
US	Proctor & Gamble	448	1,020	230	73	16·5
US	Swift	172	1,186	690	11	5·5
UK/US	British American Tobacco	445	1,050	210	105	21
UK	Unilever	541	937	173	61	11
Dutch	Unilever NV	511	—	—	52	10
UK	Imperial Tobacco	447	945	210	50	11

Source: *The Times 500 Leading Companies*, 1968.

5. CAPITAL MOVEMENTS

If the market economy is to do its economic duty of allocating resources where they are most wanted, capital must move where prices indicate that profit is highest. What has just been said about monopoly profit and the giant international company suggests that capital accumulates where it is already large. We have pointed out before in this chapter that nine-tenths of the capital raised on the Stock Exchange in Britain is raised by the top 120 companies. When we spoke of the world location of industry we recorded the CROSS-INVEST-MENT that now takes place between the already advanced

industrial lands. Again and again we have invoked the economic principle of cumulative causation. Wealth attracts and
poverty repels. It is the essential principle for understanding
the movement of capital. Because a firm has a monopolistic
position in its home market, it can set prices to give a monopoly profit; this in turn provides the accumulation of capital
for further expansion in the world market.

Historically, the role of the Stock Exchange has been to
raise money for governments and for joint-stock companies by
the issue of stocks and shares for public subscription. We saw
in Chapter 3 how this role was greatly expanded in the
middle of the nineteenth century by the protection of the
corporate identity of the company and the limited liability of
the shareholder. Nevertheless, it was only during the years
between the two World Wars in Britain that dealings on the
Stock Exchange began to be mainly in commercial and
industrial stocks, as distinct from those of governments and
public utility and railway companies. Industrial companies
were still regarded as risky investments and their ordinary
shares were generally excluded by deed from Trust and Pension funds. Ordinary shareholders are those who own the
EQUITY or property rights in a company, enjoy the profits or
bear the losses arising from its operations and can vote at an
Annual General Meeting on how these should be distributed.
To attract lenders, companies began to offer shares which
carried no voting rights but had a fixed rate of interest. These
were either tied to a MORTGAGE on the company's assets, so-
called DEBENTURE SHARES, which guaranteed repayment of
the loan, or they carried a preferential position in the shareout
of any profit that was made. Sometimes these PREFERENCE
SHARES were cumulative so that a year when a loss was
incurred and no interest was paid could be made up for in a
subsequent profitable year or years.

Between the wars, it was the practice in Britain for companies to pay out to shareholders the whole of their annual
net profits; that is to say, somewhere between two-thirds and
three-quarters of the gross profits made after payments of tax,
the remaining quarter being needed in provision for depreciation. If the company wished to expand and invest in new
capital equipment, it had to raise the necessary funds on the

market. It was up to persons who had savings to decide where to place them according to the company prospectuses. Since the war the position has changed radically. Companies now on average pay out in dividends only about one-third of their gross profits after tax and thus hold large funds in RESERVE for new capital investment over and above their depreciation provision. They are able to build up these reserves because they can charge prices which allow for a monopoly profit. Shareholders are now, moreover, quite prepared to accept even a smaller dividend, on which they must pay the full rate of tax, and to enjoy instead their CAPITAL GAINS, on which for many years in Britain they paid no tax and after 1965 paid tax at a lower rate than on dividends.

Here is the very heart of the new system of capital accumulation and, as we shall see later, of post-war inflation. The oligopolies and price leaders can set prices that give them a reserve fund for growth which when the time is ripe can be invested in new plant. More than three-quarters of the annual increase in gross assets (in plant, buildings, and purchase of subsidiaries) of the companies quoted on the London Stock Exchange has come from internal sources – depreciation funds and reserves – and only the remaining quarter from new borrowing from outside. Table V.6 gives the figures for the decade from the mid-1950s.

The result is that the large companies grow larger and find themselves with funds that are in excess of their needs for expansion in what was previously their line of business. So the process of DIVERSIFICATION begins, not only into new lines in the same field of business but into quite new fields. The Rank Organization for example went naturally from film making and cinema circuits into bowling alleys and skating rinks; but by far the greater part of its profit now derives from its purchase of the English rights to the American Xerox photocopying process. At the same time, great HOLDING COMPANIES grow up like Thomas Tilling or Powell Duffryn, which both started with capital obtained from COMPENSATION for their nationalized undertakings and today own companies that spread across the whole field of British industry. Many of the proposed mergers have seemed on the face of it unlikely marriages – Unilever and Allied Breweries, for example,

Table V.6

Sources of UK Quoted Company Finance and Its Uses, 1954–63

Year	Funds and Assets		Sources of Funds Internal Sources as % of Increase in Gross Assets	External Sources as % of Increase in Gross Assets			Uses of Funds as % of Gross Assets	
	Total Funds	Increase in Gross Assets		Total	Ordinary Shares	Long Term Loans	Expend. on Fixed Assets	Investment in Subsidiaries and others
	£m	£m	%	%	%	%	%	%
1954	1,236	820	85	15	6	9	70	15
1955	1,483	1,017	77	23	13	8	70	11
1956	1,468	1,059	75	25	12·5	10	85	13
1957	1,553	1,189	70	30	16	13	99	13
1958	1,271	945	80	20	11	8	100	16
1959	1,881	1,361	89	21	9·5	5	68	25
1960	2,327	1,528	78	22	20	2	70	26
1961	2,135	1,480	69	31	23	7	90	31
1962	1,901	1,490	72	28	9·5	14	85	30
1963	2,310	1,510	81	19	9	9·5	82	26

Note: The figures in the Uses of Funds column that add up to more than 100 are due to changes in depreciation funds and increases in debts to banks and other trade creditors.

Source: Economic Trends, February 1966.

the 1969 bid by Grand Metropolitan Hotels for Express Dairy.

In this whole process the giant companies are in effect doing what the individual capitalist did previously — switching funds from less profitable to more profitable use. There are three important differences which separate the present reality from the economists' model of a market economy:

(*a*) The giant companies are in a position, to a great extent, as we demonstrated earlier, to determine by advertising techniques how the consumer will spend at least his discretionary income.

(*b*) The size of the giants is so overwhelming and monopoly profit so easily obtained by them, if only by collusion, that large inefficient firms can survive for long where once they would have been flushed out by their more efficient rivals. The poor standing of even the large firms of British industry in international competition is some proof of this.

(*c*) The power of deciding on future lines of investment which was once dispersed amongst many tens of thousands of shareholders is now concentrated in the hands of a few men on the boards of the biggest companies. When the directors of Shell or I.C.I. decide on a major new investment they are in fact deciding on the allocation of a sizeable part of the nation's resources.

The several hundred men who direct the affairs of these giant companies have thus largely taken over the role of the market both in determining prices and in allocating resources. Once the size of plant grew much beyond that which was typical in Britain a hundred years ago, it was inevitable that this should be so, unless private capitalist control was replaced by state control. The increasingly planned processes of production faced a market that was by its very nature anarchic. The increasing role of government in managing aggregate market demand through its MONETARY POLICY and its own spending will be considered in the next chapters. The effect on the top directors of industry was not to reduce but rather to increase the power of the top men. Decisions on the timing, siting, scale and financing of new investment, including purchase of new subsidiaries, and on the WRITING OFF of old investment, had to be made not only in the light of technological change but of

what other companies were doing and what the government
was planning. Mistakes in such matters are enormously costly.
A new plant that is run below full capacity for a year or two
longer than was planned may incur losses running into millions
of pounds. Yet duplication of investment by two companies or
ignorance of the timing of government policies can easily lead
to just this happening.

To reconcile these conflicts between planned production and
market anarchy we find right across the boards of industry a
few men whose role it is to co-ordinate private sector investment and to relate it to government policies. In the United
States this co-ordination is achieved by the size of the companies and by the activities of men who move between government office and the boards of the few super giant companies,
like Mr Macnamara who moved from Chairman of General
Motors, the world's largest company, to be US Secretary of
Defense and then President of the International Bank. The
very size of an international company like General Motors
gives it a power greater than all but a few national governments possess. In Germany and Japan the Big Banks provide
the co-ordinating directors. In Britain it is the MERCHANT
BANKERS. These are private bankers who once financed
government loans at home and overseas and specialized in
foreign trade and investment. Their very names carry with
them something of the aura of Britain's long capitalist history
– Rothschilds and Sassoons, Lazards, Samuels, Hambros,
Jardine Matheson. Today their main function is as ACCEPTING
HOUSES, who arrange for the issue of new shares for companies
quoted on the Stock Exchange and themselves guarantee to
take up any that are not sold, in exchange for a premium on
those that are. In this way they are involved as advisers in
major company investment decisions and especially in proposals for mergers and take-overs. The strength of these merchant banks is that their funds can be risked; the funds are
placed with them by Trusts and private persons and increasingly by the large companies too, and with a much wider
measure of discretion allowed for their use than is open to the
Joint Stock Banks and other financial institutions.

Each of the merchant banks has directors who sit on the
boards of Joint Stock banks at home and overseas, of

G

insurance companies, of large industrial companies at home and of companies operating mainly overseas as well as of many Trusts and smaller companies. Often the merchant banker provides the Company Chairman or deputy. When directors change, the connections of one merchant bank with other banks and companies are generally maintained, so that we can find groups of banks and commercial and industrial companies associated around a merchant bank. A count in 1958 repeated in 1966 revealed about 150 merchant bankers with the following range of interests.

Table V.7

Merchant Bankers on Top Company Boards, U.K. 1958 and 1966

Major Boards	1958	1966	Notes
Number of Merchant Bankers surveyed	120	146	
Court of the Bank of England	4	3	(plus 2 ex-Governors)
Big 8 Banks	29	28	(including all eight)
Other Banks	37	55	
Top Insurance Companies	73	49	(including 12 different companies)
Top 120 Home Industrial Companies	59	60	(45 different companies)
Top Overseas Companies	39	43	
TOTAL Boards (excl. Trusts and smaller companies)	361	385	

Source: K. Coates (ed.), *Can the Workers Run Industry?* Table 13, p. 62.

For a long time in Britain it has been common practice for ex-government ministers to go onto the boards of banks, insurance and industrial companies and for top company directors to enter Conservative and even Labour administrations. Recently the ministers have been joined by top civil servants on the big company boards and also on the boards of the merchant banks. Mr Reginald Maudling, ex-Chancellor of the Exchequer, on Kleinwort, Benson and Lonsdale, and on Dunlop and AEI, may serve to illustrate the first; Sir

Humphrey Trevelyan, now Lord Trevelyan, ex-Ambassador, on Jardine and Mathesons and on the British Bank of the Middle East, British Petroleum, English Electric, Burma Mines, Ampal Tin, etc., etc., the other.[13] The implications for democratic economic planning of the emergence of the giant international company as well as of the role of these controlling directors will have to be deferred for consideration in the next chapters.

6. LABOUR MOBILITY

Where capital moves labour must follow, if only to seek higher wages. We saw in Chapter 2, when we studied the location of industry, how the pull of the largest market had attracted capital towards the south-east of England. Labour had followed, making the market still more concentrated and the process cumulative. We also saw earlier in this chapter how the social costs of congestion and building in the south-east and the under-utilized social capital in the north and west do not enter the accounts of the companies which move southwards. We may now notice that labour is not so mobile as capital. Families in Britain are perhaps unusually reluctant to move, compared say with Americans or Italians. But there are good reasons why modern industry, while it requires more mobility and flexibility of labour, in fact makes such mobility more rather than less difficult. The result is that it is a common phenomenon not only in Britain but in other advanced industrial countries that unemployment frequently remains high in areas of relatively declining industry. The Appallachians in the USA, the Borinage in Belgium match our Welsh valleys and Scottish and Durham coalfields.

Labour mobility is rendered more difficult under modern industrial conditions for four main reasons:

(*a*) Whole industries are concentrated into a few giant plants. Whereas once a man crossed the road to another works if his own closed down, he may today have to cross whole countries and even continents if he wishes to continue to practise the trade he knows.

---

[13] A full list may be found in Ken Coates (ed.) *Can The Workers Run Industry?* Table 13, p. 62 ff.

(*b*) The very fact of the location of industry near to great and growing concentrations of population makes the problem of finding house accommodation more difficult.

(*c*) The rapid pace of technological change renders the skills and experience a man has gained in one job of little use for another without a considerable period of retraining.

(*d*) As usual a cumulative process sets in by which whole communities become incapable of adaptation. Their reduced incomes from declining industries result in poorer social provision and poorer educational facilities. These in turn deprive both the present and the next generation of the means to take up the job opportunities that exist in the new industries.[14]

Of course labour mobility still exists. There are no longer the great emigrations from Europe to the empty continents of North America, Australia or Africa. But English doctors and scientists move to the United States and Indian doctors and scientists come to take their place in Britain. The concentration of capital leads to a concentration of talent, but it is a polarizing process creating wealth at one pole and poverty at the other. The pull of the market, the pull of money rather than of people, creates this result. The wants of the rich are more than satisfied; those of the poor receive little attention, unless governments interfere in the market. This is not only a moral judgment; it raises fundamental economic problems of growth and stability. It is the major problem of macroeconomics to which the next chapter is devoted.

What then is left of the economist's model of the market economy under conditions of large-scale modern industry? Wants are not apparently given but are created by those who supply them; incomes are distributed as much according to inheritance as according to performance, and wealth and poverty tend steadily to polarize; free competition is replaced by monopolistic positions at home and cartels abroad; prices are fixed rather than emerging from the free play of market forces; profit results from monopoly as much as from efficiency; capital is concentrated in giant international companies which themselves determine the allocation of the world's resources; labour follows the concentrations of capital

[14] The working of this process in the United States can be studied in Michael Harrington's *The Other America*, 1962.

as best it can. In this crude and summary picture precious little is left of the market as the reconciler of consumers' needs and producers' power. And yet perhaps the little is indeed precious, as the economists insist. All the countries with planned economies are returning to some reliance on the market, on free competition, and on the return to capital as a criterion of efficiency in providing in detail for people's needs. What was the baby that they threw out with the bath water? We shall return to the problems of planning and the market in Chapter 8. We must now look at the economist's model of economic activity that takes us out of the essentially static model of the market into the dynamic field of study of growth and decay, boom and slump and stagnation.

6 The Cycles of Economic Activity

SUMMARY

In this chapter economists' explanations of cyclical booms and slumps are examined, first in the period before governments began to intervene in the economy and later when their interventions served to damp down but not to eradicate the cycle. Four main theories are considered:

(1) Marx's theory that capital accumulation led to overproduction in relation to the spending power of the workers;

(2) Beveridge's theory that technical change created frictional unemployment;

(3) Keynes's theory of the imbalance between saving and investment and of the cumulative effect of the MULTIPLIER;

(4) Post-Keynesian theory of the rising proportion of saving in a boom.

Economists' explanations are then examined of the sequence of inflation and balance of payments crises in the period since governments intervened to match saving and investment in the economy. An attempt is made with the help of the National Income and Expenditure Accounts for the UK to build a dynamic model of the economy, which draws on both Marxian and Keynesian concepts. The key to the new as to the old cycles of boom and CRISIS is shown to be the tendency of profits to rise ahead of other incomes in periods of boom and to create unbalanced demands upon the economy. Government action appears only to damp these down but not to correct them. The reasons for this are examined in the chapter that follows next.

The economists' model of the market economy which we have just been studying is essentially a static (or at least a stable) model, in that it analyses the relationship of buyers and sellers, both of goods and services and of factors of production, at any one time. Total resources, the state of technology, and income distribution are assumed to be given. All these are, however, subject to change, and economists are interested to know what determines these changes. Since these are part of movements in the economy as a whole they are given the title of macro-economics. Until recently it was thought to be impossible for men consciously to direct such changes in the economy, except to agree with Adam Smith that it was best to remove the obstacles to the market doing the job. The changes then emerged out of a whole system of economic relations. It is these relations which we shall examine, although we shall take account at the end of this chapter of the way governments now intervene to influence the movements of the economy as a whole. In studying economic growth and change, economists have once more to build simplified models of the economy to reveal the essential relationships that are at work. The model must now be a dynamic model to show how changes take place.

1. THEORIES OF THE TRADE CYCLE

For a long time it seemed to economists that in explaining economic growth, it was only necessary to suppose that more of the factors of production were applied and that techniques were steadily improved. This increase in resources could be accommodated within the static model of the market economy. But during the nineteenth century it became clear that growth was not continuous inside any one economy but proceeded by fits and starts, or BOOMS and SLUMPS as they came to be called, and that the growth rates in different economies differed widely. The distribution of incomes changed too and all these changes required explanation.

We may start from the earliest theory, which was that put forward by Karl Marx in his great work on *Capital*, of which the first volume was completed in 1867. Marx identified the successive economic crises of the nineteenth century as realization crises, or what he called CRISES OF REPRO-DUCTION. The boom, he believed, led to an OVER-PRODUC-TION of capital and capital equipment, which in turn created the crisis and was only corrected in the subsequent slump. The whole process arose from the tendency of a private capitalist economy to polarize wealth and poverty. Marx quoted

Gladstone, later to be Liberal Prime Minister, speaking in the
House of Commons on 13 February 1843:

> It is one of the most melancholy features in the social state of
> this country that we see, beyond the possibility of denial, that
> while there is at this moment a decrease in the consuming powers
> of the people, an increase of the pressures of privations and dis-
> tress; there is at the same time a constant accumulation of wealth
> in the upper classes, an increase of the luxuriousness of their
> habits, and of their means of enjoyment.

Marx was less concerned with their luxuriousness than with
the drive of a competitive system to make them save for
further investment. As capital accumulates, Marx believed,
'so it attracts fewer and fewer labourers in proportion to its
magnitude'. Marx thought of capital as being laid out either in
labour (VARIABLE CAPITAL he called this) or in capital equipment and materials (CONSTANT CAPITAL). He expected the
proportion of the constant to rise in relation to the variable in
what he termed the ORGANIC COMPOSITION OF CAPITAL,
because of the pressure of competition on capitalists to invest
in new labour-saving equipment.

An INDUSTRIAL RESERVE ARMY of labour was thus created
which was pulled in to work in periods of sudden expansion
and thrown out again as capital accumulated. By the third
volume of *Capital* (Chapter 15) he summed the matter up as
follows:

> There is periodically a production of too many means of produc-
> tion and necessities of life to permit of their serving as means
> for the EXPLOITATION of the labourers at a certain rate of
> profit. . . . The capitalist mode of production, for this reason
> meets with barriers at a certain scale of production . . . deter-
> mined by the realization of profit, not by the satisfaction of
> social needs.

Later in Chapter 30 may be found his famous conclusion on
the abstract model with which he sought to understand cyclical crises:

> Let us suppose that the whole society is composed only of indus-
> trial capitalists and wage workers. Let us furthermore make
> exception of fluctuations of prices which prevent large portions
> of the total capital from reproducing themselves under average

conditions, and which, owing to the general interrelations of the entire process of reproduction, such as are developed particularly by credit, must always call forth general stoppages of a transient nature. Let us also make abstraction of the bogus transactions and speculations which the credit system favours. In that case, a crisis could be explained only by a DISPROPORTION of production in various branches, and by a disproportion of the consumption of the capitalists and the accumulation of their capitals. But as matters stand, the reproduction depends largely upon the consuming power of the non-producing classes; while the consuming power of the labourers is handicapped partly by the laws of wages, partly by the fact that it can be exerted only so long as the labourers can be employed at a profit for the capitalist class. The last cause of all real crises always remains the poverty and restricted consumption of the masses as compared to the tendency of capitalist production to develop the productive forces in such a way that only the absolute power of consumption of the entire society would be their limit.[1]

Marx saw the crises of the British economy in the nineteenth century as resulting inevitably from the accumulation of capital under conditions of private capital ownership. The length and rhythm of the waves of boom and slump he associated with the life-cycle of capital equipment – installation in one boom, operation through the succeeding slump and boom and then write-off in the slump that followed. Marx believed, however, that the crises would worsen, booms become more violent, slump more prolonged, as the process of accumulation polarized wealth and poverty. The result, Marx prophesied, would be the overthrow of the capitalist system by the increasingly impoverished proletarians, Marx's so called 'doctrine of increasing misery' has so often been misquoted that it is worth quoting in full.[2]

One capitalist always kills many. Hand in hand with this CENTRALIZATION, or this EXPROPRIATION of many capitalists by few, develops on an ever-extending scale the co-operative form of the labour-process, the conscious technical application of science, the methodical cultivation of the soil, the transformation of the instruments of labour into instruments of labour only

[1] Marx's economic writings can most easily be studied in R.Freedman's Penguin selection of *Marx on Economics*.
[2] For further discussion of Marx's views on this students are referred to Freedman's edition and to R.L.Meek's *Economics and Ideology*, 1967.

usable in common, the economizing of all means of production
by their use as the means of production of combined socialized
labour, the entanglement of all peoples in the net of the world-
market and the international character of the capitalistic régime.
Along with the constantly diminishing number of the magnates
of capital who usurp and monopolize all advantages of this process of transformation, grows the mass of misery, oppression,
slavery, degradation, exploitation; but with this too grows the
revolt of the working class, a class always increasing in numbers,
and disciplined, united, organized by the very mechanism of the
process of capitalist production itself. The monopoly of capital
becomes a fetter upon the mode of production which has sprung
up and flourished along with and under it. Centralization of the
means of production and socialization of labour at last reach a
point where they become incompatible with their capitalist
integument. This integument is burst asunder. The knell of
capitalist private property sounds. The expropriators are
expropriated.

Marx's predictions proved wrong. The boom of 1870 was
certainly followed by a long period of stagnation. Capital in
this period was increasingly centralized. But the workers did
not revolt. Instead of overturning the system, in fact, the
proletarians with whom Marx was most closely associated
settled down to obtain by trade union action a larger share of
the value they produced. The better organized workers
succeeded in steadily improving their position and Marx's dire
warnings of gathering crises were forgotten. Booms and
slumps, however, continued and economists became
increasingly impelled to find adequate explanations.

Marx's theories for a long time failed to enter the main-
stream of economic thought. The trade cycle was at one time
associated by W.B.Jevons and others with good and bad agricultural harvests, and its rhythm was attributed to the
cyclical appearance of sunspots and their influence on the
weather. But by the end of the nineteenth century much
evidence was collected about the timing and nature of the
trade cycle which disproved this theory. W. H. Beveridge[3]

[3] In 1908 W.H.Beveridge published his study of *Unemployment – A Problem
of Industry*. He reviewed the whole question again in his 1944 *Report on Full
Employment in a Free Society* which all students should study both for its
historical statistics and its summary of trade cycle theories (pp. 79–105).

showed in his early work that there had been many different weather cycles, few of them coinciding with trade cycles; the trade cycle could only be traced back as far as the beginning of industrialization in Britain around 1785. Unemployment was a problem of industry. His statistics revealed that in the United Kingdom from the 1850s onwards employment, foreign trade, company formation and bank rate all fluctuated together, and with them also the marriage rate, beer consumption and pauperism, this last inversely.

Beveridge's explanation for this phenomenon was that the cycle was caused by the introduction of new industries and new industrial techniques which, while they generated the booms, led also to unemployment of those whom the machines displaced. We can follow the booms and slumps since 1816 on a Chart (Table V.1) and associate the major booms with developments of industrial technology and with the opening up of new markets by Britain and other advanced industrial economies.

Table VI.1

The Trade Cycle in Britain, 1816–1968

Boom or Slump	Years	Industrial Output Index (1880 = 100)	Foreign Trade Volume Index	Industrial Changes and Foreign Trade Developments
Boom	1816–24	15–18	7–10	End of canal building. Early loco-motives.
Slump	1825–6	20–18	11–9	South American market for cotton goods expansion.
Boom	1827–30	20–23	12–13	Beginnings of Railway Construc-tion in UK.
Slump	1831–32	24–23	13–12	
Boom	1833–6	25–27	13–16	Growth of US market.
Slump	1837	28	14	
Boom	1838–41	31–33	17–19	Feverish Railway Boom in UK.
Slump	1842	32	18	Expansion of Asian markets – India and China.
Boom	1843–6	34–40	19–22	
Slump	1847	39	25	

Boom or Slump	Years	Industrial Output Index (1880 = 100)	Foreign Trade Volume Index	Industrial Changes and Foreign Trade Developments
Boom	1848–53	39–52	25–37	Electric telegraph and railway building in Europe and USA. New machine tools make the UK the 'workshop of the world'.
Slump	1854–5	52–51	36–34	
Boom	1856–60	51–63	41–49	
Slump	1861–2	60–58	48	
Boom	1863–74	61–92	49–81	US Civil War and European War. Iron and Steel Development and US railway boom.
Slump	1875–9	91–85	84–91	
Boom	1880–3	100–110	100–111	Shipbuilding boom, iron ships and Agricultural machinery and markets in Canada, Australia and South America.
Slump	1884–6	104–101	108–109	
Boom	1887–91	106–122	114–130	
Slump	1892–3	116–113	128–125	
Boom	1894–9	120–142	134–160	UK development of electric power. Tramways and house building boom. Russian, Japanese and African markets grow.
Slump	1900–4	142–141	160–175	
Boom	1905–7	151–160	182–198	Internal combustion engine. Naval and arms race. Oil and the Near East market. Rapid growth of US industry.
Slump	1908–9	152–154	187–193	
Boom	1910–13	159–184	203–232	
War	1914–18	173–149	200–127	US and Japanese arms booms – iron, steel, chemicals, motors – challenging UK trade.
Boom	1919–20	163–168	169–187	
Slump	1921	105	153	
Boom	1922–29	143–195	186–260	Motor car boom in USA with rubber, oil and electricals. US capital export boom crashes.
Slump	1930–32	183–168	226–195	
Boom	1933–37	179–240	186–286	UK housebuilding and electric grid. Arms boom including aircraft expecially in Germany and Japan.
Slump	1938	216	222	
War	1939–45	—	—	Arms industry boom especially in USA. Beginnings of industrialization in underdeveloped countries.
Boom	1946–51	227–312	184–298	Reconstruction booms everywhere. Atomic power development. Expanding demand in developing lands.
Slump	1952	304	281	

Boom or Slump	Years	Industrial Output Index (1880 = 100)	Foreign Trade Volume Index	Industrial Changes and Foreign Trade Development
Boom	1953–57	321–367	292–350	New electronics and synthetics industries. Nuclear arms and aid race – USA and USSR. Expansion in Common Market and recovery of Germany and Japan.
Slump	1958	362	340	
Boom	1959–60	383–410	356–380	
Stag- nation	1961–2	412–416	385–390	
Boom	1963–4	430–465	415–426	Use of computers in the space race. International companies' 'cross- investment'. Crisis for develop- ing lands.
Stag- nation	1965–7	476–480	450–480	
Boom	1968	505	540	

Note: In both indices the first figure gives the proportion of 1880 levels in the first year of boom or slump, the second figure the proportion for the last year.

Sources: B. R. Mitchell and P. Deane, *Abstract of British Historical Statistics*, pp. 271–2 and pp. 282–3. E. Mandel, *Marxist Economic Theory*, pp. 359–60.

This theory of Beveridge's is not so far from Marx's theory of the reserve army of labour which capitalist accumulation was for ever renewing. Economists had disposed of Marx's theory by arguing that the new labour-saving techniques, by reducing costs of production, would in the process release spending power for more goods and different goods. The production of these would then re-employ the labour saved in the first place. Beveridge believed, however, that what caused the slump after the boom was the disorganized state of the labour market and the reduction of spending power of those who were temporarily unemployed while changing jobs. If the labour market could be improved by labour exchange and if the purchasing power of the temporarily unemployed could be maintained by an insurance scheme, then the technological changes might be made without dislocating the steady growth of the economy. Beveridge was largely responsible for the Lloyd George Government's establishment of Labour Exchanges and of Unemployment and Health Insurance in 1910 and 1911. When slumps reappeared in the 1920s, and most disastrously in the crash of 1929, it was evident that new theories and new measures were desperately needed.

2. THE 'KEYNESIAN REVOLUTION'

The revolution in economic theory launched by J.M.Keynes in the 1930s was born of the unemployment in the inter-war years. From 1927 to 1939 there were never less than a million unemployed in Britain, three-quarters of them on average permanently unemployed. For three years the figure was over $2\frac{1}{2}$ million, more than one-fifth of the working population. In the great export industries – steel, coal, shipbuilding, textiles and the docks – the proportion unemployed exceeded one-third. This was something more than Beveridge's FRICTIONAL UNEMPLOYMENT. The most fundamental assumption of the market economy model, that such a self-regulating system would promote the full utilization of existing resources, was shown to be false. Keynes's revolution consisted in questioning what economists referred to as SAY'S LAW – viz. that 'supply creates its own demand', a concept developed by an early French economist J. B. Say (1767–1832). It was supported by Ricardo, whose view was that there could be no 'general glut of commodities' because in the process of producing commodities for the market enough purchasing power would always be created to buy them back. The concept had been challenged by Marx and his followers and later by the English political economist, J.A.Hobson.[4] Few other economists had listened.

Of course, there is a truth in Say's law; every sale represents a purchase and, under conditions of barter or production to order, what is produced is consumed; but in production for the market there may be a time-lag both in sales after purchases and in purchases after sales. It is also the case that, after the event, we can aggregate the National Income from different points of view and discover that (statistical counting errors apart) consumption equals production. In any year some goods produced may have gone into stock and were not consumed. What we do not know, however, is what could have been produced but was not. Yet there was massive evidence, not only of unemployed manpower, as we have seen in considering the 1930s, but of other underutilized resources. Professor J. D.

[4] See his book *The Evolution of Modern Capitalism*, written in the first decade of our century.

Bernal[5] concluded in 1939 that 'the obstacles to the achievement of plenty are real enough, but they are political and economic, not technical obstacles.' Keynes believed that the economic obstacles could be removed without political violence by extending state intervention just so far as to make the necessary adjustments of consumption and production to establish full employment. Then the classical theory, as he called the model of the market economy, 'comes into its own from that point on'.

Keynes, we must remember, was not concerned so much with the rate of economic growth as we are today but with the full use of resources – the problem of the 1930s.[6] More than once he says that he 'takes as given the existing skill and quantity of labour, the existing quality and quantity of available equipment, the existing techniques'. Thus predictions built upon Keynesian analysis, like the current Treasury economic FORECASTS, although dynamic in the sense of allowing for change in the quantity of resources utilized are extremely short-run – covering six to eighteen months only. In the long run, Keynes insisted, we were all dead.[7]

The Keynesian model of the economy starts from considering three aggregates: National Income (Y), what is spent on Consumption (C) and what is spent on Investment (I). What is spent on Investment is Savings (S). At any time $Y = C + I$ (or S). The three variables, however, mutually influence one another. The decision to consume or to invest (save) Keynes calls the propensity to consume or to invest (save) so that the use made of *extra* income Keynes calls the MARGINAL PROPENSITY TO CONSUME (MPC) and MARGINAL PROPENSITY to invest (or SAVE) (MPS), since $Y - C = S$ or I. At any level of income the MPC/MPS relationship is fairly stable for a whole economy. So Consumption and Saving are a function of Income, but is Investment a function of Income? Are Savings and Investment the same thing? When we look at the National Income and Expenditure accounts in the Blue Book for any

[5] See his book on *The Social Function of Science*, 1939.
[6] See particularly *The General Theory of Employment, Interest and Money*, 1936.
[7] Students will find it helpful to follow the argument from now on with a copy of the Blue Book on *National Income and Expenditure* in front of them because it will be referred to continually. For a detailed exposition of the terms used in the Blue Book they are referred to A. C. Prest (ed.) *The UK Economy – A Manual of Applied Economics*.

year we find what is called the Combined Capital Account. In it Savings equal Investment, but this is viewed after the event. Any differences between saving and investment is concealed by automatic adjustment. If for any reason, for example, investment had been less than savings, the level of Income would have come down until it was equal to Investment plus Consumption.

What determines the size of Income, according to Keynes, is therefore investment; but the problem lies in the relationship between Saving and Investment. We often tend to use the words interchangeably and for long economists thought of them as identical acts. So indeed they once were when the owner of a small firm was content to consume only a part of his profit, saved the rest and reinvested it in the firm. Increasingly, however, the acts of saving and of investment became separated – separated both in time and in the persons who performed them. Ownership became dispersed among thousands of shareholders who saved a part of their dividends and other income. Then when we say that they invested their savings in a company we are only saying that this is the form their savings took. Investment by the company itself means the actual purchase of assets – new plant, equipment, buildings, etc. – and to avoid confusion this is how economists use the word. In the Blue Book such investment is called GROSS FIXED CAPITAL FORMATION. The capital is fixed in an asset (even if the asset itself moves, like a lorry or crane!). We should remember here that in recent years with the increased generation of savings inside companies themselves, which we noted in the last Chapter, the acts of saving and investment have once more been brought together in common hands, if not in time. When Keynes wrote, this had still not become the usual practice.

With the separation of the act of saving and the act of investment, we can see that there is a crucial difference between decisions to consume and decisions to invest. Decisions to consume lead immediately to consumption and so to the production of consumer goods. Decisions to invest lead immediately to investment and the production of investment goods (capital equipment of various sorts). But it is the decision to save that is the obverse side of the decision to consume and this does not necessarily imply a decision to invest.

When we speak of Consumption and Investment in the economy we are really talking about the rate of decisions to purchase consumer goods and the rate of decisions to purchase investment goods, and we can illustrate these in a very simplified model following Keynes's line of thought.

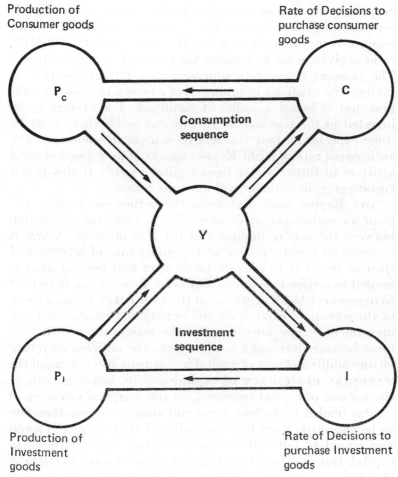

Figure 6.1. Simplified Keynesian economic model

Note: I am indebted for this diagram to an article on 'The Mechanism of Economic Instability' by Professor Arnold Tuslin (*New Scientist*, 31. October 1957).

We can think of the model as representing flows of money into
and out of a pool of income. The two sequences of consumption
and investment are self-contained. In each of them income is
spent on goods, and the production of goods generates new
income earned in the process. As income increases, some is
consumed and some saved, according to the existing marginal
propensity to save or consume. So long as what is saved is
invested all goes well, but there is no reason why this should
happen. It may do or it may not. If we assume the MPS/MPC
ratio as given, what determines the rate of decisions to invest?
The classical economists supposed that it was the rate of
saving. The existence of savings is of course a necessary condition, but it is not a sufficient condition. For savings to be
invested in the purchase of investment goods there must be
some expectation that this will be a profitable business. The
anticipated rate of profit Keynes speaks of as 'a psychological
attitude to future yields from capital assets'. If this is not
encouraging, investment will not take place.

Now Keynes took over from the earlier economists, and
from an earlier period of capitalist history, the distinction
between the rate of interest and the rate of profit. A firm is
assumed to borrow money at the going rate of interest and
then to invest it to make a profit over and beyond what is
needed to service the capital borrowed. Interest has to be paid
to overcome what Keynes called the LIQUIDITY PREFERENCE
of the owners of capital. As the anticipated return from any
investment comes down towards the rate of interest, investment becomes less and less attractive. The anticipated return
on any additional unit of capital investment Keynes called the
MARGINAL EFFICIENCY of capital and he believed that, as
the volume of capital increased, so the marginal efficiency of
capital tended to decline. Long run stagnation was therefore
to be expected. Marx had also believed that the rate of profit
was bound to fall with the accumulation of a 'plethora' of
capital. But such long term changes we must leave to the next
chapter.

Keynes' real discovery was that, if the weakness of the
market economy is the falling inducement to invest, this is
something that the State can step in and supply, in order to
assure the full use of available resources. The intervention

could be achieved by one or more of three possible measures:

(*a*) the rate of interest could be held down by increasing the money supply, and so raising the rate of profit; the rentiers, that is those living on interest payments, would suffer euthanasia but this was to be preferred to general stagnation of industry;

(*b*) the government could step in with its own schemes for investment which would take up the slack and generate incomes in a sort of pump-priming operation. Such investment could as well be in setting men to dig holes in the ground and fill them up again, as in building schools, so long as the extra incomes were generated;

(*c*) the government could increase its own consumption and its welfare payments to those who were unemployed, to the sick and the aged.

What governments then had to do was to spend their way out of crises, if necessary by so-called DEFICIT BUDGETING – that is spending more than they collected in taxes. This was recommended by Keynes at the time of the crisis of 1929–31. In fact the Labour Government did the opposite and cut its spending, thus creating still more unemployment. Post-war British governments have regarded the maintenance of near full employment as a basic requirement and have greatly increased the state's share in total investment from about 30 per cent before the war to about 45 per cent since the war. This is mainly the result of the inclusion of the nationalized industries in the state sector.

We are now in a position to improve upon the model from which we started (Fig. 6.1). We can first of all divide up the flows of income into dividends, company reserves, wages and salaries, but the main difference in our Fig. 6.2 is that we can now add government intervention to our earlier model of the economy. The Government collects DIRECT TAXES from income and INDIRECT TAXES from consumption, and it spends these in three ways – (*a*) in goods and services (Public Authorities Expenditure in the Blue Book) for maintaining the armed forces, schools, hospitals, roads, etc. These payments simply add directly to the consumption sequence; (*b*) on Transfer Incomes, that is to say, on Pensions, Subsidies and Social Security and Debt Interest payments. These transfers are what their

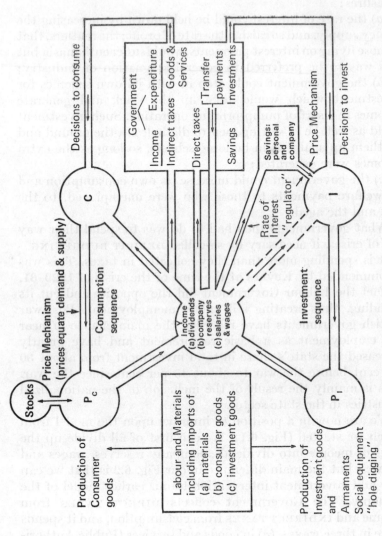

Figure 6.2. Model of a market economy with government intervention

Price Mechanism
(prices equate demand & supply)

Decisions to consume

Decisions to invest

Government

Expenditure   Goods & Services

Income

Indirect taxes

Direct taxes

Transfer payments

Investments

Savings

Savings: personal and company

Price Mechanism

Rate of Interest "regulator"

C

I

Income
(a) dividends
(b) company reserves
(c) salaries & wages

Consumption sequence

Investment sequence

Stocks

P_C

P_I

Production of Consumer goods

Production of Investment goods and Armaments Social equipment "hole digging"

Labour and Materials including imports of
(a) materials
(b) consumer goods
(c) investment goods

name implies, a form of income redistribution; (c) on Investment, that is in the Public Sector share of Gross Fixed Capital Formation (with which is generally included the public sector share of increases in stocks and work in progress). This may be in social equipment, in building schools, hospitals, roads, etc., or in the capital formation of the nationalized industries.

We have also on the new diagram to separate Savings and Investment. The rate of interest was regarded in the classical economic model as an automatic regulator. If Savings were in excess of the need for Investment, the rate would fall and the savings share of Income would be reduced. If Savings were inadequate for Investment needs, the rate would rise and attract people to save more from their incomes. But we have already seen that a fall in Investment implies a fall in the whole level of Income. Savings may be made, but if they are not needed immediately for investment this is soon shown in a general fall in their value, that is in the Stock Exchange price of stocks and shares. The self-regulating model, as Keynes insisted, might just as likely operate at a level far below the full utilization of resources, as it might with all resources fully used. The rate of interest also suffered from an inherent defect as a regulator: it tended to overcompensate. In the same way that when the governor on a diesel engine sticks, it causes the engine to 'hunt', that is to race and then to stall; so when interest rates rose, savings tended to flood in and not to be checked until too late. Then the rate tumbled and all savings were choked off, only to be overstimulated by the next compensating rise in the rate. Keynes set great store by government control of interest rates, but we shall see in the next chapter that this control proved less effective than he expected. The reason lies in the conditions upon which businessmen's anticipation of profit depends.

Keynes seemed greatly impressed by what he called 'the animal spirits' of businessmen in deciding that investment was worthwhile. Those who followed him emphasized that if Investment was the key to maintaining and expanding the level of Income, the decision to invest itself depended upon the rate of Consumption. Firms would not believe in the profitability of investment in new plant and equipment unless their old plant was being fully used or they expected the rate of consumption to increase to take up any slack. Thus the rate of Investment, far from depending on the rate of Savings, as in classical theory, depended on the rate of Consumption.[7]

Keynes' model of the economy thus consists of circular flows. Increased Investment depends upon rising Consumption, which in turn depends on extra Incomes generated by both Investment and Consumption. The two sequences depend upon the level of income, but there is nothing in the system to guarantee that the decisions to save or to consume at any time are exactly in line with the need of savings for investment. Marx had insisted that disproportion between the two departments of consumption and investment were likely to occur as capital accumulated. Keynes also believed in the declining scarcity of capital, but the central point of his thought was that as income rose the marginal propensity to save rose too. In other words, the savings proportion of total income was rising although he believed that this was rising fairly slowly. It is of course a commonplace that the proportion of income saved will be higher among the well-to-do than among the poor. For this reason Keynes favoured some modest redistribution of incomes through PROGRESSIVE TAXATION, that is to say through imposing taxes that took not just a larger amount from the rich than the poor taxpayer but took a *higher proportion* of the incomes of the rich.

We may illustrate the way the MPS rises as incomes rise by examining the way in which at any time people at different income levels spend their income in Table VI.2. As we go up the income scale we may imagine each income group laying out its extra income between saving and consumption, and thus reveal their marginal propensities as decimal proportions of unity. At the bottom, people spend more than their income; they spend their savings and run into debt; that is to say they dissave. For the first few steps up the scale the groups reduce their DISSAVING, but towards the top end of the scale they increase the share of extra income going to savings. A comparison with the United States at a much higher level of income than Britain shows that the MPS rises rather earlier

[8] Joan Robinson's little book, *An Introduction to the Theory of Employment*, 1937, perfectly describes this dependence.

Table VI.2

Saving and Consumption in the UK 1954 and USA 1950

Income Units in Tenths	Mean Disposable Income US $	Mean Disposable Income UK £	Mean Saving US $	Mean Saving UK £	MPS US	MPS UK	Mean Consumption US £	Mean Consumption UK £	MPC US	MPC UK	As % of Mean Disposable Income Saving US %	Saving UK %	Expenditure on Durable Consumer Goods US %	Expenditure on Durable Consumer Goods UK %
Bottom Tenth	479	99	−426	−20·6	—	—	905	128·6	—	—	−88·9	−30·0	10·2	4·5
Ninth Tenth	1,112	156	−45	−11·6	0·6	0·3	1,157	167·6	0·4	0·7	−4·0	−7·4	8·4	2·4
Eighth Tenth	1,653	223	3	−0·9	0·1	0·15	1,650	223·9	0·9	0·85	0·2	−0·4	10·7	2·1
Seventh Tenth	2,121	300	22	−1·0	0·05	0·0	2,099	301·0	0·95	1·0	1·0	−0·4	10·2	4·6
Sixth Tenth	2,635	365	−22	5·7	−0·3	0·1	2,657	359·3	1·3	0·9	−0·8	1·6	11·9	4·7
Fifth Tenth	3,089	424	112	12·7	0·3	0·1	2,977	411·3	0·7	0·9	3·6	3·0	12·8	4·0
Average All Units	3,233	429	278	10·9	—	—	2,955	418·1	—	—	8·6	2·5	11·7	5·9
Fourth Tenth	3,568	493	256	9·5	0·3	−0·05	3,392	483·5	0·7	1·0 5	7·2	1·9	12·1	5·0
Third Tenth	4,122	565	310	18·2	0·1	0·1	3,812	546·8	0·9	0·9	7·5	3·2	12·5	6·5
Second Tenth	4,957	666	550	6·9	0·3	−0·1	4,407	659·1	0·7	1·1	11·1	1·0	12·2	7·5
Top Tenth	8,606	1,014	2,026	100·3	0·4	0·3	6,580	913·7	0·6	0·7	23·5	9·9	11·6	7·8

Source: Oxford University Institute of Statistics, *Bulletin*, August 1960.

on the scale and shows also that the average SAVINGS PRO-
PORTION is much higher.

The figures given in Table VI.2 are old ones but they reveal
the pattern fairly clearly. They do not show the average
MPS/MPC relationship for all UK or US incomes; but
they do show that, if the economies of the UK and the
USA are regarded as comparable, then, as income rises
between the two economies from £429 to $3,233 (£1,150),
average annual saving rises from £10 18s 0d to $278
(£99 10s 0d). That is to say, of the extra £721 income, saving
takes £88 12s 0d or 12·2 per cent and consumption takes the
rest. The MPS is ·12 and MPC ·88. Saving is defined here
as long-term saving, not including savings made inside a year
for holidays or Christmas clubs. It includes house purchase
but not the purchase of cars or other durable consumer goods.
These are shown in a final column to reveal how in the 1950s
the proportion of income spent on these rose with incomes in
Britain but hardly at all in the USA. The MPS/MPC
proportions of about 1:9 are confirmed by figures of the way
extra income in Britain has in fact been distributed in post-war
years between saving and consumption.[9]

3. THE MULTIPLIER AND ACCELERATION PRINCIPLE

The importance of Keynes's emphasis on inducements to
increased investment has to be understood by realizing the
cumulative effect of investment. Extra money spent on investment goods leads to new labour being employed in the investment goods industries. The extra incomes thus generated are
spent mainly on consumer goods. This leads to more labour
being taken on in the consumer goods industries and so on
round and round the sequences we revealed in Fig. 6.1. If we
know at any time what is the average MPS/MPC relationship in an economy, we can know how the spending of an extra
£100m will be distributed between Consumption and Investment. Let us suppose the MPS to be 0·1 and MPC 0·9 then
9/10ths of the £100m will go to consumption on the first round
and 9/10ths of 9/10ths on the second round and so on. The
additions to Consumption will be £90m + £81m + £72·9m +

---

[9] These are shown in A. R. Prest's *The UK Economy*, p. 11.

£65·6m + ... giving a total of £1,000m. The MULTIPLIER, as Keynes called it is 10; £100m has become £1,000m and 10 is the RECIPROCAL of 0·1, i.e. the MPS. In fact we should have to allow for part of the extra income to be spent on imports and on indirect taxes. Taking these into account the MPC is about 0·6 in Britain today, and the MPS is 0·4 ,so that the Multiplier is 2·5, i.e. the reciprocal of 0·4

$$\left(\frac{1}{0·4} = 2·5 \right).$$

To calculate the annual effect of this additional investment we have to know the VELOCITY OF CIRCULATION of money. It is an important point in understanding the model in Figs. 6.1 and 6.2, that we are speaking of flows of income and the rate of flow. The total money supply in Britain in 1968 including credit we estimated earlier at about £6,000 millions. This can be compared in the National Income and Expenditure Accounts (Table 1) with total domestic expenditure of some £40,000 millions, including taxes on expenditure (less subsidies) of about £5,000 million. The money supply turns over about 6 times a year. A further comparison can be made by comparing the expansion of money supply at about £1,000m a year between 1965 and 1969[10] and the growth of domestic expenditure at about £2,000 million a year in this period. We shall return to this question of money supply in the next chapter.

The multiplier effect is a further example of the central economic principle of cumulative causation which we have met so often before. It is because of its multiplier effect that government action in stepping up public investment can be so important in maintaining aggregate demand for consumption goods, when otherwise the savings proportion would be reducing this. It is especially important because the multiplier can as easily work in reverse as it can in forward gear. A reduction in employment as a result of technological change, if it is not compensated by redundancy pay, unemployment benefit and other social security payments, or by rapid redeployment of the unemployed, leads to reduced earnings; the general level of income is lowered; consumption is cut back; those employed in consumer goods industries become

10 See *Economic Trends* for May 1969, p. xxv.

unemployed and their earnings are reduced; investment is cut back and still more workers are unemployed and their earnings reduced; and so it can go on in a declining spiral of activity unless action is taken to reverse the process. The collapse of interest rates, caused by falling incomes and savings, may well not be enough to encourage new investments, for demand has fallen away so far, surplus capacity has become widespread and no need for new plant presents itself until old plant is written off and losses have been absorbed.

This then was Keynes' theory of the INCONSISTENCY of decisions about saving and investment, because of the unresponsiveness of each to changes in interest rates. Keynes emphasized that this was made worse by speculative hoarding of money in anticipation of further price falls – what came to be called the liquidity trap. There was in fact no self-adjusting full-employment mechanism, as classical economic theory had supposed.

We are now seeing the implications of Keynesian thought for our earlier study of the trade cycle. Keynes' own thinking about investment decisions involved three main elements: rate of interest, cost of investment, i.e. of capital goods and anticipated return from use of investment on capital goods. His followers, as we saw, emphasized also the level of demand for the product. The influence of demand for consumption goods upon decisions to invest in capital goods was described by Alvin Hansen and Paul Samuelson (both American Keynesian economists and the latter the author of the most popular text book on Economics in the world) in terms of an ACCELERATION principle. This is fairly simply explained as meaning that quite small changes in Consumption can lead to quite large relative changes in Investment. The reason is best understood by looking at an imaginary individual firm's sales and investment decisions over a period of years, as in Table VI.3.

It is assumed that the firm, starting from a sales figure of £50 million, enjoys increased sales of £25 million a year for three years and adds to its capital stock within the year the same proportional increment, i.e. half as much again the first year; a third the second year, and a quarter the third year. If the

[11] A comprehensive study of Keynes' thought with empirical evidence to support it will be found in Gardner Ackley's *Macro-economic Theory*, 1961.

Table VI.3

Acceleration Principle in a Firm's Sales and Capital Investment

Year	Sales a year Increment %	Actual £m	Capital Stock at beginning of Year £m	Investment in year (in £m.) Replacement (Capital Consumption)	Net Investment	Gross Investment
0	−0	50	20	1	0	1
1	+50	75	20	1	10	11
1	+33⅓	100	30	1·5	10	11·5
3	+25	125	40	2	10	12
4	0	125	50	2·5	0	2·5

firm's REPLACEMENT policy, that is to say its regular orders for plant to replace old plant, so called CAPITAL CONSUMPTION, was based on a twenty-year depreciation provision it would replace capital stock of £20 million at the rate of £1 million a year. This would be the total of its order for investment goods before sales began to rise. But a rise of 50 per cent in sales leads to new orders for capital equipment at ten times the level of previous orders; and when the rise in sales stops these orders fall away almost as sharply as they rose. For the acceleration principle has as its obverse a deceleration principle.

Real life is never so neat and clear as economists' examples, but the following figures taken from the Accounts of the Associated Electrical Industries in the 1950s do show the principle at work. (Table V.4.)

Depreciation provision is not of course the same as replacement or capital consumption, since the provision is what is set aside in the Depreciation Fund for future replacement each year and not what is paid out of the fund each year for replacement. The figure is given because no other is available and the difference in sums will not affect the principle being illustrated.

Table VI.4

Annual Turnover and Investment of Associated Electrical Industries, 1954–62.

Year	Sales Turnover £m	Sales Increment %	Capital Assets £m	Deprecia-tion	Investment (£m) Net	Gross
1954	96	0	14	1·5	3·0	4·5
1955	128	+33	23	2	9	11
1956	133	+34	34	3	11	14
1957	150	+13	42	4	8	12
1958	182	+21	53	5	11	16
1959	208	+14	59	6	6	12
1960	215	+ 3	60	6	1	7
1961	214	0	61	6	0	6
1962	210	−2	61	6	0	6

Source: AEI *Annual Accounts.*

4. THE INVESTMENT CYCLE – FLOOR AND CEILING

If each individual firm had a cycle of investment related to sales, such as we have been looking at, but these were all staggered according to a rise and fall of demand for particular products, the acceleration principle would be relatively unimportant for the economy as a whole. If, however, all firms tend to move together to increase investment as demand expands and business expectations rise, and then cut back as demand falls and expectations collapse, an important elemen⁺ in the business cycle is explained. This is that the cycle has a much greater amplitude in the capital goods industries than in the consumer goods sector. Steel workers know only too well which were the years of boom and good money after the war – 1947–9, 1956, 1960–1, 1964–5 and 1968 – and which the years of slump and short time – 1950–1, 1957–8, 1962–3, 1966–7. Steel is used primarily in capital goods – buildings and new plant – and these years of boom and slump indicate a general bunching together of investment.

We can take from the Blue Book a series of annual figures of Consumption and Investment to illustrate what is evidently an INVESTMENT CYCLE in the post-war years. In Table VI.5 the annual changes are shown in personal consumption and in private investment apart from that in dwellings. We notice at once that in 1951–2 a small annual cut in consumption of around 1 per cent led to a 10 per cent cut in investment; the 4 per cent annual increases in consumption that followed led to annual increases in investment of over 16 per cent. Later periods of boom or of slow growth in consumption produced correspondingly large or small increases in investment. There tends naturally to be a time lag of about a year between the one and the other. We may notice also that, while Public Authorities consumption remained almost static from 1952 to 1961, there was some attempt by governments to balance private investment changes by public investment changes in the opposite direction, particularly in the years up to 1958 and again in 1967–8.

It is clear that the multiplier and acceleration principle, in forward and reverse gear, provide valuable explanations of the way booms swing up and slumps swing down. There remains to be determined what starts the boom off and then brings it to a crisis. We have seen that in the post-Keynesian world national governments had much to do with the starting and stopping of the investment cycle, but what of the 150 years prior to the 1940s? We may start by noticing a weakness in Keynesian analysis, which some of his followers have detected.[12] Keynes thought of the marginal propensity to save or to consume as remaining stable over the period of a few years and rising slowly as incomes rose. In fact there are good reasons for supposing that it changes rapidly over the period of a trade cycle. This is because profits tend to rise faster in a boom period than do other incomes and to fall faster in a slump. Profits if paid out in dividends go to those with higher incomes whose propensity to save is higher than those with lower incomes. A rise in the savings proportion thus takes place over the period of a boom. This will be exaggerated by the tendency of firms to increase their own savings (reserves), rather than raising dividends, in a boom.[13]

For an explanation of why profits rise in a boom we have already noticed that, as production comes up towards full

[12] Jan Pen's Pelican on *Modern Economics*, 1958, deals with the point admirably.
[13] The point is discussed in R. C. O. Matthews' excellent introductory book. *The Trade Cycle*, 1959.

Table VI.5

Annual Changes in Consumption and Investment, UK 1948–68 (in real terms 1958 prices and % changes on the previous year)

Year	Consumption Personal		Gross Fixed Capital Formation (Investment)					
					Private Total Other Private		Public Total	
	£m	% change	Public £m	Dwellings £m	£m	% change	£m	% change
1948	12,531	—	3,070	65	1,095	—	975	—
1949	12,765	+1·5	3,255	79	1,141	+4·5	1,113	+14
1950	13,116	+3	3,255	71	1,208	+4·5	1,180	+6
1951	12,941	−1·5	3,500	72	1,123	−8	1,274	+8
1952	12,876	−1·0	3,856	112	1,003	−10·5	1,364	+7
1953	13,450	+4·5	3,963	192	1,032	+3	1,524	+12
1954	13,995	+4	3,948	258	1,209	+17	1,515	−1
1955	14,559	+4	3,832	286	1,405	+16·5	1,487	−6
1956	14,682	+1	3,808	305	1,542	+10	1,456	+2
1957	14,985	+2	3,748	304	1,660	+8	1,506	+3·5
1958	15,362	+2·5	3,675	322	1,690	+1	1,484	−2
1959	16,080	+4·5	3,744	400	1,772	+5	1,580	+7
1960	16,735	+4	3,824	484	2,009	+12·5	1,639	+4

1961	17,117	+2·5	3,964	527	2,230	+11	1,767	+8
1962	17,517	+2	4,091	515	2,151	−3·5	1,834	+4
1963	18,375	+4·5	4,153	512	2,144	−0·5	1,926	+5
1964	19,082	+4	4,221	625	2,483	+16	2,258	+18
1965	19,421	+1·5	4,391	616	2,604	+4·5	2,360	+5
1966	19,811	+2	4,516	553	2,579	−0·5	2,537	+8
1967	20,211	+2	4,747	530	2,530	−2·0	2,884	+14
1968	(20,600)	+2	(4,800)	(530)	(2,760)	+9·0	2,950	+2

Note: Figures in brackets = estimates from *Economic Trends*, April 1969.

Source: *National Income and Expenditure*, Blue Book, 1968, plus for 1948–51 National Institute *Economic Review*.

capacity in any firm, unit costs will fall, and as, demand overtakes supply, prices will rise. Falling costs and rising prices mean increased profits unless wages are pushed up very sharply. We are thrown back to an examination of the relative bargaining strengths of employers and workers and to Marxian theories of capital accumulation. The very essence of private capital ownership, with or without monopoly, is, as we saw in the last chapter, that profit is maximized. A firm that does not show good profits will fail to attract the new capital it needs to keep up in a competitive market. The facts are in any case not in dispute.

Table VI.6

Indices of Output, Wages and Profits in Manufacturing Industry in the USA 1919–33 (1919 = 100)

Year	Manufacturing Output	Employment	Output per worker	Average Annual Money Earnings	Prices	Real Earnings	Corporate Profits paid in Dividends Money	Real
1919	100	100	100	100	100	100	100	100
1920	103	100	103	120	115	104	110	96
1921	78	77	101	100	103	94	101	98
1922	103	85	121	98	96	101	101	105
1923	119	97	123	108	98	110	127	130
1924	112	90	124	109	98	111	131	134
1925	125	94	133	110	101	108	154	152
1926	132	95	139	112	102	109	170	167
1927	130	93	140	113	100	113	183	183
1928	136	93	145	114	98	116	198	202
1929	153	100	153	115	98	117	226	230
1930	125	88	142	105	94	112	215	228
1931	104	75	139	84	85	99	160	189
1932	79	66	118	74	76	97	101	133
1933	95	72	132	66	73	94	80	110

Note:

1. Corporate Profits are for all industries.

2. 'Real Earnings' and 'Real' Dividends respectively are found by dividing Money Earnings and Dividends by the Price Changes.

Source: *Historical Statistics of the United States, 1789–1945,* US Dept. of Commerce.

We need only to look at the decade prior to 1929 in the United States Economy, in Table VI.6, to find that profits rose in real terms seven times as fast as earnings and then fell right back by 1933. Since output per worker rose far ahead of earnings, while prices remained stable, it is not surprising that profits increased. J. K. Galbraith comments:

> The profits sustained the spending of the well-to-do, and they also nourished at least some of the expectations behind the stock market boom. Most of all they encouraged a high level of capital investment. . . . A large and increasing investment in capital goods was, in other words, a principal device by which the profits were being spent. It follows that anything that interrupted the investment outlays – anything indeed which kept them from showing the necessary rate of increase – could cause trouble. When this occurred, compensation through an increase in consumer spending could not automatically be expected.[14]

This last sentence may be regarded as something of an understatement, but the comment stands.

We are now in a position to sum up the causes and stages of the trade cycle as it was before Keynesian measures began to be adopted by governments. We can take from Beveridge the belief that technological advances provide the initial stimulus for the boom. As costs are brought down, consumer spending power is increased and this is spread by the multiplier throughout the economy. The increase in consumption encourages new investment at an accelerated rate. New spending power is generated and again spread by the multiplier, encouraging still more investment. Meantime the savings proportion has been growing with rapidly rising profits, but by this very fact the propensity to consume has been falling. New opportunities for profitable investment suddenly dry up, a crisis is reached, aggravated possibly by a speculative stock exchange and credit boom. Investment is then cut back with the acceleration principle working in reverse. The multiplier too goes into reverse as unemployment rises and earnings fall, first in the capital goods sector and then in consumption goods also. Firms are forced to cut their prices, to sell off their stocks and to write off some of their more obsolete plant. When the losses

[14] See *The Great Crash 1929*, 1954, pp. 157–8.

H

have been absorbed their more modern plant remains, with which output can be produced at lower unit costs. With prices cut as costs are reduced spending power recovers and the cycle starts again.

There is in other words a floor and a ceiling to the investment cycle. In Keynesian thought the ceiling is set by the rising propensity of firms and individuals to save as income rises; the floor is set by the dissaving that takes place as income falls. We saw this in Table VI.2. Individuals maintain their consumption levels despite the changes in income. This is sometimes referred to as the RATCHET EFFECT or Duesenbery effect after the economist who first developed the idea.[15] Consumption goes up and comes down by steps. This is true also of company investment. Income rises some way before consumption is increased and this increases savings; but once a certain level is achieved it is held on to at the expense of saving. The whole relationship is referred to by Keynesian economists as the CONSUMPTION FUNCTION. It can be studied in detail in Gardner Ackley's book on *Macro Economic Theory*. What we have added is a Marxian explanation of why profits should rise faster than other incomes in a boom.

We can now see the whole sequence of events on a graph, which shows for an imaginary period of years the respective movements of demand for consumption goods and services, and of industry's capacity to supply from investment. Acceleration of investment follows each upward movement of demand and deceleration follows collapse of demand (Fig. 6.3).

The length of the cycle, it will be noted, corresponds with the writing off of plant and equipment over a twelve-year period. This is shorter than the period over which depreciation provision has generally been supposed to be calculated, but there is evidence to show that much plant has always, in fact, been written off before the end of its expected life. The more rapid the rate of technological change the shorter the period over which plant will be kept in operation before becoming obsolete. It is a significant fact that the length of the cycle has tended, as we can see from the earlier Table VI.1, to get shorter. Some economists have discerned a longer SECULAR CYCLE moving with the major technological advances which we

[15] J. Duesenbery, *Income, Saving and Consumer Behaviour*, 1949, Harvard.

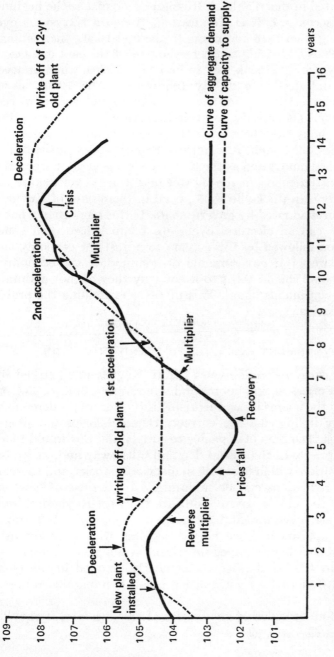

Figure 6.3. Diagrammatic stages of the trade cycle

indicated in that Table. A Russian economist at the beginning of this century, N.D.Kondratieff, traced a sixty-year cycle, starting from 1843 and rising to the mid-1850s, then falling to the 1880s and rising again to the end of the century. On this theory the next peak was to be in the 1920s, which indeed it was and decline certainly followed in the 1930s. Joseph Schumpeter[16] developed the idea of larger and smaller waves of activity. The steady, and indeed rapid, economic growth throughout the 1950s and 1960s has somewhat upset these theories, although it confirms Schumpeter's insistence on technical innovation as the main cyclical generator. Something evidently remains of the shorter investment cycle, as we have already seen (in Table VI.5), even in these days of Keynesian measures adopted by governments. Is this more than what the cynics call an electoral cycle – a boom before each general election followed by three years to adjust the economy again in between? If governments do manipulate the economy so readily we should want to know why they cannot maintain a more continuous boom. This involves examining the problem of inflation.

5. GOVERNMENT INTERVENTION AND INFLATION

The history of trade cycles before Keynes was marked by a rise in prices during booms and a fall during slumps. The price rise in the booms is not surprising if the curves for demand and supply in Fig. 6.3 are correct. Demand keeps bumping up against the limits of capacity to supply and this would tend to raise prices. In the slump demand falls away and, as we have seen, prices will first be cut to dispose of stocks, and thereafter price reductions can be maintained by the use of new plant when the old is written off. In the post-Keynesian world, however, government intervention to maintain full employment appears to have been associated with a steady rise in prices. This has averaged in Britain over 3 per cent per annum, so that the retail price index nearly doubled in the twenty years after 1948 – an increase previously unparalleled in peace time.

Before considering the causes of this increase, it should be

[16] *Business Cycles*, 1939.

set in historical context. It is generally believed that prices have risen fairly consistently over a long period of history. 'Johnny shall have but a penny a day because he can't work any faster.' So runs the old nursery rhyme and it is many years since a penny a day could have kept Johnny's body and soul together. He could have bought a 4 lb loaf in London for 1*d*, and in some areas for less, throughout the fourteenth and fifteenth centuries, but prices more than trebled in the sixteenth century, doubled again at the end of the eighteenth century and during the Napoleonic Wars the 4 lb loaf cost 18*d*. Prices however, fell steadily in the nineteenth century, although with ups and downs in booms and slumps, and the loaf could be bought for 5½*d* or 6*d* in London just before the First World War. Prices trebled in the First World War but fell back again in the inter-war years. They doubled in the Second World War and have doubled again since. Today you would pay 3*s* 6*d* for a 4 lb loaf if you could find one. More general indices of prices can be constructed, but they are, as we saw earlier, somewhat arbitrary constructions over a long period since the quality of goods being priced inevitably changes.[17] They all show price increases over a long period, but none of them show increases for any peacetime period since the sixteenth century that compare with those in the last twenty years. The steady rise is quite different from the wartime situations after 1800 or 1914, when prices shot up, stayed up for the period of the war and just after and then collapsed.

There were certainly price increases in famines and wars before the sixteenth century.[18] How do economists explain this long history of what we now call inflation? The first explanation is the proclivity of rulers for DEBASING the coinage, even clipping bits off it to pay their bills. The second is that coins wear down and get lighter and in the words of the famous law of a sixteenth century banker, Sir Thomas Gresham, 'bad money drives out good'. William the Conqueror took over the Saxon penny, originally struck by King Offa in AD 760 – two hundred and forty of them to a pound of silver – and set the

---

[17] Such indices may be studied in the tables in Mitchell and Deane's *Abstract of British Historical Statistics*.
[18] The student can learn of them from E. V. Morgan's fascinating Pelican *A History of Money*, 1965, and in R. F. Harrod's textbook on *Money*, 1969.

STERLING standard at 925 parts of silver to 1,000. But by the fifteenth century there were 480 to a pound and only 250 parts of silver per 1,000. Then came the voyages of discovery and the import into Europe by the Spanish government fleet alone of 200 tons of gold and 18,000 tons of silver. This great increase in the quantity of money provides the third explanation. Price increases are but the obverse of a fall in the value of money. An increase in quantity, unless offset by an equivalent increase in demand, will reduce the value of anything. To the increase in supplies of gold and silver was soon added the increase in credit and paper money. Bills of exchange, which are but promises to pay a certain sum in three or six months' time, if accepted by a financial house of good standing, can be exchanged like money. So too can a paper note on which the Governor of the Bank of England promises to pay the Bearer £1, which today means just another paper note.

The expansion of the money supply need not necessarily mean a rise in prices. This depends on the corresponding increase in the production of goods and services which people want money to pay for. Inflation is generally associated with the situation in wartime or in the aftermath of a war, when productive capacity is concentrated on armaments or dislocated or destroyed, and money is being paid to people to buy goods which do not exist. Periods of galloping inflation occurred in Germany and Austria and Greece after both world wars, when governments aggravated the situation by continuing to pay their soldiers and civil servants with paper money that declined in value as soon as it was run off the printing press. The important point to notice is the relation between the money supply and the capacity to produce. If surplus unused capacity to produce goods exists, an expansion of money supply may be useful in evoking actual increased production. A moderate degree of inflation is encouraging also to businessmen since it both enhances the value of property (plant, machinery, buildings, etc.) in relation to money (hence the current preference for ordinary shares as a HEDGE against inflation) and at the same time assists the writing off of old plant against the value of new sales. By contrast inflation is detrimental to those who have no property and particularly to those whose incomes are fixed. For an economy as a whole inflation is harmful too, if prices rise much faster in it than in the economies of competitors in international trading.

The wartime and immediate post-war types of inflation which we have been considering are well characterized by the phrase about 'too much money chasing too few goods'. The pressure on prices comes from the demand side and economists refer to this as DEMAND-PULL INFLATION. We should expect to find it today, as we have in the past, in periods of boom, when demand exceeds the capacity to supply. It is frequently argued that this is indeed the condition in which the British economy has found itself since the war. Because of full employment, it is said, the new situation is the very opposite of what we saw occurred in the USA from 1919 to 1929; and now wages are pushed up faster than output per man. Again and again, it is said, governments have been forced to deflate the booms because of the inflationary pressure of wage increases. There is a certain truth in this line of argument, but there are two important weaknesses. In the first place, demand on the nation's resources comes from many other sources as well as from wages.

Indeed, if we draw up a Table as in Table VI.7 of effective demand, that is of spending power in the economy, we then find that wages, after tax, insurance and savings are deducted, only account for about 30 per cent net of total demand, salaries another 10 per cent; wages, account for only half of private consumption and there are also the pulls of investment (public and private sector capital formation) and of public consumption, taking 20 per cent or so each.[19]

Apart from the fact, however, that wages only form a part of effective demand, a more serious objection to demand-pull arguments must be faced. This is that if we divide up the post-war years into periods of boom and periods of stagnation, as in Table VI.8, we find that prices rose faster in the periods of stagnation than in the periods of boom – almost twice as fast in fact: 3·4 per cent p.a. compared with 1·9 per cent (Table VI.8, column 2). Only in the immediate post-war years of 1947–52, which included the Korean war boom of 1949–50, could one speak of demand-pull inflation with prices pulled up

[19] Students should study the Blue Book carefully to see how this Table is built up.

Table VI.7
Effective Demand UK 1960 (£m)

Sources of Income Items	Before Direct Tax	Direct Tax +NI	After Tax +NI	Personal Saving	Indirect Tax less Subsidies	Net Total Demand	%
I. PRIVATE CONSUMPTION							
Wages	8,630	−620	8,010	−420	−1,150	6,440	29
Salaries	5,060	−412	4,644	−630	−520	2,494	11
Forces Pay	455	−30	425	−40	−40	345	2
Self-Employment	2,007	−853	3,494	−960	−500	2,084	9
Rent, Dividend, Interest	2,340						
Govt. Transfer Payments	1,650	−16	1,634	−50	−240	1,954	9
Private Superannuation	650	−40	610				
TOTAL	20,790	−1,970	18,790	−2,100	−2,450	13,270	60
NI Contributions							
Employers		424					
Employees		487					

II. SAVING for CAPITAL FORMATION	Personal Saving	Net Total Demand		%
Personal	1,494	Prvt. Cap. Fm.	2,443	
Private Superannuation	603			
Company	2,067	Pub. Cap. Fm.	1,660	
Company Tax Reserves	452			4,691	21
Public Corporation	292	Stck. Increase	591	
Central and Local Govt.	690			
Foreign (Dis) Investment	−344			−2

III. TAXATION for PUBLIC CONSUMPTION

Sources of Income Items	Before Direct Tax	Direct Tax +NI	*Deduct*	After Tax +NI	Personal Saving	Indirect Tax less Subsidies	Net Total Demand	%
Company Taxes	—	705	*Deduct*	1,650				
Direct Taxes on Persons	—	1,970	Trans. to Per	690	Defence	1,597		
Capital Taxes	—	236	Capt. Form.	1,158	Ed. and Health	1,848	4,189	19
Indirect Taxes	—	2,939	Debt Interest	489	Other	744		
NI Contributions	—	911	Subsidies	86				
Rates	—	764	Grants Abroad					
Other Income	—	886						
TOTAL		8,381	TOTAL	4,073				
Error							440	2
TOTAL GNP							22,316	100

Note: Estimates have been made for the distribution of savings and indirect taxes between wages and salaries and other incomes on the basis of a study made by K. Alexander and J. Hughes in *A Socialist Wages Plan*, 1958, Appendix I.

Source: *National Income and Expenditure*, Blue Book, 1961.

Table VI.8
Wages and Profits in Growth and Stagnation in the UK 1947-1967
(All figures are average annual changes for the period)

Year/Period	(1) Growth in GNP	(2) Price Changes	(3) Real Growth	(4) Real Growth per Person Employed	Weekly Wage Rates		Weekly Earnings		Company Profits	
					(5) Money	(6) Real	(7) Money	(8) Real	(9) Money	(10) Real
Boom 1947-50	8·5	4·4*	4·5	4·0	3·0†	-1·5	4·0	-0·5	7·6	3·0
Stagnation 1950-52	9·5	8·5	1·0	0·5	7·7	-0·7	9·2	0·9	2·5	-5·0
Boom 1952-55	6·5	2·5	3·9	2·5	5·2	3·0	8·0	5·2	11·0	8·0
Stagnation 1955-58	4·5	3·6	0·9	0·5	5·5	2·0	5·3	1·9	4·0	0·3
Boom 1958-60	5·5	1·0	4·4	3·5	2·8	1·6	5·6	4·5	10·0	9·0
Stagnation 1960-62	4·5	3·0	1·5	1·3	3·6	0·5	4·6	1·5	0·5	-2·2
Boom 1962-64	7·0	2·2	4·9	3·5	4·2	2·0	5·6	3·0	10·2	8·0
Stagnation 1964-67	5·3	3·6	1·8	1·8	4·2	0·1	5·6	1·8	5·1	0·0
1952-67 Average	5·5	2·6	2·9	2·1	4·2	1·6	5·8	3·0	6·5	4·0
7 Boom Years	6·5	1·9	4·4	3·1	4·25	2·5	6·5	4·5	1·03	8·5
8 Stagnant Years	4·7	3·4	1·4	1·1	4·4	0·8	5·1	1·7	2·5	-0·5

Notes: 'Real' figures are deflated by capital goods price increases for profits and by consumer price increases for the rest. Wage rates are for all Industries. Weekly Earnings exclude agriculture, railways, coal mining, docks and distribution.

Sources: *National Income and Expenditure* Blue Book 1968. National Institute, *Economic Review.*

* 8 per cent price rise in 1948.   † Wage freeze in 1948.

all over the world by post-war shortages and stock piling. In the next fifteen years the pattern is inescapable. We can see that real weekly earnings (column 8) rose faster in the boom periods than productivity (column 4) and much faster than real wage rates (column 6). These increases in weekly earnings, however, were apparently absorbed, presumably because wage rates rose so slowly; and company profits showed very rapid increases. It was in the stagnant years that prices rose, and real earnings rose much more slowly.

We must be careful with these figures, however, since the Ministry of Labour Weekly Earnings Surveys exclude earnings in agriculture, on the railways, in coal mining, docks and retail distribution; that is, they cover mainly the industries where the possibility exists of pushing wages up through premia and higher piece-work rates in a period of boom. The figures for basic wage rates by contrast cover nearly all industries and services. Remembering these qualifications we can detect a gap in times of boom between the rise in weekly earnings, many of them subject to increases made at the point of production, and the rise in wage rates mainly negotiated nationally. The gap is referred to as WAGES DRIFT and is regarded by many economists as an important element in inflation. The fact remains that the main price increases have been in periods of stagnation and not of boom. Some other explanation than 'demand pull' is required and the theory offered by economists is referred to as COST PUSH INFLATION.

The increases in money wages resulting from trade union pressure, it is argued, are passed on in higher prices by firms with monopolistic positions. We noted earlier how many firms include in their costs an allowance for the extra cost of replacement of old machinery on the assumption that prices will go on rising. They thus help to create the very inflation they are preparing against. Reduced unit costs, moreover, made possible by full capacity operation, are not necessarily passed on in lower prices to the consumer. This kind of price fixing is certainly one cause of inflation as well as of high profits in the booms. It is clear from Table VI.8 that, as far as wages pressure is concerned, wage rates rise faster in the periods of stagnation than of boom, often almost as fast as weekly earnings in these periods. What is happening, it is said, is that increased earnings enjoyed in the boom are being consolidated in new rates, and those workers whose wages are based on nationally negotiated rates are catching up with their fellows who could push it in the boom. But the important point is that these increases in wage rates cannot be absorbed when firms are working below capacity in the period of stagnation, prices are raised sharply to cover higher unit costs and even so company profits rise slowly if at all. We thus have the following position: when demand is being held back by government action, the unit costs of firms are bound to rise as total costs have to be spread over a reduced output. Higher costs are then passed on in higher prices, But when demand is expanding and firms are working near full capacity, the lower costs are *not* passed on in lower prices.

Governments which have succeeded in maintaining full employment by expansionary measures have found the expansion threatening to get out of hand. All firms still expand together in the manner of the old style booms, but with profits and investment accelerating they have to be cut back by government action long before an old style crisis could occur. In doing this, moreover, governments have used measures which have the effect of directly raising prices – higher interest rates, increased indirect taxation, and so on – all designed to make some things more expensive for us so that we buy less of other things. To reduce pressure on the economy and bring the boom to an end, governments in Britain have by these means been able to hold back or actually reduce home market demand; but the cure has been more inflationary than the illness that was being treated.

We need, therefore, to clarify precisely the condition of the economy in the boom periods in which government deflationary activity was required, although apparently prices were not rising or not rising immoderately fast. What was it that was getting out of hand? The answer is that booming demand was drawing in a huge quantity of additional imported goods – far beyond what could be paid for by exports. These extra supplies kept prices from rising, but a balance of payments crisis, actual or threatened, forced governments to act to check the boom before it reached the stage of raising prices. Of course, governments might have acted at many different points of the economy to direct output and increase efficiency and solve the balance of payments as a by-product, but this would have been a slow business and would have meant rather more intervention than they were prepared for. This will be the subject of the next chapter.

As it was, in filling up the slumps by maintaining aggregate demand, governments were forced to cut off the tops of the booms also. A steadier growth has been achieved but not at a much faster long-term rate than the combined booms and slumps provided in earlier periods. This is revealed by Table VI.9. Students will notice from this Table that growth in the 1950s was evidently to a great extent the result of increased employment, since the growth rate of GNP per occupied population was lower than that per total population. By contrast growth in the 1960s has been less the result of increased employment than of increased productivity, since growth per occupied population was faster than growth per total population. This is certainly an important change whose implications will be further examined in the final chapter.

We can now sum up our study of the post-war cycle with an additional graph (Fig. 6.4) this time bringing government action into the picture, and showing actual changes year by year for 1957 to 1965. The kind of Budget, the level of bank rate and the presence or absence of HP controls are all shown on the graph. We shall take up in the next chapter the whole range of government measures designed to obtain growth without inflation. Here we need only to note the remarkable persistence, despite so much official intervention, of the apparently underlying cyclical trend of economic activity.

In Fig. 6.4, the line showing home supply capacity can only be a guess, but it must include those imports that can be paid for by exports. The graph indicates the way demand first catches up with capacity as a result of government expansionary measures: in this period unit costs of firms are reduced, prices are stable, profits and earnings rise; but then after a few months demand (home and export) rises ahead of capacity. The investment boom only follows after expanding demand has shown the need for it and is too late then to meet the new level of demand. Extra imports that cannot be paid for by exports are pulled in to fill the gap and a balance of payments deficit arises. The government takes deflationary measures to hold home demand

Table VI.9

Average Long-term Rates of Growth, Great Britain and UK 1801–1959 (Compound per cent per annum)

A. *Decades over 30 years*	*Growth of National Product (1913–14 prices)*	
Great Britain	(*a*) per occupied population	(*b*) per total population
1801/11–1831/41	1·5	1·5
1811/21–1841/51	1·4	1·5
1821/31–1851/61	0·9	1·1
1831/41–1861/71	0·9	1·0
1841/51–1871/81	1·4	1·3
1851/61–1881/91	2·0	1·9
1861/71–1891/1901	2·2	1·7
United Kingdom		
1875/84–1905/14	—	1·5
1890/99–1920/29	—	0·3
1900/09–1930/39	—	0·5
1905/14–1935/44	—	0·9
1920/29–1950/59	—	1·3
B. *Individual Periods*		
United Kingdom		
1857–67	1	2·4
1867–75	2·7	2·6
1875–81	—	0·9
1881–89	2·5	2·9
1889–1909	—	1·0
1909–1913	—	2·0
1857–1913	1·6	1·8
1913–22	—	1·5
1922–29	1·6	2·3
1929–37	1·6	1·9
1937–50	—	0·0
1950–59	1·7	2·7
1960–69	2·3	2·0
1857–1959	1·2	1·4

Sources: Phyllis Deane and W. A. Cole, *British Economic Growth, 1688–1959.* National Institute *Economic Review* for 1960–69 figures which are based on 1963 prices.

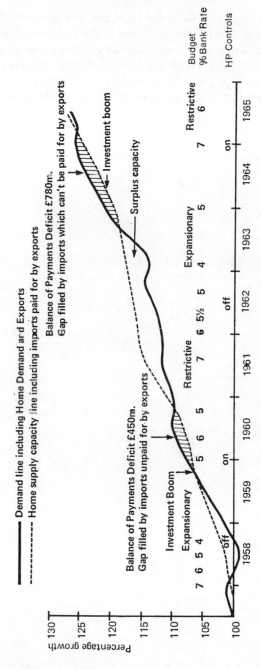

Figure 6.4. The cycle of activity in post-war Britain

down below capacity, in order to check the growth of imports and encourage firms to export, until the balance of payments is righted. Then a new expansionary phase begins with the same result and an even larger foreign deficit. This is the problem of 'stop and go', which recent Governments have promised to solve. But that is the subject of the next chapter.

7 The Instruments of State Intervention in the Market Economy

SUMMARY

In this chapter we consider from British experience four types of government intervention designed to manage aggregate movements in a market economy, and draw conclusions about their effectiveness:

(1) MONETARY AND CREDIT CONTROL, no longer as effective as it was and more effective in checking expansion than encouraging it;

(2) Foreign exchange management, designed to correct foreign payments imbalances but stopping short of full capital export control;

(3) Budgetary and FISCAL POLICIES, used increasingly to encourage economic activity, and especially through the investment of the nationalized industries, but involving a rather regressive tax system and heavy borrowing from the private sector;

(4) The use of physical controls, especially through building licences, these have so far been very limited in range although with them we may include the direct controls involved in certain recent Prices and Incomes policies.

Economic planning is left until the next chapter. On British experience such planning is considered by many economists to be increasingly necessary because of the inadequacy and undiscriminating nature of other measures. Government power to influence the working of a market economy is shown to be very considerable, but the many individual measures of government intervention are seen to require an overall strategy if they are to avail against the growing power of the large international companies.

In the last chapter we described how governments had

begun to intervene in the market economy in order to ensure that resources were fully utilized and, in doing so, had encountered problems of inflation and balance of payments crises. These crises arose on account of the particular measures which were used by governments to maintain the country's aggregate demand for goods and services and to manage it in relation to aggregate supply. Results have fallen below expectations. While we saw that the depths of slumps have been averted, at the same time the tops of the booms have been chopped off, so that the underlying growth rate, despite some increase in output per man employed, remains much the same as before. This could be due to the inadequacy or inappropriateness of the measures applied, or to mismanagement and mistiming, or to more fundamental causes in the whole structure of the market economy. We need to look more closely at the armoury of measures open to governments for managing the economy. What follows can only serve to introduce a complex subject.[1]

Gunnar Myrdal[2] has spoken of economic planning as the 'co-ordination of government intervention in the economy'. The various measures listed above have naturally to be co-ordinated to some extent; but it is their co-ordination under some overall strategy that deserves the term economic planning. This implies a situation, where an economic plan becomes an important determinant of economic decisions, even where it is not, as in a planned economy, the chief determinant. After the Labour Government's aborted National Plan of 1965 economic plans have not been important determinants of economic decisions in Britain. The same Government's later 'economic assessment to 1972'[3] opened by emphasizing that 'this is a Planning Document not a Plan'. Since it is British Governments' interventions in the economy that we shall be studying in this chapter, we can safely stop short of economic planning.

[1] Students who want to master some of the detail should start with Sir Oscar Hobson's *How the City Works* and go on to Samuel Brittain's *The Treasury under the Tories*, 1964.
[2] See *Beyond the Welfare State*, 1960.
[3] Entitled *The Task Ahead* and published in 1969.

1. MONETARY AND CREDIT CONTROL

We have already described the increase in money supply made possible first by the use of notes of credit and private bills of exchange, and then in the nineteenth century by the extension of bank overdrafts and loans and by the Bank of England printing banknotes well beyond any reserves of gold or silver which it had in its vaults. Originally, under the 1844 Act, this so-called FIDUCIARY ISSUE of notes not backed by gold was limited to £14m. Today the link between the Bank's gold holdings and note issue has been broken. £1,000 million of gold and other currency reserves are held by the Exchange Equalization Account for managing the rate at which sterling exchanges with foreign currencies. The issue of £3,000 million and more of notes at home is varied simply for the convenience of the public. But this is not the end of the credit system in Britain today. Since 1890 and increasingly since the First World War, governments have also been able to obtain short-term credit (apart that is from the issue of long-term securities) by issuing TREASURY BILLS. These are like bills of exchange normally repayable in three months. They add at any time another £1,000 million to the money supply. Finally, a whole new range of financial intermediaries – HP Finance Houses, Building Societies, Trusts, Insurance Companies and other institutions including merchant and foreign banks – now provide loans in addition to those of the main joint-stock deposit and clearing banks. A study in 1961 by J. Revell[4] revealed that on the basis of some £80,000 millions of physical assets in Britain a structure of financial claims amounting to twice that figure was erected.

The Bank of England, which was nationalized in 1949 but still retained a certain independence of the Treasury (as we learn from the speeches of recent Governors) is entrusted with the task of managing this vast structure of credit. Since the banking system is not nationalized, it has to be managed by financial incentives and penalties and not by government orders, although the forms of persuasion applied sometimes contain a veiled threat of 'or else'. For many years the joint-stock banks – that is mainly the Big Five CLEARING BANKS – did

[4] *Wealth of the Nation*, 1967.

most of the lending, and their accounts consisted of Bank of
England notes, Treasury Bills and government long-term
securities. While this was so, the task of the Bank of England
was complicated but not difficult.

A chart showing the distribution of the Joint Stock Banks'
DEPOSITS laid out in different ways and the connection of
each with the Bank of England will help to explain the
process (Fig. 7.1).

What made it complicated was the continuing intermediary
role of the DISCOUNT HOUSES between the joint-stock banks
and the Treasury. The basis of the system up to 1958–9 was
that the banks laid out their deposits in order of liquidity as
the chart shows: CASH at one end, ADVANCES at the other. To
be able safely to meet their customers requirements, they kept
8 per cent in cash in hand or at the Bank of England, and
another 7 per cent on call, or short notice. But on the
cash, of course, they earned no interest and on the money on
call a very low rate. Another 15 per cent was lent to the
Discount Houses who took up Treasury and other Bills
for them. On this they earned the Bill rate, which is fixed
just below bank rate. Altogether this 30 per cent of their
deposits provided their LIQUIDITY RATIO. The rest was up
to 1959 divided between, first, government securities – about
25 per cent to 30 per cent of their deposits – at long-term
interest rates, and, secondly, advances to customers – 35
per cent to 40 per cent – the most lucrative part of the
business, at a 5 per cent minimum interest rate or 1 per
cent above bank rate.

Now supposing the government wished to expand the money
supply and lower interest rates it could act both at the short
end and the long end. At the short end, the Treasury could
issue more Treasury Bills. This both reduced the rate paid and
increased the Banks' liquid holdings. The banks would then
wish to expand their advances (like a concertina) to maintain
the liquidity ratio at about 30 per cent. At the same time, at
the long end the government BROKER could buy up some of the
government's own securities and pay cash for them. This
would expand the public's overall cash holdings and also raise
the value of the stock and thus reduce the yield, i.e., the rate
of interest divided by the price, on government stock. It is

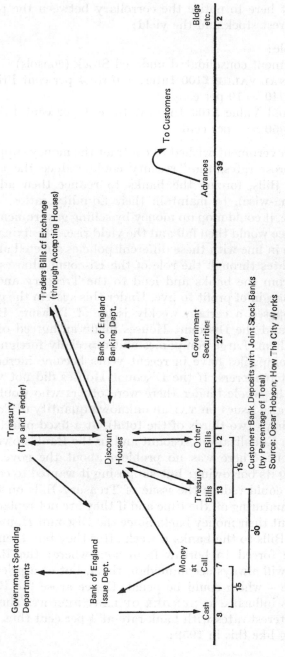

Figure 7.1. Movements of cash and securities in the British banking system, 1959

Source: Oscar Hobson, *How The City Works*

important here to notice the corrollary between the price of fixed interest stock and the yield:

Example:
Government consolidated undated Stock (consols)
(a) NOMINAL VALUE £100 Interest Rate 4 per cent Price £40
   Yield 4/40 = 10 per cent
(b) Nominal Value £100 Interest Rate 4 per cent Price £50
   Yield 4/50 = 8 per cent

If the government wished to contract the money supply and raise interest rates, the Treasury could reduce the issue of Treasury Bills, forcing the banks to reduce their advances (concertina-wise), to maintain their liquidity ratios. At the same time, it could mop up money by selling government stock whose price would then fall and the yield rise. The fixing of the bank rate in line with these different policies affected all other interest rates through the role of the Discount Houses. They borrow from the banks and lend to the Treasury and must make a margin of profit to live. Under this system the government proposed a certain weekly issue of Treasury Bills on TENDER and the Discount Houses made an agreed offer for most of them. Large companies and especially foreign banks and oil companies have in recent years become increasingly important tenderers. If the Discount Houses did not wish to take up the whole tender there were others who would. The Treasury also issues on TAP an unknown quantity of Treasury Bills (perhaps two-thirds of the total), at a fixed price, to the Exchange Equalization Account and to the Bank's own Issue Department. There was no problem about the government expanding its borrowing; but supposing it wanted to contract credit, it could reduce the issue of Treasury Bills on tender. Bills are maturing all the time and if they are not replaced the banks want their money back. Since the Discount Houses only sell their Bills to the banks a week after they buy them, they would be forced to borrow from somewhere; the Bank of England will always accommodate them, but at a price – the bank rate – which could be penal. Hence arose the Bank of England's influence as LENDER OF LAST RESORT. The structure of interest rates with bank rate at 4 per cent thus looked something like this in 1959:

Table VII.1

Structure of Interest Rates, UK 1959

Mortgages from Building Societies	5½
Yield on Industrial Securities	5¼
Bank Advances	5
Yield on Consols (2½%)	4¾
Bank Rate	4
Tender Rate for Treasury Bills	3 to 3½
Short Loans from Banks to Discount Hosues	2⅞

All this changed after 1959 because, in the first place, the pattern of the gross deposits of the Clearing Banks had changed in the following ways by 1968:

Table VII.2

Use of Funds by London Clearing Banks 1959 and 1968
(Percentage of Total Deposits)

Use of Funds	December 1959	December 1968
Cash	8	8
Money on Call	7·5	14
Treasury Bills	13	5
Other Bills	2	5·5
Liquidity Ratio	30·5	32·5
Government Stock	27	13
Advances	38·5	47
Special Deposits	0	2
Buildings, etc.	4	5·5
TOTAL	100	100

Source: *Bank of England Quarterly Bulletin.*

Money on call and advances greatly increased while holdings of Treasury Bills and Government Stock were halved. The government's control over the banks was correspondingly reduced.

In the second place, the public's deposits with different types of banks and financial institutions changed as follows:

Table VII.3

Deposits with the UK Banking System 1958 and 1968

Institution	Deposits (£m) Dec. 1958	Dec. 1968	Increase 1958 to 1968 (1958 = 100)
London Clearing (Joint Stock) Banks	7,199	10,736	150
Scottish and Northern Ireland (Joint Stock) Banks	940	1,300	140
Accepting Houses (Merchant Banks)	220	1,880	850
Overseas and Foreign Banks	922	11,710	1,270
Finance Houses	128	1,050	850
Building Societies	2,617	7,850	300
Insurance Companies Assets:			
Life Funds	4,042	11,830	295
General Funds	399	1,335	335
Pension Funds Assets	1,658	3,850	230

Source: *Bank of England Quarterly Bulletin.*

All the institutions listed under the Joint Stock Banks, London, Scottish and Irish, advanced their positions ahead of them. This further reduced the influence of governments in acting through the liquidity of such banks. For these reasons new measures had to be adopted by the Treasury to control the expansion of credit, viz: direct restrictions on Hire Purchase, the use of a SPECIAL DEPOSITS scheme which in effect freezes 2 per cent of the banks deposits and a general pressure on banks to reduce credit, all combined with a régime of much higher interest rates.

Monetary measures were always favoured by economists as instruments of economic management for three main reasons:

(*a*) they were sure: interest rates could be moved; banks could be squeezed;

(*b*) they did not discriminate: all enterprises were supposed to be equally affected by changes in rates and in credit availability;

(*c*) they provided a delicate instrument that allowed of small movements which could be adjusted according to the response of the market.

It had always been recognized that monetary measures were more effective in controlling a boom than in averting a slump, like the cables that hold down a balloon but will not hold it up. Even very low interest rates will not encourage a firm to expand if it already has unused surplus capacity. It became true also that very high interest rates would not discourage a firm either, if it was anxious to expand. The reasons advanced for favouring monetary measures corresponded less and less to the facts of the economy, when large firms relied increasingly on generating internally most of their own capital requirements and thus largely immunizing themselves from the effects of interest rate changes and credit control. Nevertheless, of course, it remained true that personal spending could still be influenced by HP restrictions and credit squeezes.[5]

2. FOREIGN EXCHANGE MANAGEMENT AND THE BALANCE OF PAYMENTS

Before 1930 the exchange rates of most national currencies moved according to the demand for and supply of them in the international currency markets. Under the GOLD STANDARD all rates were related to the price of gold and, if rates moved beyond a certain range, gold was shipped from one country to another to redress the balance. The theory was a beautiful one – that prices would fall in the country having to export gold, since the domestic money supply would thereby be reduced, and rise in the country receiving the gold, for the opposite reason. These movements in relative domestic prices would keep exchange rates adjusted to the real purchasing power of the different currencies. Of course, the system was advantageous to countries with the largest stores of gold and, since sterling was regarded as being as good as gold, particularly advantageous to Britain. The system also failed to take into account the difficulties we noted in Chapter 3 of any developing country establishing its own infant industries in a world of free trade and free capital movements.

From the 1930s onwards more and more countries imposed

[5] For a complete study see J. C. R. Dow, *The Management of the British Economy 1945–60.*

tariffs and other protective devices on their trade and proceeded to intervene in the currency market, to protect their
foreign exchange rates. These 'beggar-my-neighbour' policies
led to a vicious downward spiral of international trade and also
to a complete collapse of primary product prices, since these
could be less easily supported by restrictive policies than the
prices of manufactures. After the Second World War, with the
advice of Lord Keynes, exchange rates were fixed by an international agreement signed at Bretton Woods in the USA;
a GENERAL AGREEMENT ON TARIFFS AND TRADE (GATT)
was also signed committing the parties not to raise but to
attempt to reduce all tariffs and other trade restrictions; and at
the same time two funds were set up – the INTERNATIONAL
MONETARY FUND (IMF), to help tide countries over temporary deficits on their foreign accounts, and an INTER-
NATIONAL BANK to provide AID for long-term structural
economic readjustment and development.

The conditions which underlay the acceptance by the
nations of fixed exchange rates were (*a*) that governments
whose economies earned persistent surpluses on foreign trade
should revalue upwards, (*b*) that those with persistent deficits
could devalue, (*c*) that ample sums would be available from
the two funds – automatically in the case of funds from the
IMF. In the event, this last condition has never applied. In
relation to the growth of world trade the growth of INTER-
NATIONAL LIQUIDITY has always lagged behind and was still
likely to lag behind even after the introduction of SPECIAL
DRAWING RIGHTS on the IMF (SDRs) agreed upon in
1969. Between 1956 and 1968 the value of world trade more
than doubled from about $100b a year to $240b while the
value of all the nations reserves of gold and convertible
currency, including those held by the IMF, rose by only
35 per cent from $56b to $76b. The SDRs were designed to
add another $9,5b or $12\frac{1}{2}$ per cent by 1972. But by that time
world trade could well have grown by another 30 per cent.

It must be emphasized that the problem of world liquidity is
not a problem of financing trade exchanges. Lack of such
finance may have limited trade before the war; today the
enormous improvements in communications, the establishment of branches of national banks all over the world and the

CREDIT GUARANTEES provided by governments, all ensure that the world is one market. Some countries are regarded as better credit risks than others and much capital equipment is today so large and costly as to require special credit arrangements which only governments can supply. The problem of world liquidity remains that of providing a cushion of reserves for countries which run into balance of payments difficulties. Without such a cushion, governments are bound to take emergency measures to try to correct their foreign payments deficits by reducing their imports and expanding their exports. They have three main alternatives:

(*a*) DEVALUATION of the currency, so long as this does not lead to the devaluation of other currencies, will probably work, albeit rather slowly, because its effect is to raise the prices at home of imported goods and to lower the prices abroad of exports. These price movements should discourage imports and encourage exports as long as there is some spare capacity in the economy; but the effectiveness of devaluation will depend on the price elasticities of the products imported and of those exported by the devaluing country. If the sales of its products abroad can be greatly increased by a reduction in price – and this is true of most manufactured goods entering world trade – then exports will rise. If the purchase of imported goods is equally affected by a rise in their price, then imports will fall and devaluation will certainly work. If, however, purchases of imported goods are very little affected by a rise in price, that is, they are price-inelastic, then on balance devaluation will still work through increased exports. This seems to have been the case with Britain's devaluation in 1967. Obviously, for a country with only goods to offer for which demand is inelastic – the position of many underdeveloped countries – devaluation is not likely to be helpful. Most governments avoid devaluation because it seems to be a national humiliation; and economists dislike it because it raises home prices and protects inefficient producers.

(*b*) Imposition of higher tariffs, forbidden under GATT, or of import controls, can be very effective so long as they do not lead to retaliation. The danger of such restrictions is that they protect monopoly and inefficiency and create problems of discrimination that we shall consider later.

(c) DEFLATION of the whole economy, in order to reduce imports and encourage firms to export by generally reducing demand at home, is effective in the short run. A long check to expansion, however, would tend to leave the economy at the end even less competitive than at the start.

The difficulty with all these measures and particularly with the last, is that one country's imports are another's exports. To redress an imbalance by cutting imports means cutting someone else's exports. He will then have to do the same, and the whole level of world trade will tend to be balanced at less than its optimum. Short of planned trade exchanges, a very large cushion of reserves is necessary to sustain trade expansion. The problem for the poorer countries in this respect has become especially acute. Their share of the world's liquid reserves fell from about 29 per cent to 15 per cent of the total between 1955 and 1968. Moreover, just seven of the poorer countries with only 60 million population held in 1968 10 per cent of the reserves, while the remainder with 500 million population held 5 per cent. The seven were Spain, Israel, Venezuela, Malaysia, Thailand, Saudi Arabia and Kuwait.

By comparison, Britain's reserve problem is less serious, although as a major trading partner with many of these poor countries British trade has suffered indirectly from their embarrassment. The main problem posed for British governments by its narrowing margin of reserves has been that of maintaining growth without running into balance of payments deficits. Since the post-war devaluation in 1949, Britain's gold and currency reserve has been held at between £800m and £1,000m, plus £400m rising to £900m available from the IMF. During this period the value of Britain's imports has, however, risen from £2,000m to £6,000m. This may be compared with the 1930s when £600m to £800m of imports were covered by reserves of about half that sum. What is more, since 1949 the debts to overseas holders of sterling – private citizens and governments – have rarely been less than £3,500m. In the 1930s they averaged £500m.

These debts can be seen in two ways: on the one hand, they have provided essential short-term finance including hard currency for British investors to turn into long-term capital. For several years many of these debts or STERLING BALANCES as they are called, were almost forced loans imposed upon colonial territories by the Sterling Area system of banking all dollar earnings in London and tying colonial currencies to a fixed Sterling Reserve. Colonies on obtaining their independence generally drew down immediately their balances in London; only Malaysia and Kuwait had major holdings in 1969. On the other hand, the interest charges on these balances have been amounting to between £150m and £200m a year. Moreover, since most of the colonies are now independent, UK interest rates have had to be kept up in order to attract such funds and the funds of other large sterling holders to London and to hold them there. Even with high rates there has been a continual threat of this so-called 'HOT' MONEY leaving London whenever fears of the pound being devalued spread around.

The problem has been made more difficult by the fact that many countries carry on their trade in sterling and even hold reserves in sterling, so that sterling and the dollar have become what are called 'key' currencies. Indeed it has been a major aim of the City of London to keep it that way since this meant extra funds banked in London, and not in Bonn, New York or Zurich. It has to be made clear, however, that movements of 'hot' money are not primarily the result of speculation by the gnomes of Zurich, as the mythology has it, but are mainly due to transfers in the accounts of the large international companies. In the difficult weeks of March 1968 when the French franc, and with it the pound sterling, were under heavy pressure, *The Times* reported (20 March 1968) that Unilever, BP, ICI, and British American Tobacco, which are all firms that have operations in every part of the world, had been moving funds out of London and mainly to Bonn where revaluation of the mark was anticipated.

The startling increase in banking outside the joint-stock banks, shown in Table VII.3, was in the deposits of overseas and foreign banks. These include a certain amount of interbank lending and an overwhelming proportion of deposits by overseas residents, some of whom may be overseas affiliates of British-based international companies. These deposits were built up after the relaxation of exchange controls in 1957–8. Many of them are in foreign currencies and EURO-DOLLARS, that is to say dollars which can be used more profitably in Europe than in the USA. They have little effect on the domestic money supply; but, together with the sterling balances, they have made the government's use of monetary measures that much more difficult, because any lowering of interest rates tends to lead to an outflow of funds and speculation against the pound.

All this has contributed an important element in the British balance of payments crises. On top of the deficits on goods and services occasioned by booming demand there have been very large government payments and large movements of long-term capital.

Table VII.4

UK Balance of Payments, 1959–67

	Annual Average (£m) 1959–64			Annual Average (£m) 1965–67		
	In-come	Out-flow	Net	In-come	Out-flow	Net
Goods and Services Account						
Balance on Goods	+9,371	−4,216	−245	+4,969	−5,317	−348
Balance on Services (incl. Private Transfers excl. Govt. and Property Income)	+1,566	−1,420	+146	+1,920	−1,715	+205
Balance on Goods and Services			−99			−143
Government Account						
Government non-Military Transfers and Administration	0	−142	−142	0	−203	−203
Military Expenditure	+138	−224	−186	+25	−292	−267
Government Balance			−328			−470
Capital and Property Income Account						
British Overseas Inward Property Income (+) and Outward Investment (−)	+739	−352	+387	+1,013	−416	+597
Foreign Inward Investment (+) and Outward Property Income (−)	+205	−435	+230	+307	−575	−268
Long-Term Capital Balance and Property Income			+157			+329

	Annual Average 1959–64			Annual Average 1965–67		
	Income	Outflow	Net	Income	Outflow	Net
Overall Account						
Combined Net Balance (Total so far)			−224			−284
Met by Monetary Movements						
Sales from $ Portfolio			0			+173
Borrowed from IMF			+15			+60
Sales from Gold Reserve (+)						
(Increase = −)			+54			−100
Increase in Sterling Debt			+142			+155
Increase in non-Sterling Debt						
Decrease = −)			+56			−31
Balancing Item and Miscellaneous (net)			−43			+27
Total of Monetary Movements			+224			+284

Source: *UK Balance of Payments* and see M. Barratt Brown, *Labour and Sterling*, 1968, Institute of Workers Control.

In Table VII.4 the Long-term Capital Account and the Property Income Account have been combined together so as to show the net inward and outward movements. On long-term investment, outward flows of £350–£400 million have been not quite balanced by inward flows of £200–£300 million. The justification for the outflow of capital is, of course, the return in property income by dividends and interest from it. This is indeed considerable. Property income paid out to foreigners on their investments in Britain at £430m to £570m has been much more than balanced by inflows from British investments abroad at £700m to £1,000m. The net credit from the combined capital and property income movements was £150m in 1959–64 rising to £330m in 1965–7. After the mid-1950s, although foreign holders of sterling were allowed to convert freely into other currencies, some control was retained over British citizens' conversion of sterling into foreign currencies, even of the foreign currencies British companies earned abroad. In fact, however, the increase in overseas investment by British companies was encouraged by tax concessions. Property income increased rapidly its contributions to the balance of payments. This was historically the way in which the British overseas payments account had been balanced and a surplus for further overseas investment achieved.[6]

[6] The process may be studied in detail in M. Barratt Brown's *After Imperialism*, 1963.

The differences between the great outward movements of British capital in the nineteenth century and those today are: that the earlier movements were primarily of loans to governments and railway companies for the economic development of the then developing countries (mainly the United States and the British dominions), whereas today the movements are either into oil production in otherwise barren lands or into other advanced industrial lands as part of the process of cross-investment of which we spoke in Chapter 3. The result is that, while the nineteenth-century capital movements certainly generated and financed British exports, particularly of capital equipment, there is now more than a little doubt whether the present outflow of capital may not actually reduce British exports. This is because overseas subsidiaries of British companies begin to manufacture goods which were previously exported. It raises a crucial question about the role of the international company.[7]

It cannot be doubted that there has been a most rapid expansion in the total of world trade in the 1950s and 1960s averaging a rate of increase of around 9 per cent per year. The proportion of this trade, however, which is accounted for by the already developed industrial countries rose from 60 per cent pre-war to 70 per cent; over a half instead of a third consisting of exchanges between themselves. It is trade increasingly dominated by the international company. The international flow of private capital has created serious problems indeed for British governments, with the attendant military expenditure amounting to two or three hundred millions a year, which is said to be required to protect this capital from communist and other subversion. This flow of capital is said by some to be the cause of Britain's payments deficits. Those who argue in this way[8] have to answer the question as to how they would replace the present dependence on private investment and military spending in generating international trade. This might be done by some form of international economic planning which we shall consider in the last chapter. Here it is necessary only to emphasize that maintaining

[7] The argument is considered at length in a report by W. B. Reddaway, *The Effects of UK Direct Investment Overseas*, 1967 and 1968.

[8] T. Drinkwater in his very valuable little *Guide to the Balance of Payments*, 1966.

a balance of imports and exports of goods and services apart from these capital flows has been a real problem for Britain. Excluding the capital movements and military expenditures, Britain's imports of goods and services were rising faster in the 1950s and 1960s than exports. This was particularly the case of manufactured goods which are Britain's main stock in trade. We may see this from Table VII.5.

Table VII.5

Movements of UK Imports and Exports of Goods and Services 1948–68

Goods and Services	Volumes (1958 = 100)					Value (£m)
	1948	1953	1958	1963	1968	1968
All Goods and Services						
Imports	73	78	100	125	158	8,130
Exports	66	84	100	118	147	7,910
All Goods						
Imports	72	86	100	128	174	6,060
Exports	72	86	100	121	153	6,180
Manufactured Goods						
Imports	49	70	100	202	415	1,470
Exports	71	85	100	120	152	5,800
GDP						
TOTAL	79	90	100	117	136	35,100
Industrial Output	65	89	100	119	139	19,500

Sources: *National Income and Expenditure* Blue Books and *Reports on Overseas Trade*.

Once more we must notice that running a balance of payments surplus or deficit very easily becomes a cumulative process. The government of a country such as Britain which finds the economy in deficit on its foreign payments and deflates demand at home, to hold back imports while exports catch up, and thus creates a check to growth, is inevitably delaying thereby important schemes for capital investment at home. By contrast the government of a country like West Germany, which enjoys a surplus on its foreign trade, can

ɪ

allow growth to continue at a faster rate and need not delay its schemes of capital investment. In this way Britain could and did fall rapidly behind West Germany in productivity, with all the repercussions on relative prices that were bound to follow.

We can sum up by saying that government policies of permitting a large measure of freedom to both foreign and British-based international companies, wishing to change sterling into foreign currencies, required a régime of high interest rates in Britain. The high rates were necessary to attract the holders of funds to sterling. This provided funds for overseas investment, but it meant, first, that British firms at home which had to borrow funds were forced to pay higher interest rates than their foreign competitors; and second, that the room for manœuvre of British governments in altering the rate of interest was severely limited. Lowering rates enough to encourage expansion over a long period was out of the question.

3. BUDGETARY AND FISCAL POLICIES AND THE NATIONALIZED INDUSTRIES

Monetary controls we have concluded at best provide a serviceable brake upon economic activity. For an accelerator to encourage expansion governments have increasingly relied upon stepping up their own expenditure. Keynes' advice to governments in the depression years of the 1930s was to spend their way out of a slump by DEFICIT FINANCE, that is by spending more than they collected in taxes. This they certainly most persistently did in every year but one (1958) between 1951 and 1968, as we may see from Table VII.6. A budget surplus (shown in Column 2 on the Table) was achieved in each year after current account spending was covered; but only in the years 1948–51, in 1958 and again in 1968 did this surplus wholly provide for the gross fixed capital formation of central and local government. The rest of the investment had to be met by borrowing. Sometimes this involved large sums, as in 1953–5, in 1959–61 and in 1963–5. The dates coincide with major booms in output, as the first column shows. They also coincide with general elections. What Michael Kalecki, a distinguished Polish economist, already foresaw in the 1940s as

Table VII.6

UK Public Sector: Saving and Capital Formation 1948–68

Year	Real Change in GDP over Previous Year (%)	Central and Local Government Current Surplus £m (current prices)	Public Authorities Gross Fixed Capital Formation £m (current prices)	as % change over previous year (real terms)	Public Corporations Saving/ Gross Fixed Capital Formation £m (current prices)
1948	—	585	491	—	77/–
1949	+3	671	498	+1	86/264
1950	+3	742	535	+5	128/288
1951	+4	659	615	+3	171/358
1952	−0·5	424	740	+9	183/414
1953	+4·5	316	826	+11	194/488
1954	+3·5	350	759	−8	204/538
1955	+3·5	614	730	−7·5	166/570
1956	+1·5	542	787	+4	205/592
1957	+2	692	814	+0	166/660
1958	−0·5	792	789	−5	149/694
1959	+3·5	699	834	+6	185/758
1960	+5	447	860	+2	309/788
1961	+3·5	563	919	+4	364/905
1962	+1	887	1,020	+7	402/933
1963	+4	509	1,108	+10	577/1,024
1964	+6	826	1,393	+22	608/1,187
1965	+3	1,183	1,505	+3·5	661/1,293
1966	+2	1,602	1,683	+7	644/1,455
1967	+1·5	1,488	1,979	+15	655/1,662
1968	+3	2,178	2,172	+7	796/1,647

Source: *National Income and Expenditure* Blue Book.

a 'political cycle' has come to be expected. It is a tribute to the success of governments that they can manage it, whatever the consequences for themselves or their successors in the years of deflation that follow.

Borrowing has not only been required for central and local government investment in Britain since the war; it has equally been required for the investment of the nationalized industries. We can see from the last two columns of Table VII.6 that up to 1960 the public corporations provided for only about one-third of their gross capital formation out of their own savings. This meant that several of them were failing to cover their depreciation charges and were in effect showing losses on their trading accounts. This itself resulted from the deliberate policy of governments, which did not at that time permit public corporations – the National Coal Board in the 1950s was an outstanding example – to raise their prices to the level the market would bear and so not only to cover their losses but to build up capital reserves for future investment. Only after a new policy, on the Financial and Economic Obligations of the Nationalized Industries, was enunciated in 1961 were the public corporations required to cover both HISTORIC COST depreciation and make allowance for REPLACEMENT COSTS and for some contribution towards future development. Thereafter, as Table VII.6 shows, they covered about a half of their annual investments from saving. The rest was still met by borrowing.

This borrowing requirement by the public sector, to cover the difference between the saving of public authorities and public corporations and their spending on fixed capital formation, rose steadily (see Table VII.6) from about £500 millions a year in the 1950s to over £1,000 millions a year in the 1960s. In 1967 it was £1,500 millions, the difference between £1,488m plus £655m saved and £1,979m plus £1,662m spent. Although the borrowing may be arranged by the government, the funds must come from the issue of long-term stock or of Treasury Bills – usually the latter – to the public. What has been happening is that in the private sector individuals and companies, and particularly the large companies, have been lending to the government from the internal reserves they have built up. Until these companies are ready to use their reserves for their own expansion, Treasury Bills provide a safe home and at the high reigning interest rates a profitable resting place for their funds. While the enlarged public sector of investment has given to governments great power to influence the economy, it has involved a continuous transfer of wealth from the public to the private sector. Professor James Meade[9] has spoken of the British economy in 1960, in which the State's

[9] In a book referred to frequently before, *Efficiency, Equality and the Ownership of Property.*

debts exceeded its assets, as an 'anti-Socialist economy'. The position had changed somewhat by 1966 under a Labour Government, but the transfer of funds through the NATIONAL DEBT from the public to the private sector remained overwhelming, as the following figures reveal:

Table VII.7

Public and Private Property in the UK 1960 and 1966

Figures in £ billions	Total		Private		Public	
	1960	1966	1960	1966	1960	1966
Real Property	50	82	29	48	21	34
National Debt	—	—	28	31	−28	−31
Annual Debt Interest	—	—	1,2	1,8	−1,2	−1,8

Source: *National Income and Expenditure* Blue Books.

It would be easy, however, in this way to underestimate the influence of British governments on the national economy. Table VII.8 reveals that something near to 50 per cent of the national product passed through public hands in 1967.

Table VII.8

Share of the State in the British Economy 1938–1967
(All figures are percentages of GNP except in C.)

Year	1938	1948	1957	1965	1967
A. *Types of Government Expenditure*					
All Government Expenditure					
(Current and Capital)	31·2	42·4	39·2	43·0	48·9
Payments to Persons –					
Debt Interest	5·4	5·5	4·1	4·3	5·0
Pensions/Subsidies	5·9	12·5	8·9	11·1	12·6
Current Goods and Services –					
Arms	4·9	7·1	7·8	6·7	6·7
Health/Welfare/Education	5·8	5·4	6·5	7·8	8·6
Other	4·3	4·6	4·0	4·5	5·2
Fixed Capital Investment	4·4	4·8	4·0	4·9	5·7
Loans and Capital Grants	0·5	2·5	3·8	3·7	5·1
B. *Public Corporation Expenditure*					
TOTAL	—	13·9	18·2	17·7	18·8
Current Goods and Services	—	5·1	7·2	6·4	7·1
Wages and Salaries	—	6·4	7·0	6·7	6·9
Fixed Capital Investment	—	2·4	4·0	4·4	4·8

Years	1938	1948	1957	1965	1967
C. *Public Share of Consumption and Investment*					
Government and Public Corporation's Investment as % of all Capital Investment	30	46	44	46·5	51
Government Current Civil Purchases* and Public Sector Housebuilding as % of all Consumption and Housebuilding	12·5	13	13·5	15·7	16·5

Note: * i.e., excluding military and overseas expenditure.
Sources: *National Income and Expenditure* Blue Books.

One part of this is the huge proportion of capital formation for which central and local government authorities and the public corporation are responsible. The share of the state in consumption is much less, although some personal consumption is financed by state funds because of the large proportion of old people for whom the state is responsible. The influence upon the British economy of these payments to persons becomes clearer if we compare the shares of the state in the national product in the USA and the UK;

Table VII.9

Share of the State in the Economies of the UK and USA, 1964

Items as % of GNP	USA	UK
Payments to Persons	7·5	14·25
of which debt interest	2·0	4·25
Goods and Services	15·5	18·25
of which military	9·5	6·5
Capital Investment	6·0	10·5
of which Public Corporation	—	4·0
TOTAL	29	43

Source: R. Williams (ed.) *May Day Manifesto 1968*, p. 115, derived from US and UK official figures.

While the share of the state in the British national product was much above that in the USA in 1964, and had risen still further by 1968, we should here notice the remarks of a Labour Government Chancellor of the Exchequer, Mr James Callaghan, in 1967:

In the early 'sixties the switch towards developing our public services was started by the previous Conservative Government . . . and has been continued by the Labour Government. We have now reached a point where we should try to hold a balance between the collective needs of society and the personal needs of the individual. *(Hansard,* 30.6.1967, Column 1139.)

The view has since then been widely expressed in Britain that until we have more growth we cannot have more public services. This is to assume that the level of taxation in Britain had already reached in 1967 the maximum that was politically acceptable. For it is a fallacy, however widely believed, that there is some economic law that says that you can only spend more money on social services when you have first spent more on motor-cars. There is nothing special about increases in manufacturing production that alone makes possible increases in education. If anything it is the other way round. Of course every technological advance introduced into industry,which makes it possible to spend less time and effort on providing our basic needs of food, clothing and shelter, makes available more time and effort for other things. But in an advanced economy like ours at least a half of our income is what we have called 'discretionary'. Whether we spend it on cars or schools is not an economic but a political decision.

The political decision will, however, depend very much on the way in which taxes are collected and on the weight of them that is borne by different groups in society. Economists refer to this as the INCIDENCE OF TAXATION. They speak of a PROGRESSIVE TAX structure where people pay a higher proportion of their income, not just more but a higher proportion, the richer they are; and they speak of a REGRESSIVE TAX structure where people pay a higher proportion or the same proportion of their income the poorer they are. For a LINEAR relation between income and tax, that is with the tax rising proportionately to income, would still be regarded as inequitable for the lower group. There are many different kinds of taxes which have to be considered in these respects, and it will also be necessary to consider the incidence of benefits from state expenditure. It is naturally on some estimate of what he pays and what he gets that the citizen

votes for more or less public services, but we shall not forget
that he may be influenced by the advertising of suppliers of
goods and by the practical difficulty of persuading others to
vote with him when he wants public services rather than
personal goods.

Adam Smith long ago laid down four canons of a good tax
system: (a) the incidence should be according to ability to pay;
(b) the amount levied on each citizen should be certain and
understandable and not arbitrary; (c) the form of collection
should be convenient; (d) the costs of collection should be
minimal.

Unfortunately the canons may easily conflict. There can be
little doubt that the most convenient and the cheapest taxes
to collect are the so-called INDIRECT TAXES, that is taxes on
expenditure. In the case of these taxes, whether they are levied
on drink, tobacco or petrol, on goods liable to PURCHASE TAX
or on the employment of labour, the supplier makes the payment to the government and the consumer is put to no in-
convenience. He may even enjoy paying his taxes when the
process involves drinking a pint of beer or smoking a cigarette.
But he may not understand how much of the cost of his pint
(nearly half in 1969) or of his cigarette (nearly three-quarters
in 1969) goes in tax. Indirect taxes have furthermore a very
regressive incidence. It may be argued that people can do
without alcoholic drink and tobacco, whose taxation provides
over one-third of all indirect taxes. The fact is that they do not
go without them but, as we saw in considering income elasticities of demand in Chapter 2, spend the same proportion of
their income on these items at all different income levels.
Indeed this is one of the main reasons why drink and tobacco
are made to bear so great a weight of taxation. The demand for
these products is very inelastic. People go on buying the
same number of pints or cigarettes whatever the price. If
they did not, the Chancellor would lose money by raising the
tax.

The direct taxes include national insurance contributions
but these are even more regressive than indirect taxes.
National Insurance Contributions were in fact for long a POLL-
TAX, the same for everyone whatever their income, until
the graduated scheme was introduced. Other direct taxes

however, on personal income, earned or UNEARNED, on company income and on capital have certainly the advantage of being imposed according to ability to pay and therefore tend to be the most progressive part of the tax structure. For most people with earned incomes on PAYE schemes they are moreover, understandable, certain and easy and cheap to collect. Self-employed income, unearned income and company income present much greater problems. A great army of inspectors is required to work out what may be set against takings before taxable income is determined. Medical practitioners have always been careful to come under the self-employed schedule for this reason. The major taxes on capital – death duties – which could be the most progressive tax, can be avoided by anyone who does not suffer an accident or hate his children, by the simple expedient of passing on the estate five years before death.[10]

Table VII.10

The Structure of Taxation in the UK 1938–67

(As Percentage of GNP)

Type of Taxation	1938	1948	1957	1967
Taxes on:				
Employment Income	1·1	4·4	4·7	7·2
Property and Self-employment Income	4·6	8·3	7·3	4·0
Corporate Income	1·8	2·8	1·2	3·6
Taxes on Capital	1·5	2·1	0·9	1·0
TOTAL of Direct Taxes	9·0	17·6	14·1	15·8
Taxes on Expenditure	8·0	16·6	12·0	13·2
National Insurance Contributions	2·1	3·3	3·4	5·6
Local Rates	4·1	3·1	3·2	4·3
TOTAL of Indirect Taxes and National Insurance Contributions	14·2	23·0	18·6	23·1

[10] Other methods of tax avoidance for the rich are examined in Richard Titmuss's *Income Distribution and Social Change*.

Type of Taxation	1938	1948	1957	1967
TOTAL All Taxes	23·2	40·6	32·7	38·9
Other Government Income		2·7	3·1	4·3
Raised by Borrowing (+)	+8·0	−0·9	+3·4	+5·7
or offset by Debt Repayment (−)				
TOTAL GOVERNMENT EXPENDITURE	31·2	42·4	39·2	48·9

Note: Taxes on Shareholders' income from company profits are shown with Property Income and not Corporate Income throughout.

Source: *National Income and Expenditure* Blue Book.

Examination of Table VII.10 reveals that the main increases since before the war have been in taxes on employment income, in national insurance contributions and in indirect taxes in that order. The CORPORATION TAX introduced in 1967 raised the contribution from company income. Previously, such income was assumed to belong to the shareholders for tax purposes and was included with personal income. Companies only paid a small PROFIT TAX and sometimes an EXCESS PROFITS TAX. The purpose of the change to a corporation tax was to make possible different rates of tax on persons and companies with a view to encouraging companies to plough back their profits into new capital equipment. Direct taxation as a whole still provided in 1967 about 40 per cent of the total of taxes collected, as it had done before the war.

The resulting incidence of taxes and also of benefits for a standard household of a man and wife and two children in Britain in 1967 is shown in Table VII.11. The total of taxes paid moves first regressively downwards as income rises and then moves up in households with over £40 a week. This is because the proportions of income going to indirect taxes and National Insurance Contributions fall faster than the rise in the proportion of income paid in direct taxes. Comparing benefits with taxes, however, there is a steady rise in net benefits as income falls. Cash benefits and subsidies can easily be attributed to the recipients but benefits in kind (mainly for health and education services) are assumed to be equally divided throughout the community. Many authorities, like Richard Titmuss, have questioned this assumption and believe

Table VII.11

UK Taxes and Benefits in Relation to Household Income, 1967 (Percentage of Income for Household of Man, Wife and Two Children)

Pre-Tax Income Range (£.s.)	Proportion of Households Surveyed (%)	Income Tax and Surtax	NI Contributions	Indirect Taxes	Total Taxes	Benefits Received (as % of Income)	Difference: Benefits *minus* Tax (as % of Income)
		Taxes as % of Income					
10.15–13.10	1	1	10	37	48	65	+17
13.10–15.15	3	3	10	25·5	38	48	+10
15.15–19.0	10	3	10	24	37	32	−5
19.0 –23.0	16	4	9	20·5	33·5	22	−11·5
23.0 –28.0	21	5·5	8	19	32·5	20	−12·5
28.0 –34.0	21	8	6·5	18	32·5	19·5	−13
34.0 –41.0	14	10	5·5	16·5	32	14	−18
41.0 –49.10	7	14	4·5	15	33·5	12	−21·5
49.10–60.0	4	15·5	3·5	16	35	10	−25
60 plus	3	23	2·5	12	37·5	7·5	−30
Average	100	9·5	0·5	17·5	33·5	19	−14·5

Note: Benefits include cash benefits, housing but not farming subsidies and benefits in kind from education, health and welfare services. Other State expenditures on defence, police, prisons, parks, roads, museums and administrations are excluded.

Source: *Economic Trends,* February 1969.

that the middle classes benefit disproportionately from the social services.

A study of comparative tax systems in Europe in the 1950s, from which Table VII.12 is taken, showed Britain as having about the average proportion of direct and indirect taxes and of social insurance contributions in its tax system, as well as about the average share of national product going to the State. The United States government received a high proportion of taxes from corporations; other West European countries have subsequently moved in this direction. The main difference between Britain and the others was found to lie in Britain's more progressive system of direct taxation. Table VII.12 shows the differences not only in terms of average tax rate at different levels but, even more noticeably, in terms of MARGI-NAL TAX RATE – that is the amount that a person cannot hope to keep of extra income above a certain level.

Table VII.12

Average and Marginal Income Tax Rates for Standard Families in Four Countries in the 1950s

Income before Tax (£ equivalent)	Britain		Sweden		W. Germany		USA	
	Average	Marginal	Average	Marginal	Average	Marginal	Average	Marginal
500	1	4	9	23	12	12	3	3
1,000	10	32	17	35	18	18	5	22
1,500	15	39	22	42	22	24	7	20
5,000	36	61	42	61	25	40	19	32
10,000	52	76	52	67	33	49	29	49
20,000	67	89	60	69	40	53	40	63
50,000	81	89	66	69	48	53	62	85
100,000	85	89	68	69	50	53	75	91

Source: L. Needleman, National Institute *Economic Review*, March 1961.

According to the average tax per income figures, the UK taxes its very rich citizens much more heavily than the other similarly advanced countries do. However, the income taxes of the UK, and of Sweden too, begin to bear heavily upon marginal income at quite low levels. Around one-third of any extra income was already mortgaged to tax for a standard family with £1,000 p.a. in both countries in the 1950s, and about 40 per cent of it for the family with £1,500 p.a. It is frequently argued that an increase in direct taxation provides a disincentive to earning and that this is damaging to the economy both in respect of workers and of businessmen. Workers refuse to do overtime and businessmen lose interest in chasing export orders.[11] There is much evidence, however, that points in the exactly contrary direction, that most people set themselves a certain living standard and if taxes go up will work harder or longer to maintain it.

The fact that the British believe that they are the most heavily taxed nation on earth does mean that there are definite limits to the proportion of the national income which

[11] This point is argued by Paul Einzig in *Decline and Fall?*, 1969.

the government can lay its hands on. This proportion was undoubtedly raised very sharply between 1957 and 1969 as Table VII.8 clearly showed. If the proportion were raised above the 1969 level of 49 per cent it would probably have to be done by some kind of wealth tax, as Professor James Meade suggested, which bore most heavily on the recipients of inherited wealth rather than on the donors. Writers like Mr Paul Einzig would complain that we should be 'killing the goose that lays the golden eggs' – the reference being to private investors whose capital we rely upon for industrial investment. Since these are rapidly being replaced by giant corporations generating their own funds, and by institutional investors, the argument is weakened. There are still those who fear a 'strike of capital' and remember the rumblings in the City of London when a Labour Chancellor, Mr Hugh Dalton in 1946, set the bank rate at 2 per cent. In the last resort, however, governments have now the power to step up their own capital investment to replace any deficiencies of private capital. This is what they have, in fact, been doing in the 1960s, in making loans and grants to the private sector to the tune of some £1,500 millions or about 5 per cent of the 1967 national product.[12]

No one should doubt the power of government today through fiscal measures to influence the economy. With such a large proportion of the national income passing through its hands the government can influence the whole level and pattern of production. There are important public gains, not only in education, health, welfare and amenity, that must be set against the costs in taxation. Criticism of the so-called 'burden' of taxes comes partly from the rich and partly from all those who feel that they have little or no say in the decision on how the money is spent and in the direct management of the spending. This is a political rather than an economic question and will be considered again in the next chapter. Criticism is likely to remain, however, both so long as the incidence of taxes seems to be unfair, and great inequalities of income remain, and so long as government spending seems to be undiscriminating in its effects.

[12] These are listed in Table 1 on p. 25 of K. Coates (ed.), *Can the Workers Run Industry?*

Two examples only can be provided here of the undiscriminating nature of government decisions. First, increases
in pensions for the aged and in many other social services have
frequently been held back on the ground that the balance of
payments did not permit an increase in spending power at
home which might generate a higher level of imports. Yet there
is little evidence that old-age pensioners have a high marginal
propensity to spend on imported goods or that other social
services generate a high proportion of imports. Little or no
study has, in fact, been made of the relative import propensities of different forms of personal or government spending.
Secondly, increases in grants (or tax concessions) have been
made to firms in particular industries and areas. This may
seem to be an attempt at discrimination, but the result has
generally been to help all firms in those industries and areas,
whether they were doing what the government wished or
not.

Grants for capital investment in the areas of higher than
average unemployment were offered by the Labour Government after 1965 at twice the rate (20 per cent) available to
firms elsewhere. This was naturally an encouragement to
capital-intensive industries to go to these areas. Such
industries may generate some secondary employment opportunities; but by their very nature they do little directly to
create employment. In one case, moreover, that of the oil
industry, which had already decided on deep-water terminals
for refineries in Scotland, the extra grant earned by the oil
companies did much to offset other policies being pursued by
the government to protect the coal industry. The grants
encouraged capital-intensive investment and were received by
the oil companies for doing what they would have done
anyway.

Although it was designed to discourage the employment of
labour in service industries and in areas of labour shortage,
this was the case also with the introduction of a SELECTIVE
EMPLOYMENT TAX (SET) in 1966. It was selective in that it
selected industries, e.g. manufacturing, and in 1967 whole
regions also – those with above average unemployment –
where the tax was not only remitted but a premium was paid
per employee. The problem that arose with SET was that

employers received this premium whether they were doing something for the first time or only doing what they would anyway have done. There was no extra carrot for those who took on *extra* labour or for those who *increased* their manufactures for export rather than for the home market. The INVESTMENT GRANTS, which were also paid at a higher rate in the regions of above average unemployment, worked in the same way. Firms received the grants for what they might anyway have done. Since the government was at the same time deflating the home market, and many firms had unused capacity as a result, such firms were not likely to invest in new capacity even with the prospect of an investment grant for doing so. Many of the government's advance factories, built in Scotland and the North of England to encourage businessmen into these areas, remained empty for years after they were built. It was because a policy of carrots proved so unrewarding that governments turned increasingly to the use of sticks as well as carrots; that is to applying physical controls to the economy. Monetary measures provided a brake, fiscal measures an accelerator for the economy, but the use of the two together (even at the same time!) was no substitute for a steering wheel.

4. THE USE OF PHYSICAL CONTROLS AND PRICES AND INCOMES POLICIES

Governments have for long applied physical controls in certain areas of the national life, through Mines and Factory Acts, housing standards, sanitation and health control, road and street regulations and some town and country planning. In war time controls have been widespread – on imports, foreign exchange, prices, rents, profits and building and through food rationing, the direction of labour and raw material allocations. When peace came there was soon a bonfire of controls in the interests of the free working of the market; and we have already noticed earlier the problems that economists insist such controls bring with them.[13] Controls may be effective in the short run, but in a market economy they tend in the longer run to worsen the very situation they are designed to cure.

[13] They are wittily dealt with in E. J. Mishan's *Twenty One Popular Economic Fallacies*, 1969.

Control over rising prices due to shortages – whether of goods, land, labour or capital – leads to falling incomes where the controls are imposed and so to less and not more resources being allocated there. Control over rising imports due to uncompetitive products at home gives protection to such products and reduces rather than increases the incentive to make them competitive. Direction of labour and rationing of other resources in short supply both require a large and costly force of highly skilled persons to manage and police.

Not all the criticisms of such controls are economic. Many are political. An army of bureaucrats is established to operate the controls. Then who will control the controllers themselves? In wartime, experts from the largest companies move into the new government offices and their chairmen become ministers. In the last war such ministers included Lord Leathers of Wm. Cory's Shipping Lines at the Ministry of Transport, Lord Woolton of Lewis's at the Ministry of Food, Lord Chandos of the London Tin Corporation at the Ministry of Production, Sir Andrew Duncan of the Iron and Steel Federation at the Ministry of Supply, Lord Waverley of Vickers as Co-ordinator of the Home Front. Even without suggesting corrupt practices, we may recognize that the allocation of materials tended to go to those who were already the largest firms in the business.[14]

Controls create other problems; for example, the detail of controls is enormously complex. Attempts to control capital investment, as through the post-war CAPITAL ISSUES committee, had either to cover every decision, however small, or set a minimum limit; whereupon enterprising firms would raise capital through a hundred subsidiaries each taking up less than the minimum. Attempts to control prices face tens of thousands of firms each deciding its own price ranges. As the size of firms grows and price leadership or monopoly develop, this ceases to be such a problem, but the difficulty remains of controlling changes in quality that are concealed in a controlled price. Standard specifications can be laid down, as with the war-time utility clothing and furniture. But here as elsewhere

[14] A new kind of feudalism emerged which is well described in Peter Shore's and A. A. Rogow's study of the *Labour Government and British Industry 1945-51*.

people rebel against the restrictions on their free choice. The direction of labour challenges a freedom that all people will wish to preserve most ardently, and owners of property will have the same feelings of wishing to be able to do what they will with their own.

None of this is to say that for short periods in wartime, and in emergencies in peacetime, controls do not have an important place in the economic armoury of the State. Most governments limit themselves, however, to those which have the least effect on what the public regards as essential human freedoms. Thus, building controls through licensing have been the main physical weapons of governments wishing to direct the location of industry. Incentives to firms to go where government wishes are best combined with restrictions on them building where they may wish. Such building controls at home must be supported by foreign exchange controls, or firms will simply transfer their capital to other countries where they believe it to be advantageous to do so. Control over international companies with funds in many countries becomes exceedingly difficult in these circumstances. Governments may have to reassure themselves that at least flights of capital do not take out of the country any capital plant or skilled workers; but they may be forced in the end to set these to work themselves.

The main controversy over controls in Britain in the 1960s was over the power of governments to control prices and incomes through a Prices and Incomes Policy.[15] Several major attempts were made to use powers of persuasion upon employers and trade unions to agree on limits to the growth of both prices and incomes in order to curb inflation. But the prices and incomes policies pursued by the Labour Government after 1965 combined intervention in the market through government influence on the process of wage and price determination with direct controls over wages and prices. A succession of legislative acts required industries and unions to register proposed increases in prices and incomes. A Prices and Incomes Board was established to investigate increases that the government referred to it. The chief successes claimed for these

[15] A good introduction to this is J. Corina, *Incomes Policy – Problems and Prospects*, 1966.

acts arose not from attempts at persuasion but from government administrative orders. A number of price increases were delayed by order, a number of wage demands reduced and for six months in 1961 and in 1966 a wage freeze was imposed. The difficulty of imposing such restrictions, especially upon workers unwilling to give up their freedom to negotiate wage increases when they saw the opportunity to do so, led to the threat of legal sanctions against unofficial strikers. The government withdrew the threat, contained in the White Paper *In Place of Strife*, only when the TUC agreed to act as policeman to its own members.

In the controversy over prices and incomes a main issue at stake was the bracketing of the two together in one policy. Many trade unionists maintained that there were important distinctions between the two which allowed that prices might properly be controlled but incomes should be the subject of voluntary agreement.[16] The distinctions included the following:[17]

(*1*) Prices can be raised unilaterally, wages cannot.

(*2*) Prices are not the subject of long negotiation and public inquiry, wages are.

(*3*) Prices raise profits and hence property incomes, but even if the profits are not paid out in dividends the extra wealth accrues to property owners in the form of increased real assets, whereas other incomes once forgone are lost and not deferred.

(*4*) Taxing profits differs from taxing other incomes in the possibilities open for evasion and allowances.

(*5*) Prices of goods, though they seem to be concerned with 'things' and to be the result of economic forces beyond human control, are in effect the prices set by groups of powerful employers upon the labour of others; wages are the price of a man's own labour.

(*6*) Employers have more funds and more support in the Press to put their side of an argument than do the unions.

(*7*) In the last analysis employers can hold out longer in

---

[16] See R. Blackburn and A. Cockburn (eds.), *The Incompatibles*, 1967.

[17] For detailed development of this argument see M. Barratt Brown and R. J. Harrison, 'Incomes Policy – A Reply' *New Left Review*, No. 37 May–June 1966.

bargaining than workers can, however well organized the latter are and however well filled their strike funds.

Trade unionists who argued in this way still recognized that inflation cut severely into their monetary wage demands and was particularly damaging to those living on fixed incomes. They recognized that the continuance of deflationary policies to check rising prices and imports was as damaging to themselves as to others in the community. They favoured an incomes policy, however, only as part of an overall economic plan. They rejected the planning of wages alone. In the words of Frank Cousins, leader in the 1960s of Britain's largest union, 'In a free for all, we are part of the all.'

The great number of measures of government intervention in the market economy which we have considered in this chapter have been seen to be valuable in themselves, but to require increasingly an overall strategy to make them effective. The next step for British governments after the 1960s seemed to be necessarily either a return to the free market, with all its distortion by the power of giant companies, or the extension of government intervention into the realm of economic planning. The choice can be seen as a political one, but an understanding of the measures available for strategic planning of the economy and the economic problems involved in such planning are necessary for the proper exercise of that choice. These are the subject of our last chapter.

8 Economic Planning or a Planned Economy?

SUMMARY

Plans in economics as in other matters are Man's attempts to prepare for and arrange for change in the future. In economic affairs they are particularly concerned with making good the failure of the market to go beyond a static and local equilibrium and to provide for future economic development in a world-wide context. Economic planning has to try to reconcile those divergences of interest of producers and consumers which we have seen in the market. Where the means of production are owned by a few private persons, these interests are inevitably antagonistic; and government planning is limited by the power of the firm. Where ownership is social, the interests of productive enterprises and of the general body of consumers may still conflict, but the conflicts should be capable of being reconciled within a framework of government social planning. We may distinguish these two cases as economic planning in a market economy and a planned economy based on social ownership. Plan and market may, none the less, have to be combined under social ownership to allow for individual choice within social resource allocation.

Since economic growth is now regarded in most societies as a main objective of planning, the nature and processes of such growth are examined here with special attention given to its effect on income distribution. Where ownership of capital is mainly in private hands and the market remains intact, the role of government economic planning in both developed and developing economies is found to be concerned primarily with co-ordinating investment for future growth both in time and place. The problems arising in various forms of planning – INDICATIVE, CO-ORDINATIVE and RESOURCE PLANNING – are illustrated from the British government's National Plan of 1965, and the Regional and Fuel Policies associated with it.

In a planned economy based on social ownership there are

great advantages in centrally managed investment of an
EXTENSIVE type. These advantages may be illustrated at a
low level of national income from the experience of the Soviet
Union; so may the disadvantages at higher levels of income.
INTENSIVE INVESTMENT is seen to require a new economic
framework of decentralized decision-making where people
manage their own resources. Attempts to marry the plan and
market under Socialism are, therefore, being explored both in
the writings of the Czech economist, Dr Ota Sik, and in the
experience of Yugoslav self-management. In both the aim is
seen to be to harness broad social decisions about future
TRENDS with flexible responses to current local and individual
needs.

1. WHAT IS PLANNING?

If planning simply means preparing for the future by arranging things beforehand, this does not mean that the arrangements necessarily work. 'The best laid plans of mice and men
gang aft agley,' said Robert Burns. Family planning is an
example. Four separate stages can be distinguished in any
kind of planning: (*a*) deciding on your aims with other parties
who must be consulted – what it is you want, when and how
many; (*b*) understanding the processes involved in realizing
your aims; (*c*) making some arrangements to increase the
likelihood that your aims will be realized; (*d*) considering the
results of your arrangements for all those who may be involved.
Each of these stages is inherent in any kind of economic
planning, and we shall have to hold each of them in mind
throughout this chapter. We have first to remember what
economic questions are concerned with.

We have already noted the scale, duration and complexity
of planning required in a large industrial enterprise using
modern techniques of production. Increasingly, technology
determines the production of the firm and is half-way to
determining the allocation of national resources in our kind of
private capitalist economy. This was supposed to be the role
of the market, but we saw in Chapter 5 how giant international
companies now dominate the market, disposing of greater
resources than most national governments. Their plans for

production increasingly decide what we shall have to consume. Their technological advances determine the growth path of our economy. If motor-car production proves more amenable to technological advances than, shall we say, house-building, then more motor-cars will be built by the most modern techniques of automated assembly lines, and house-building will remain technically backward. If, moreover, the market for private goods can be more easily managed than the market for increased educational provision, and if the protection of amenity – clean air and parks and unpolluted rivers – is more difficult to organize than the motor-car lobby, then we shall have that private affluence amidst public squalor which we hear reported from the United States.[1]

Economic questions have become involved in technical questions and the reason is clear. You cannot have planned production without some planning of the distribution and use of what is produced. We noticed in Chapter 5 how bankers and other controllers sitting across the boards of several giant companies supply some co-ordination of their investment in what would otherwise be market anarchy. The investment decisions of large companies, however, as we saw earlier, increasingly involve more than just co-ordination with other companies' plans; they require co-ordination with government plans, both as regards the timing of growth and the distribution of government taxation and spending. For even though governments may eschew strategic economic planning, they too, like the giant companies, have to plan their own operations.

We can list references throughout this book to the increasing role of government intervention in the market – in the location of industry, in controlling monopoly, in redistributing incomes and in other ways influencing prices and incomes, in encouraging labour mobility, in maintaining full employment, in curbing inflation, in balancing foreign payments, in stimulating economic growth. In Chapter 6 we dealt generally with government intervention in the trade cycle and with the expansionary implications of full employment for prices and imports. In Chapter 7 we saw, however, that governments have been required, not simply to correct inadequacies,

[1] J.K.Galbraith has written most wittily about this in his book *The Affluent Society*, 1968.

injustices, inequalities, imbalances, but to take more positive action; in effect to develop an overall strategic plan.

2. THE OBJECTIVES OF PLANNING

We have already noted a number of plans that have been worked out by British governments in order to solve particular practical problems. Increasingly, however, economic planning involves questions about the choice of objectives which go rather wider than specific aims like maintaining full employment, rectifying the balance of payments or curbing inflation. Sometimes this is because there is a logical conflict of objectives involved. With given resources, more of one form of government spending – on arms for example – must mean less spending on another – schools or hospitals. More often the conflict lies in the economic system of a market economy as we have seen it working. The benefits of full employment and economic growth seem to involve the costs of inflation and balance of payments crises. To reduce these costs, governments stop growth and deliberately create unemployment. There are other methods, of course, of dealing with the problem – prices could be controlled, capital exports prevented and imports restricted by QUOTAS. But such measures would create other problems of black markets, corruption and loss of incentives for investment. More than this, they would involve decisions by some authority about the proper level of controlled prices and the proper allocation of the restricted imports. This would mean that governments would have to interfere in a discriminatory way in the economy. As soon as a government does this, it opens itself to criticism, unless the objectives are clearly understood and generally agreed. In wartime, objectives are simplified by the overall requirement of winning the war. In peacetime, a consensus of opinion can also develop but it will tend to exclude the interests of important minorities and to be moulded by dominant economic interests such as, for example, those of the international companies.

Welfare economics is the branch of economic theory in which economists have attempted to define economic objectives in relation to optimum resource allocation, through ensuring that goods and services are charged for and output adjusted to long-run marginal cost. The classic statement can be taken from A. C. Pigou.[2]

> 1 Any cause which, without the exercise of compulsion or pressure upon people to make them work more then their wishes and interests dictate, increases productive efficiency, and, therewith, the average volume of the national dividend (income), provided that it neither injures the distribution, nor augments the variability of the country's consumable income, will, in general, increase economic welfare.
>
> 2 Any cause which increases the proportion of the national dividend received by poor persons, provided that it does not lead to a contraction of the dividend and does not injuriously affect its variability, will, in general, increase economic welfare.

The second proposition Pigou thought was fortified by the diminishing marginal utility of income (that is by the way we meet less urgent demands as our incomes rise). The first proposition had the crucial corollary attached to it that in any given state of technology, available resources should be allocated so that the social net product of a unit of these resources was equal in money values at the margin of each and every use. This was the economist's test of efficiency and this was supposed to be achieved by the market; but we have seen that there are many limitations to the working of the market. I. M. D. Little lists the following:[3]

(*a*) monopoly positions will raise some prices above marginal cost;

(*b*) taxation distorts costs if it is at all discriminatory;

(*c*) the marginal unit may be too large for easy division and often too large for an individual; e.g. a park or road, where the marginal cost, that is the cost of an extra person using it, may be zero;

(*d*) a firm's marginal costs take no account of external economies or diseconomies, in location, foreign trade and alternative structures of production;

(*e*) factors in elastic supply will be underpaid compared with those in inelastic supply. Land and capital have for this reason earned a rent on top of their marginal cost; whereas the

[2] See his book *Economics of Welfare*, 1932.
[3] See his book *A Critique of Welfare Economics*, 1950.

marginal costs of under-employed or unemployed labour may be zero;

To these we may add two points from earlier chapters:

(*f*) social costs and benefits will not be allowed for in a firm's costings, and social choices may thus be limited as regards both alternative goods and services and alternative methods of production;

(*g*) adaptation to new consumer demands may be costly and slow, especially where these cannot be EXTRAPOLATED from past trends.

Most of these points are hard for governments to get around without major interference in the market, amounting to a strategic plan. Welfare economics has therefore mainly confined itself to calculating the costs and benefits of particular schemes in pounds, shillings and pence. The cost of air pollution can be measured in terms of house-painting and stone-repairing costs and of the value of days of work lost and of hospital charges for cases of bronchitis. The benefits of a new road or underground railway line can be measured in the value not only of the fuel and the vehicles' wear and tear but of time saved, which must include some estimate of the valuation people put on their leisure. We are left with the problem that we met in Chapter 2 of how we are to compare one man's gain with another's, or one man's loss with another man's gain. The market leaves it to individuals to put their own price on this; but where incomes and market power are most unequally distributed we have seen that this leads to results which are regarded as unsatisfactory. This does not mean, however, that we should assume that no comparisons of costs and benefits to individuals can be made. Firstly, if it is true that wants diminish in urgency as they are satisfied, then any increases in benefits to the poor at the cost of the rich must be regarded as net benefits. Secondly, compensation could be offered to those who, when granted legal rights, to amenity for example, were prepared to waive them at a price. In this way, as Dr E. J. Mishan suggests,[4] some inter-personal costs and benefits could be adjusted.

Such methods of preserving the market mechanism, by altering the legal framework in which it operates, seem to be

[4] See *Growth: The Price We Pay*, 1969.

rather complicated ways of discovering popular preferences in
the economy. Simpler methods of developing social choices are
needed. The advantages of cost-benefit studies, according to
two leading exponents of them[5], are probably limited in their
usefulness to comparisons between projects in the same field,
say one road project as against another or one fuel as against
another. Here they may be of great value in supplementing
straight market accounting methods. We shall return to this
point later.

If welfare economics can give us little help in determining
economic objectives in the light of the efficiency of resource
utilization, then we must abandon positive economics and ask
some normative questions. This will mean considering some of
the objectives that governments have set themselves and
allowing readers to judge, as voters must, whether the objectives are what they would wish and are adequately realized.
The objectives can be listed briefly.[6] The list that follows is not
in an order that will please every reader or in a form that is
very precise. In some cases we can distinguish conservative
and radical policies where change could go in different
directions:

(*a*) economic growth at a faster rate;

(*b*) full employment, or at least a low rate and short duration
of average unemployment;

(*c*) more stable prices, or at least less inflation;

(*d*) a balance of foreign payments and a surplus for overseas
investment or aid;

(*e*) a change in composition of the output of goods and
services (Conservative: more private goods; Radical: more
public services);

(*f*) more freedom of choice in the mix of goods and services
and leisure;

(*g*) a change in the distribution of income (Conservative:
more incentives; Radical: more social security);

(*h*) more control over the processes and over the distribution
of production. We should perhaps add (*i*) the winning of the

[5] A. R. Prest and R. Turvey, 'Theories of Cost Benefit Analysis' in *Surveys of
Economic Theory*, Vol. III.

[6] A good introduction to the problem of ordering economic objectives will be
found at the beginning of Michael Lipton's book, *Assessing Economic Performance*, 1968.

next election, since the timing of the post-war investment cycle has already suggested that this has been a manageable objective of governments.

These objectives although separated here are closely interconnected. We saw in the last chapter that planning involved an overall strategy of government interventions, since several of the objectives tended to be hard to reconcile and often proved to be mutually contradictory. Full employment with stable prices and balanced foreign payments was one example. It is not that there is a logical contradiction here as there might be between more leisure and more output or between more goods *and* more services. The contradiction we saw was one that required an alternative framework of economic relationships. Governments would have to find a way of maintaining aggregate demand so that it does not lead to inflation and balance of payments crises. One way suggested was to step up the rate of economic growth. Here the influence is mutual. Economic growth can be faster if not interrupted by periods of deflation. The problem, as so often in economics, is to get on to an upward circle of causation. Moreover, if economic growth is speeded up, changes in the composition of goods and services, in the range of choice and even in income distribution might be easier to make, since the total resources available would be increased. It may be well to start, then, by examining the processes involved in economic growth as they are understood by economists.

3. THE PROCESSES OF ECONOMIC GROWTH

It is first necessary to define what is meant by economic growth. The first point to emphasize is that, as we have just seen, economic growth does not necessarily mean an increase in economic welfare. E. J. Mishan has written at length[7] on the social costs in dis-amenity and human conflict of growth at any price. The chief example for him is the increase in motorcar production. This can be measured as economic growth but it brings with it what he calls the SPILL-OVER effects of noise, stench, congestion, danger to life and limb, ruin of cities and countryside alike, the much longer-term pollution of land, sea and

[7] See particularly *Growth: The Price We Pay*, 1969.

air, and the encouragement of a debilitating and anti-social way of living. Some of these costs can be measured – like the 7,000 dead and the 15,000 hospital beds required for road accidents each year; other costs are not subject to any kind of measurement let alone a financial one. Altering the growth path of an economy is likely to present a more intractable problem than altering the growth rate.

The other problems of measuring economic growth are more easily solved. Annual statistics of GROSS NATIONAL INCOME or of NET NATIONAL INCOME, that is after deducting CAPITAL CONSUMPTION, are generally used by economists as the basis for an index of growth in market economies. In planned economies, for reasons associated with a Marxist view of economic surplus, which we shall examine later, work in the so-called non-productive spheres, of state administration, defence, community and personal services, banking and insurance, is not included in the social accounts. In either case two adjustments have to be made to the annual totals in order to provide a 'real' index of this general sort of growth.

The first is that prices may have risen (or fallen) from year to year. The adjustment is usually made, as we noted in the second chapter, by discovering the price changes for every item since a base year and adjusting all current values for these price changes. The result is an index of growth at constant prices. In the *National Income and Expenditure* Blue Book 1958 was used as the base year for the period up to 1968. From time to time, the base year has to be changed as the mix of goods and services in the national income changes, entirely new goods like TV sets appear and the products being priced may change in quality. All this means that indices become less and less reliable the longer the period of time over which they are extended.

The second adjustment that has to be made to an index based on annual national income statistics arises from changes in the population of the country among whom the income is distributed. The usual practice is to divide the economic growth index by an index of the growth in population to give a *per capita* growth rate. Changes in the structure of populations (more old people, for example) have led some economists to prefer an index that assumes not only constant prices but a constant population structure.[8] This is obviously more important over long periods of time than over short periods. The best solution to these problems of indices is to use average annual *per capita* growth rates over short periods like five years or a decade, remembering, first, that these are cumulative and must be compounded like compound interest to reveal long-term growth, and secondly that productivity or growth per person employed provides an important supplementary index (see Table VI.9 above).

Economic growth as we have now defined it, can only occur either through more people working, or through people working harder, on richer land or with more equipment, or through people working more effectively. Economists and politicians in recent years have tended to emphasize the importance for economic growth of investment in extra equipment. They call the methods of increasing factor inputs – of land, labour and capital – extensive development, and those of improving their mix and organization – intensive development. In Chapter 3 we saw that the great changes in output since the Industrial Revolution have been the result of adding mechanical power to human labour and exploiting a combination of the division of labour and the economies of large-scale production. In the first stage most of this was extensive development. We noted that this was easier in the case of industry than of agriculture and that the very fact of the transfer of labour from agriculture to industry resulted in major gains in output per man. We can see from Table VIII.1 that this transfer was a main explanation of the more rapid rates of economic growth in the 1950s in Germany, France, Italy and Japan than in Britain, where we had no longer much agricultural labour to transfer. Today, therefore, with near full employment and no new lands to discover, it may seem surprising that the proportion of a country's resources set aside to new extensive investment in capital equipment has been the first source of economic growth to which economists have drawn attention. It did not, however, as Table VIII.1 shows, account for more than a fifth of the annual growth rates of the USA and Western European countries in the 1950s. The extra labour applied was also important, but even more important were

[8] See M. Lipton, *Assessing Economic Performance*, Chapter II.

Table VIII.1

USA and Eight West European Countries Relative National Incomes per Person 1960, Growth Rates 1950–1962 and Factor Contributions to Growth Rates

	USA	UK	W. Germany	Seven N.W. European Countries	Italy
National Income 1960 Relative per head	100	57	56	54	26
Annual Average Growth Rates 1950–62 TOTAL %	3·3	2·3	7·3	4·8	6·0
A. *Contribution of Factor Inputs* TOTAL %	1·95	1·1	2·8	1·7	1·7
Labour	1·1	0·6	1·4	0·8	1·0
Capital	0·85	0·5	1·4	0·9	0·7
B. *Contribution of Changes in Output per Unit of Input* TOTAL %	1·35	1·2	4·5	3·1	4·3
Resource Shifts					
from Agriculture	0·25	0·06	0·8†	0·45	1·04
from Self-Employment	0·05	0·04	0·15	0·15	0·22
from Trade Barrier changes	0·0	0·02	0·1	0·08	0·16
Economies of Scale					
from Size of National Market	0·3	0·2	0·6	0·4	0·55
(including that part contributed by Growth of National Market	0·3	0·3	1·5	0·9	1·1)
from Growth of Local Markets	0·06	0·05	0·07	0·07	0·07
from Different Consumption Patterns	0·0	0·0	0·9	0·45	0·51
Demand Fluctuation Losses	−0·04	−0·09*	0·0	−0·01	0·0
Residual Gains					
Application of Knowledge, etc.	0·75	0·8	1·6	1·3	1·65
Residual Gains as a % of TOTAL Changes in Output per unit of Input	55	64	36	42	37

Notes: 7 N.W. European Countries = UK, W. Germany, France, Belgium, Denmark, Netherlands, Norway.

*Loss through Demand Fluctuation in UK 1955–62 = −0·29.

†Gain through shift of resources from agriculture in Germany took place mainly before 1955.

Source: E. F. Dennison, *Why Growth Rates Differ*, Brookings Institution 1967.

the ways the extra inputs were organized – i.e. in intensive development by applying new knowledge more effectively.

Investment may be in many different kinds of capital equipment: roads, railways, ports, communications and transport equipment, schools, universities and hospitals – all these the economists call INFRASTRUCTURE development—and in plant and machinery for primary production in mining and agriculture, for manufacture and for the many service industries. At different stages of economic development each of these may be more important than others in generating increased output: but extra investment will have very different effects on output according to the form which it takes. At a low level of development a quite small increase in investment will, moreover, lead to a much greater relative increase in output than at higher levels. The effects of extensive investment is much greater at a low level than at a high level. This means that different economies will have different capital – output ratios or INCREMENTAL CAPITAL-OUTPUT RATIOS (ICORs), as economists describe the ratio of the share of current output invested to extra output achieved.

Table VII.2 reveals different ICORs for European countries and the USA in the 1950s. The Western European countries are listed in order of their growth rates in gross domestic product over the decade, but if they were ranked according to gross investment as a percentage of GDP the ranking would be rather similar. The statisticians call this a CORRELATION. Each additional 1 per cent in investment gives on average an extra 0·3 per cent of GDP. The correlation coefficient is 0·7. But the ICORs depend, as can be seen in the Tables, upon the overall level which the economy has attained. The higher the *per capita* GDP, the higher the ICOR has to be for a given increase in GDP. The East European countries, and others at much lower *per capita* GDP, do not need higher gross investment ratios to get higher increases in growth of GDP. On the other hand, it is much more difficult for them to achieve these higher rates of investment, since saving a fifth of national income every year for them means cutting much more heavily into current spending on essential items than it does in richer countries.

This is the great problem of the developing economies, that

Table VIII.2

Economic Growth and Investment (in 24 countries), 1949–1959 (at constant prices)

	1	2	3	4	5	6
		1949–1959		1949–54 Average		
	1950	Growth Rates		Gross Investment		
	Relative	(% p.a.)		as % of GDP		ICOR
	Per Capita		of Pro-		Public	Col. 4/
Country	GDP	of	ductivity	Total	Sector	Col. 2
	(USA = 100)	GDP	of Labour			
W. Europe						
W. Germany	56	7·4	5·7	24·2	10	3·3
Austria	40	6·0	4·8	23·3	17	3·9
Greece	(15)	5·9	4·3	17·8	—	3·0
Italy	26	5·9	4·8	21·9	14	3·7
Turkey	(15)	5·9	3·4	(15·0)	—	(2·6)
Iceland	50	5·4	3·8	30·9	—	5·7
Spain	(20)	5·2	4·3	(16·3)	—	(3·1)
Switzerland	69	5·2	3·7	(23·7)	2	(4·5)
Netherlands	45	4·8	3·6	25	7	5·2
France	51	4·5	4·3	20·6	11	4·6
Finland	32	4·2	3·4	30	16	7·2
Portugal	14	4·1	3·5	16·2	—	4·0
Norway	48	3·4	3·1	32·6	7·0	9·5
Sweden	67	3·4	2·9	21·4	13*	6·3
Denmark	55	3·2	2·2	17·5	8*	5·5
Belgium	53	3·0	2·7	16·9	4	5·6
UK	57	2·4	1·8	16·1	8	6·7
N. America						
Canada	72	4·2	2·1	25·5	5	6·0
USA	100	3·3	2·0	18·1	4	5·5
E. Europe						
Bulgaria		10·2	—	18·8	18*	1·8
Hungary		6·7	—	19·9	19*	3·3
Poland		8·1	—	21·5	21*	2·6
USSR	(35)	8·2	—	27·8	27*	3·4
Yugoslavia	12	5·5	4·4	23·2	20*	4·2

Notes: *Including Co-operatives. Figures in brackets are estimates.

Source: United Nations Economic Commission for Europe, *Some Factors in Economic Growth in Europe during the 1950s.*

jam tomorrow really means going without bread today. A brief look at the process of economic growth in underdeveloped countries may help us to understand why economic planning is now so widely canvassed in them. For an industrial revolution to succeed, the 'iron heel of primitive capital accumulation', as a Russian economist called it in the 1920s,[9] has always had to be imposed whether by a capitalist class or a Stalin. PEASANTS on the borderline of starvation will not voluntarily give up the little extra they win from the land today to feed industrial workers in the towns, so that they may make machines for tomorrow. In Britain's industrial revolution capital was accumulated by individual capitalists out of the sweated labour of women and children. The capitalists probably neither preferred to do it that way, nor had they any wider social objective of economic growth in mind. As Keynes put it, 'Like bees they saved and accumulated, no less to the advantage of the whole community because they themselves had narrower ends in prospect.'[10] Today in many underdeveloped countries the local capitalists are too closely tied to their role as clients of the giant international companies from the advanced economics to plough their capital back into industrial development in their own lands. New groups and leaders will have to emerge to do this, but one way or the other they will have to accelerate the accumulation process for increased investment.

With the growing scale of production in modern industry, the role of government in economic development becomes ever more important. In Britain's industrial revolution the capital required for a mill or forge was not beyond the range of one man to find with a few partners. Railway building required the formation of joint-stock companies. Nuclear power requires giant CONSORTIA of companies with government finance. Underdeveloped lands today cannot be expected to go stage by stage from small-scale to large-scale industrialization, as Britain did, if only because their products would be hopelessly uncompetitive with the products of modern industry. They have to make a giant leap into the twentieth century, or not move at all. Government economic planning,

[9] E. Preobrazhensky, *The New Economics*.
[10] J.M.Keynes, *Economic Consequences of the Peace*, p. 16.

K

therefore, is required, not only to assign the necessary funds and to organize the collection of food, but to bring together the various elements in the industrial structure. Without such planning private owners of resources will delay their development until they see other complementary development occurring. Thus electric power and irrigation, steel plants and chemical by-products, transport and communications, research and education, have all to be developed in an integrated way, where a modern large scale of operations is adopted.

It has not been too difficult for extensive development to be achieved by private owners of capital in an unplanned market, since it consists mainly of mere cumulative additions to capital equipment. Intensive development, involving rationalized organization and harnessing of external economies, needs more planning if great wastage of resources in booms and slumps and in delayed development are to be avoided. Governments and giant companies can influence this by the expenditure and encouragement they give to education and research. In Britain investment by the public sector accounts, we saw, for half of the total of annual gross capital formation. It is indeed the 'external economies' of integrated location and timing of investment which are the main object of economic planning.[11]

It may be noted from Table VIII.1 that the countries with planned economies, where most investment was public investment, had high rates of growth in the 1950s. There is some evidence that even in the advanced private capitalist economies there is a correlation between the proportion of public investment and the rate of growth. One international economist, Mr Angus Maddison, has stated categorically that, 'The countries where government has saved most are those with the highest investment rates', and high investment rates are one factor in economic growth, as we have seen.[12] At the same time it is very evident that the rapid rate of growth of the planned economies in the 1950s was not sustained in the 1960s. The most obvious example was Czechoslovakia. It

[11] An excellent introduction to such problems of economic growth and planning is W. Birmingham and A. G. Ford, *Planning and Growth in Rich and Poor Countries*, 1966.

[12] E. A. G. Robinson (ed.), in *Problems of Economic Development*, Chapter IV.

seems that for extensive development the planned economy
gave rapid rates of growth, but difficulties arose in them, too,
with intensive development. To these we shall return. We need
first to look at economic planning in market economies where
capital is privately owned.

4. ECONOMIC PLANNING IN A MARKET ECONOMY

In the last chapter it became clear that governments in the
market economies were being driven into some overall
economic planning by the inadequacy and failure of monetary,
fiscal and even physical controls to disaggregate the different
elements in national income, and thus to achieve a balance of
growth between boom years and stagnation, between home
demand and exports, between one region and another.

Keynes taught economists to aggregate demand and supply,
consumption and investment, and governments to influence
the aggregates to ensure a fuller use of resources. A major task
of economists today is to disaggregate again within the aggregates. Keynes distinguished the marginal propensity to save
and to consume. Economists are now concerned with the
marginal propensity to import and to buy at home, the marginal propensity to consume private goods and public services,
the marginal propensity to expand output in the old industrial
areas and the new. The moment, however, that we begin to
break down the elements of consumption and investment into
imports and exports, private and public or north and south, the
problems of discrimination which we met in the last chapter
emerge. The blunt weapons of monetary and fiscal management become inadequate. Physical controls also require an
overall plan within which they can be operated.

Even more difficult is the problem of anticipating future
demand in a market economy. Economic plans for the future
growth path of an economy can start from one of two assumptions: that the previous growth path will continue, or that it
will be changed deliberately in certain respects. The Labour
Government's National Plan, adumbrated in 1965, was based
on the extrapolation of past trends of consumption but it
sought to increase the rate of investment in manufacturing
equipment at the expense of commercial investment and to

raise the share of exports in the national output while reducing the share of imports. This was an uneasy mixture from the start, since the growth path in consumption to a large extent determines both manufacturing investment and the ratio of imports and exports. The hope was that the publication of the Plan itself would step up the overall growth rate of output from under 3 per cent p.a., to nearly 4 per cent p.a. and that from a larger output more would be available for manufacturing investment, for exports and for replacing imports with home products. The major changes indicated in Table VIII.3 were not impossible, but they were unlikely if the previous growth path of the economy was not radically altered; and this involved major shifts in resource allocation and income distribution.

It is necessary at this point to describe the different degrees of economic planning for future demand, which shade off at one end into what we have called a planned economy. Economists distinguish between (*a*) indicative planning, (*b*) co-ordinative planning, and (*c*) resource planning.

We can take them one by one. Indicative planning implies a statement by governments of the rate at which the growth of the whole economy is expected to proceed, and what this will mean in output terms for each sector of the economy. The idea of this kind of planning is to encourage the belief among individual firms in a faster rate of growth, still extrapolating past trends for particular products. The firms, it is hoped, will then step up their own investment plans and create in fact the faster growth rate that was indicated in the plan. When we considered the nature of the investment cycle in Chapter 6, the chief reason why this created problems for the economy was seen to be the fact that all firms expanded together in the boom and cut back together in the slump. One of the main arguments for indicative planning is that firms will have more faith in a steady growth rate and will not delay their investment plans until they actually see demand growing up to their levels of capacity. So long as the indications of the Plan are fulfilled, this kind of planning can be very effective. If, however, for any reason, such as in Britain the balance of payments crisis in 1966 and 1967 and the subsequent devaluation and deflation, or because of changed trends in demand, the

Table VIII.3

The UK National Plan 1965
Shares in National Product and Growth Rates by Sector

	GNP Shares 1954 (%)	Annual Growth Rates or Changes — Actual 1954–60	Actual 1960–64	Planned 1964–70	GNP Shares 1970 (%)
Resources available at Current Prices	100	—	—	—	100
(after Balance of Payments on Current Account)	= £17·8 billion				= £40·75 billion
Output	—	2·8	3·4	3·8	—
Employment	—	0·5	0·7	0·5	—
Output per head	—	2·4	2·7	3·2	—
Consumption					
Personal	68	3·0	3·1	3·2	63·5
Personal per head	—	2·2	2·4	2·6	—
Public	17·5	−0·6	2·4	4·0	15·8
Gross Investment					
Total	14·3	5·5	6·6	5·5*	19·8
Public	7·3	1·5	8·6	5·8†	8·9†
Private	7·0	10·1	5·3	5·4†	11·6†
Nat. Industries	3·0	4·0	8·4	4·5†	3·65†
Housing – Public Sector	2·35	−2·5	13·5	6·0†	1·8†
Housing – Private Sector	1·25	14·0	6·5	4·6	2·15
Manufacturing	3·3	6·0	2·4	7·0	4·6
Distribution and Services	1·55	15·0	8·9	4·0	2·85
Foreign Trade					
Imports	16·8	5·8	5·9	4·0	17·7
of which finished Mfgs.	0·9	21·0	12·4	9·1	3·8
of which Fuels (net)	1·85	13·0	9·5	6·1	1·45
Exports	14·9	3·0	3·4	5·6	15·0
Terms of Trade	—	+2·4	+0·5	+0·5	—

Notes: *Excluding stockbuilding.

†Based on estimate that the public and private sectors of housebuilding by 1970 will be respectively £730m. and £865m. The Plan only gives public sector figures for budget year 1969–70.

Sources: *National Income and Expenditures* Blue Book 1965; *Report on Overseas Trade; The National Plan*.

indications are falsified, then firms which were caught once by raised expectations will be even more cautious in the timing of their investments in future.

Since the demise of the National Plan, economic planning exercises in Britain have been limited, first to the Treasury's short-term (six months to one year) estimates of future movements in National Income and Expenditure, upon which the Chancellor bases his budget, and second, to the somewhat longer-term (three years) indications of 'a possible future course for the economy on the basis of past trends'.[13]

Co-ordinative planning goes somewhat further than indicative planning and suggests ways in which complementary or competitive industries might work together. A good example was the British Government's Fuel Policy,[14] laid down late in 1967 after consultation with the chairmen of the boards of the nationalized coal, gas and electricity industries. The government indicated certain measures of support for the coal industry, in order to phase its run-down to 1975 in relation to the increase of natural gas supplies, particularly as a fuel for electric power generation. The oil industry, which was not directly involved in the consultations, was expected to maintain its previous rate of growth, subject to the continuation of the fuel oil tax and other short-term measures of discrimination against oil users. Thus, although some element of government co-ordination was introduced into the supply of fuel to meet the economy's growing energy requirements, the share of oil, which was expected to rise from 36 per cent to 43 per cent of the total between 1966 and 1975, was left to the free choice of consumers in the market. The arguments deployed by the coal industry against such a large measure of market freedom included the rising cost to the balance of payments, expected to be of the order of £500 millions net by 1970, and the social cost of unemployment in mining areas, in some of which up to 50 per cent of male employment opportunities were in mining.

The aim of Government Fuel Policy in Britain was in fact that of assisting a declining industry to compete in the market

[13] The quotation is from the Preface to *The Task Ahead – An Economic Assessment to 1972*, published by the Department of Economic Affairs in 1969.
[14] See *Fuel Policy*, Ministry of Power White Paper, 1967.

by measures of protection, including the writing off of a large part of the capital debt, and at the same time giving temporary assistance to the men made redundant by pit closures. It has not primarily been a positive co-ordination of fuel supplies. The story, however, illustrates very well the problems of co-ordinative economic planning. Government studies can indicate possible dangers in the future, for example in shortages affecting the balance of payments or, at the other extreme, in excess capacity in relation to expected demand. But co-ordination implies in the last resort taking action. The government could order the Electricity Generating Board to use solid fuel rather than oil or natural gas; it could not order the oil companies to raise their fuel oil prices or to ease off on their advertising campaigns for oil-fired central heating.

Moreover, although the nationalized industries can be given their marching orders by the government, if these orders involve them in extra costs their boards may reasonably complain that they should be paid a subsidy to cover them. Otherwise, their individual customers are paying for what should truly be a charge on the whole community. In a matter like fuel policy, government decisions have to be based on a study of social costs and benefits and these have to include an estimate of who pays and who gains. It is strongly argued in favour of a subsidy to the coal industry, for supplying for example free house coal to old-age pensioners, that, while the structure of taxes, from which the subsidy must come, is moderately progressive in Britain, the proportion of fuel costs in the budgets of OAPs is much higher than in those of the average tax payer. Such a subsidy would therefore certainly involve a transfer of income from richer to poorer households, and could be regarded as ensuring a net beneficial effect.

Government co-ordination to compensate for the results of relying on free competition in the market is seen as a matter mainly of intervention with taxes and subsidies rather than of administrative orders. It may nevertheless have to be backed up by orders – at least negative orders – or the carrots may need to be unreasonably large and juicy to encourage the right actions, as we saw in the case of regional policies. Private industry cannot easily be given orders of what it should positively do, although it can be told negatively what it must *not*

do. We shall see in a moment that similar problems arise in
ordering even publicly owned industry to do what it does not
want to do, in a planned economy as much as in a market
economy. You can take a horse to the water but you cannot
make him drink.

Attempts to overcome the many difficulties surrounding
government intervention in the market through indicative and
co-ordinative planning have led to the proliferation of bodies
in which consultation takes place between the private and
public sectors of industry, the government and the trade
unions. In Britain this process of consultation takes place
through the Regional Economic Planning Councils and the
National Economic Development Committee and its many
sub-committees, including committees for each of the several
major industries. It is to initiate discussions by these bodies
that the indications of broad future trends in a document like
The Task Ahead are formulated. But the more detailed the
discussions become in the regional councils and the industry
committees, the more the process of consultation moves in the
direction of resource planning. This has been the main
experience of the French Planning Commission which has
developed the most intricate pattern of vertical and horizontal consultation. Out of this emerges a detailed plan for
economic development in every sector and region. This is
ultimately given by Parliament the force of law. The power of
Parliament to enforce is in fact reserved to specific contracts
signed by the government with particular firms to supply at
controlled prices. The effectiveness of the Plan lies in the
detailed studies of resource development on which it is based.[15]

Some beginnings in resource planning have occurred in
Britain as a result of the setting up of a Central Unit for
ENVIRONMENTAL PLANNING originally placed in the Department of Economic Affairs, and of the FEASIBILITY STUDIES
which it has been asked to make. The first of these was a study
of the possibilities of development in the Humberside area.
Starting from the existing economic development and the
given physical assets, amenities and restraints, this study put
forward comprehensive proposals for future development of

[15] A good survey of French planning can be found in J. and A. M. Hackett's
Economic Planning in France, 1963.

the Area's potential. The study of Severnside, the South-East Joint Planning Study and the plans for new towns like Milton Keynes, share with the Humberside Study their origins in the need to find new locations for Britain's expanding population. Nevertheless, the questions raised in considering the long-term future location of population and industry must increasingly involve governments in overall resource planning. Decisions on road and railway building, port modernization and deepwater terminals require decisions on the future location of the steel industry, oil refining, electric power generation, coal mining, chemicals and associated manufacturing.

Integrated location decisions provide many of the external economies which we saw earlier that economists regard as so important to growth. Governments will also be required to prepare for changes in employment in any locality by training and retraining schemes, by research into local assets which could be developed, as well as by arranging for the integrated activities of different firms. This is indeed precisely where a planned economy is so effective in preparing for joint economic development which no individual firm would be able to do. Location decisions also involve questions of the timing, scale, capacity and type of plant. Estimates of future demands for different goods and services have to be made by separate firms. Extrapolations of past trends often mean, as we have seen, nothing more nor less than leaving the growth path essentially to be determined by the technological considerations of a few giant companies. The problem remains that of replacing choices in the market by some other system of voting for the way technological advances are to be used. We may now consider how this is done in a planned economy.

5. THE PLANNED ECONOMY

The basis of a planned economy is that the main means of production, distribution and exchange are in public hands; producing enterprises can be ordered what to produce according to a plan, taking an estimate of present and future consumer needs into account, instead of such enterprises producing what gives them the best return they can obtain from the market. Marx supposed that private ownership of capital would develop technology to the point where it needed this kind of public ownership and planning, and where the workers would understand that they had to take over from the private owners to assure this; but he assumed that the revolutionary change would take place where the failure of the old system of private ownership to use the new technology led to total breakdown in the system. In the event, workers took over the system of ownership in Russia, where it had certainly broken down but where it had broken down as a result of war and defeat and not as a result of the advanced development either of large productive forces or of a large self-conscious proletariat. The result was the Stalinist system, of central administrative directions buttressed by what was really a pseudo-Marxist theory. This theory was that under Socialism labour would become social labour just because it was consciously directed instead of being as under capitalism unconsciously, or indirectly market-directed. Adam Smith's 'invisible hand' and Marx's law of value both provided for the social co-operation of individual workers through money-commodity relations in the market, where the worker lost control of his labour power to the capitalist. Marx, however, expected labour as a market commodity to be replaced by consciously directed social labour under social ownership, but on the assumption of very highly developed productive forces that would both require this and make it possible.

What has in fact happened has been a series of communist inspired revolutions in countries at quite low levels of economic development. Stalin explained the perpetuation of money-commodity relations in Soviet society in terms only of the continued role of peasant collectives in agriculture. In fact, the conflict of interest of commodity relations continued also between the socially owned industrial enterprises, as we shall see. In Russia the Communist Party had to stand in as 'care-taker' for the PROLETARIAT, in a phrase of the historian of the Bolshevik revolution, E. H. Carr.[16] The Red Army itself stood in for the proletariat in the revolutions that followed the Second World War in most of Eastern Europe. The result was

---

[16] Part of his great works on the *History of Soviet Russia* are neatly summarized in his two little books, *The Soviet Impact on the Western World* and *The New Society*.

that planned economies were established by communist governments in Eastern Europe and then in China and Cuba, not so much to manage productive forces that had burst the bonds of capitalism but to promote industrial revolutions in countries where these had been held back by the kind of distorted development we described at the end of Chapter 3. What we may learn from the planning of such underdeveloped economies for the problems of advanced industrial economies like Britain's may therefore be misleading, but Soviet experience may have an important bearing on the still underdeveloped two-thirds of the world.[17]

A planned economy requires plans for all branches and sectors of the economy, covering different time-scales – long, medium and short – and different balances – physical, labour, regional, financial, and export/import. In the Soviet Union most emphasis was put on the medium-term, Five-Year Plan, for outputs of broad categories of goods; but it was set within a 15-year perspective of even broader growth trends and was itself broken down into concrete one-year plans for the actual output of all enterprises. These plans were not of course arbitrary constructions. They were based on a kind of national inventory of what enterprises were producing and what they estimated they could produce with more labour and equipment over a period of years. To these estimates were added the plans for new enterprises. All these had then to be reconciled. Physical inputs and outputs of materials and equipment had to balance, with allowance made for balanced imports and exports. Labour requirements had to be balanced by labour availability. Prices and incomes (plus credit) had to be in balance so that what was produced could be sold. Finally, all these balances had to be examined by region and in the light of transport capacity.

Such planning was a formidable undertaking, which required a great army of officials, administrative, technical and specialist. In the early years of the Soviet Union no calculating machines or computers were available for assisting in marshalling and analysing the vast mass of statistical data. The task was only possible with the limited manpower available,

[17] The best single book on the history of the Soviet planned economy is Alec Nove's, *An Economic History of the USSR*.

because in fact the range of goods and services available was
severely restricted and the greater part of the plan was concentrated upon a few major projects for building a base in
heavy industry which was developed extensively by new

Table VIII.4

Growth of the Gross National Product of the USSR, 1928–55
(based on Index 1937=100)

	1928		1937		1950		1955	
	Index	%	Index	%	Index	%	Index	%
Consumption								
Personal	98	79·5	100	52·5	130	45·7	197	48·0
Communal	27	4·6	100	10·5	145	10·2	178	8·7
Government	41	2·1	100	3·2	200	4·3	142	2·1
Defence	10	1·3	100	7·9	245	12·9	358	13·1
Gross Investment	30	12·5	100	25·9	155	26·9	236	28·1
GNP	62	100·0	100	100·0	150	100·0	216	100·0
Industry								
Output A	26		100		191		315	
Output B	36		100		138		218	
Employment	38		100		170		200	
Agriculture	95		100		113		141	

Note: All Figures are based on 1937 Rouble Factor Cost except for variant A of
Industrial Output which is based on 1955 Rouble Factor Cost.

Source: A. Bergson, *The Economics of Soviet Planning*, Table 13.2, p. 209, and
R. W. Davies, 'Planning for Rapid Economic Growth in the USSR' in *The Economics
of Planning*, Oslo.

capital investment. We can see the picture in Table VIII.4.
Personal consumption barely expanded in the period of the
first two Russian Five-Year Plans of 1928–37. There was a
rapid expansion in communal consumption and also greatly
increased expenditure on defence; but gross investment took
nearly one-half of the annual increment in GNP in this period
and three-quarters of this investment was in heavy industry.

The result of the stepping up of the rate of investment in the
Soviet Union was that in the mid-1930s around one-quarter
of the national product was being ploughed back into fixed
capital formation. This was a fearsome achievement for a
country at a level of *per capita* income that corresponded to
something under one-quarter of that in Britain, even after the

ravages of the 1914–18 war and the Civil War had been repaired. Since the workers in industry and in offices were still but a small percentage of the occupied population and had to be rewarded for their contribution to economic growth, the greater part of the capital accumulation for investment came inevitably from the agricultural sector. Collectivization of farms was speeded up by Stalin in 1929, mainly because villagers who received land in 1917 were eating better than before and the previous output of grain from the larger pre-war estates was simply not coming on to the market to feed the new industrial workers in the towns. The imposition on the collective farms of a system of compulsory deliveries to the State, at prices equivalent to about half of the average price for all grain marketed, not only ensured that the grain was delivered but was in effect a form of taxation which provided for the necessary capital accumulation.

The result, however, was to leave little incentive for collective farmers to improve their output from their collective efforts. They concentrated instead upon their remaining individual plots of land and their sales from these in the local markets. According to the figure in Table VIII.4 agricultural output rose by only 5 per cent between 1928 and 1937. The transfer of labour from the land during this period provided an increase in industrial employment of eight millions; but since this was about the size of the increase in the total labour force there can have been little increase in agricultural productivity beyond the increase of agricultural output. Major price reforms occurred in 1953, 1958 and 1964 which greatly improved agricultural earnings and output. The continuing backwardness of Soviet agriculture right down to the mid-1960s, however, provides powerful criticism of a pricing system that destroyed incentive. Alternatively it may be regarded as the inevitable result of the rapid pace of industrialization.

A more serious criticism of the Soviet planned economy must now be considered. This is that it encouraged both irrationality and gross wastage in the use of resources. Irrationality, it is argued,[18] followed from a quite arbitrary pricing system and

---

[18] Most vehemently by N. Jasny in his *Soviet Industrialization*, 1961, but much earlier by Von Hayek and Von Mises in their book *Collectivist Economic Planning*.

from the failure to charge a rate of interest. The early critics
of the Soviet Plans like Von Mises and Von Hayek emphasized
the absence of free price movements as the essential indicators
of demand and supply in the market; but prices as terms on
which alternatives are offered could still have been utilized for
allocating resources in a socialized economy. Prices in the
Soviet economy were in fact based, not on market supply and
demand, but on VALUE ADDED in production plus a TURNOVER
TAX that was varied according to the nature of the product.
Thus the tax was high on consumer goods and nil on heavy
capital equipment, the object being to encourage the use of
machinery and mop up consumer spending power for new
investment. The relative cheapening of capital equipment
meant, however, that there was a high incentive for enterprises to extend capital investment and a lessened incentive
to introduce more efficient capital-saving equipment. The
relative expensiveness of consumer goods meant that there
was a reduced incentive among individuals to increase their
output. We discussed earlier the disincentive effect of taxation
in market economies. The problem in the Soviet economy was
rather the subjective nature of the decisions about prices,
unrelated to the real labour costs of investment. This was a
very un-Marxist development, Marx having always emphasized that labour – present and past – was the determinant of
value.

The failure to make a charge (i.e. an interest rate) for the
capital provided to enterprises not only resulted in wastage of
resources, through labour hoarding, excessive capital investment and inadequate stock control, but meant that schemes
were simply not judged according to their capital cost. The
effect of a rate of interest, as we saw earlier, is to build a time-
scale into capital investment. A high rate of interest, like a
short repayment period, means that an investment must pay
its way quickly, that is through the charging of high prices out
of current spending. A low rate, like a long repayment period,
means that the price charged today can be kept down and the
investment is allowed to pay its way over a long period.
Without a rate of interest, long-term schemes are favoured,
often tying up capital for years before any results are to be
seen. Without a rate of interest, indeed, it is in effect im-

possible to compare schemes according to their real capital cost.

Wastage of resources[19] comprises the most serious criticism of the Soviet Planned Economy and was beginning to be recognized as such in the moves towards economic reform in the mid-1960s. In the early Soviet Plans enterprises were set an output target each year with an allowance of labour and materials and funds for capital equipment with which to reach it. The important thing was to fulfil the plan in physical terms – so many shoes, tractors, pistols or what have you. Incentives were offered to each enterprise for fulfilment of its plan; and there were fines for non-fulfilment. The manager of the enterprise had a fund, depending in size on plan fulfilment, from which to distribute individual incentives for all who worked in the enterprise. Since plan fulfilment was the overriding aim, managers were naturally quite prepared to conceal the real potential of their plant, to hoard labour, extend investment and stock up fuel and materials, to fulfil the plan at almost any cost. In this they had the support of the Communist Party and trade union representatives in the enterprise and of all the workers in it too.

In the course of successive Soviet Plans more sophisticated indicators were used to encourage increases in labour productivity, stock control and saving of capital, primarily by charging a rate of interest. The banks became important instruments of control in these matters. But the overriding aim of physical plan fulfilment remained. This aim was quite appropriate, so long as capital-extensive development and an increase in sheer quantity of goods really were the most important requirements, and the goods produced were mainly not such as to involve variation in quality to meet individual needs. As the proportion of personal consumer goods in the national product and the need for capital-intensive development increased again, however, after the savage cuts of the first few plans and the privations of the war (see Table VIII.4), the fulfilment of purely quantitative plans became increasingly inappropriate. Dissatisfaction was first openly expressed in the early 1960s, when the Soviet public stopped increasing its purchases of

[19] These are well described in the case of Polish enterprises in an article in *The British Journal of Industrial Relations* for March 1965.

many consumer goods and especially of clothing. Production soon outstripped sales and by 1962 the Soviet press reported that warehouses were carrying unsold stocks of consumer goods valued at £4,360 millions or about four months' supplies. Prices were sharply marked down, but only half the stocks were sold and stocks of clothing in 1963 rose to three times the 1959 level. Similar developments took place in Czechoslovakia, where economic growth and productivity actually came to a halt in the early 1960s.

In 1965 an economic reform was introduced into the Soviet planned economy which followed the lines proposed by a Soviet economist, Professor V. Liberman. The new system was tried out in the clothing industry, but within three years it had been applied to enterprises producing about two-thirds of total industrial output. The new system had two elements:

(a) The target for each enterprise was set in terms of profit – not of course, as the Russians wish always to insist, to a private owner of capital. The profit target was a certain per cent return to the capital provided by the banking system and from internal reserves. Bonuses and fines were applied according to profit target fulfilment.

(b) Enterprises had henceforth to sign contracts with their customers, whether they were selling consumer goods or capital equipment. The contracts specified qualities, standards and delivery dates and there were penal clauses for non-fulfilment.

There remained the danger that enterprises would try to keep down their profit targets to make plan fulfilment easier. This could be met in two ways: either by lengthening the period over which the profit target applied, beyond the one-year period generally in use; or by doing away with the target system altogether and leaving enterprises to get on with producing what they could sell. The government would then retain control only of the overall allocation of resources between sectors and groups of products, between branches of industry and between regions. It would control certain basic prices and impose taxes to provide for public services. By 1969 decentralization of decision-making in the Soviet Union had gone a certain way in devolving upon the regions and upon individual ministries some of the planning that was once concentrated at the centre. It had not reached the point of decentralizing such major decisions upon the enterprises. This was the further step taken in the Yugoslav economic system and the direction in which the Czechoslovak reforms were moving up to the summer of 1968.

6. RECONCILING PLAN AND MARKET

At the end of Chapter 5 we posed the question of whether countries, which had adopted both public ownership of capital and planned economies, had not thrown out the baby with the bathwater. By this we meant that, in ending the system in which economic activity was determined according to the profit to private capital from market sales, they had gone too far in ending also the role both of the firm's profit motive and of the market. From what has just been said about the Soviet Union it would certainly seem to be so. In one sense this is a political problem about power to manage the market. This may, as in Britain, be in the hands of the international company holding giant concentrations of capital with subsidiaries all over the capitalist world, or it may be in the hands of a group of all-powerful Party functionaries in the central ministries of the Soviet Government with their satellites throughout the Communist world. The political problem is of control by the people over the controllers themselves and of finding new ways in which as workers we can all increase our control over our working conditions and in which as consumers we can take a greater part in influencing the choice of goods and services available.

If there is still an important role for the market to play in relating what is produced to what in fact we want, now and in the future, this is an economic problem. It has been most effectively explored by Professor Ota Sik, the Czechoslovak economist, who was Vice-Chairman of the Economic Council in the Czechoslovak Government prior to the Russian invasion in 1968.[20] Professor Sik starts from several basic assumptions. These are:

(*a*) that he is speaking about planning for an economy

---

[20] See his study *Plan and Market under Socialism*, summarized in 'Socialist Market Relations and Planning' in C. Feinstein (ed.), *Socialism, Capitalism and Economic Growth*, 1967.

in which capital has been taken out of private hands and is held socially as the means for production, distribution and exchange;

(*b*) that work is not yet an end in itself providing its own satisfaction, that is to say for most people apart from a few writers, artists and scientists. Therefore, most work is done to acquire the necessary use values (Sik uses the Marxist terminology here) that are produced by others on the basis of an advanced division of labour;

(*c*) that there is no better judge of whether products are in fact use values, that is, goods of the kind required, than the consumer himself, including here the enterprise consuming the produce of other enterprises; the conflict between producer and consumer does not on this assumption end with social ownership; a system of administrative directions to producers, as we have seen, easily led them to maximize their gains at the expense of actual consumer demands;

(*d*) that commodity production continues even under social ownership, so long as there is a distinction between exchange value and use value. This is Marx's distinction of goods that exchange on the basis of the socially necessary amount of labour time for their production at a particular stage of technological development but concretely incorporate a certain actual amount of labour time that may well be greater than is socially necessary (see earlier Chapter 4);

(*e*) that, in exchanging his actual labour time for commodities, the worker will want to receive equivalent use values for the labour he expends, but his actual labour may not be socially necessary labour because he is not working with the tools of the average technological level of his times;

(*f*) that enterprise groups are bound to remain the major units of production, having a common interest for those working together, in maximizing their own wages fund, but an interest that is narrower than that of the whole of society;

(*g*) that competition between enterprise groups is essential both to ensure consumer choice and the formation of relative prices which reflect socially necessary labour time;

(*h*) that, while such competition is essential, the role of planning is to provide the framework within which social purposes as well as individual choices are realized.

From these assumptions Professor Sik's argument proceeds as follows: since enterprise groups will wish to ensure that their labour time is exchanged for equivalent use values, they have an interest in reducing their labour time down to and beyond what is socially necessary, that is to say above-average productivity levels. Prices in the market provide the only means of testing use value and rewarding above-average productivity; but an abstract model of price structures or 'SHADOW' PRICES can and must be elaborated by government planners. This model will indicate the long-term average equilibrium prices over the planning period, against which to test the actual prices emerging in the market. Where actual prices diverge from the model's 'shadow' prices, monopolistic positions and temporary shortages of supply for future demand will be indicated and the government will have power to intervene. In formulating the model prices, account will be taken not only of actual current labour time but of 'dated' labour materialized ('stored up' as Marx called it) in capital equipment both in the past and in the period for which plans are being made. In determining the value of this materialized labour, differential interest rates will have to be assigned, since interest rates, as we saw earlier, affect the way in which costs are distributed between today and tomorrow. This must be a political decision which brings society's overall interests to bear upon enterprise prices, instead of being an arbitrary decision of planners, as it was in the Soviet Union, or of the state of capitalists' liquidity preference as it mainly is in an economy like Britain's today.

To the weapons of 'shadow' price surveillance and interest rate management as described above, the government would have to add taxation and certain broad decisions on resource allocation and the general rate of growth of the economy. This framework of socialist planning is essential in order to control monopoly and temporary short supply positions, in which prices could be raised, and in order to provide for redistribution of incomes between regions, to balance foreign trade and to ensure an increasing area of free social provision as well as the covering of administrative costs, defence and so forth. But government, in Professor Sik's view, should not use planning to set enterprise targets and to control their fulfilment. It should concern itself with managing basic economic priorities and relationships in the interest of achieving social co-operation on an agreed line of economic growth. Such long-term perspectives should be put forward, in Professor Sik's view, in the form of two or three mutually consistent variants for free discussion and democratic decision.

Something approaching Professor Sik's programme has been developing in Yugoslavia. An example taken some years ago from a Yugoslav enterprise manufacturing electronic equipment may serve to illustrate the theoretical analysis we have just made. Enterprises in Yugoslavia are owned by the work group themselves who elect their own managers and workers' council. They operate competitively within a framework set by government taxation and interest rate policies. For

Table VIII.5

Distribution of Income of a Manufacturing Enterprise in Yugoslavia 1960

Items	Value (million Dinars)*	As % of Receipts	As % of Net Profit	As % of Clear Profit
Total Receipts	6,280	100		
Cost of Materials	2,160	34·4		
Overheads: Amortization (at assigned interest rates)	205	3·3		
Other charges	836	13·3		
Federal Turnover Tax	353	5·6		
Total Expenditure	3,554	55·6		
Net Profit	2,726	43·4	100	
Contributions to Social Needs (Local and Regional)	1,300	20·7	47·7	
Clear Profit	1,426	22·7	52·3	100
assigned to: Personal Incomes	1,155	18·3		81·1
Reserve Fund	93	1·5		6·6
Capital Assets Fund	130	2·1		9·1
Social Welfare Fund	45	0·7		3·2

*Note: For million Dinars read £000s to get a rough approximation.

Source: M. Barratt Brown, 'Workers' Control in a Planned Economy', *New Left Review*, No. 2, 1960.

national expenditures and for the purpose of regional redistribution of income, some taxes are paid to the federal government; the rest go to local and regional authorities. Table VIII.5 shows how an enterprise's clear profit, as the Yugoslavs call it, is arrived at. This comes into the hands of the enterprise to assign as they wish, taking into account present personal and social needs and future capital requirements. It must be noticed that taxation and interest rates are based on gross income and not on profit; or enterprises would not maximize sales and would reduce profits to a minimum. In effect taxes have to be flexible but a firm's management will have to know for some time in advance what rates they must pay so as to respond adequately to the government influences on general economic development within which they have to operate.

Table VIII.6

Deductions from Personal Incomes in a Yugoslav Enterprise 1960

To the budget	11%	
To Social Insurance	24%	
To House Building Fund	7%	
TOTAL DEDUCTIONS	42%	= 485,000,000 D.
Leaving Net Personal Income	58%	= 670,000,000 D.

Source: as for Table VIII.5.

Basic personal incomes in the Yugoslav enterprise are established by the Workers' Council at the beginning of each financial year subject to deductions shown in Table VIII.6. But these incomes are later increased from any Clear Profit that is achieved, according to the assignments made at the end of the accounting year. In this way Yugoslav workers will speak of having received, for example, thirteen months' income, meaning that they received on top of their basic income, a bonus of one-twelfth out of the 'Clear Profit'. The additions will be distributed by departments and shops according to the contribution of each to total profit. These bonuses provide the necessary incentives for individual and enterprise endeavours to raise the productivity of their labour.

In fact the Yugoslav have not yet adopted Professor Sik's 'shadow' price surveillance system and have attempted to curb the monopolistic positions of some of their large modern enterprises by exposing the Yugoslav economy to international competition. At one time they imposed a tax on enterprises enjoying monopoly positions, but, without a price model of Professor Sik's type these taxes were regarded as unacceptably arbitrary and uncertain and had a strong disincentive effect on investment. In fact, also, the small size of the Yugoslav economy has made its exposure to international competition, including international capital flows, exceedingly difficult for the government to manage. Large modern enterprises in effect increased their pre-eminent position in the economy both in their power over smaller enterprises and in the level of their earnings. Professor Sik's ideas suggest the solution, which includes a continuing firm framework of social planning.

So long then as work is not done for its own sake and goods and services are not in such ample supply that they can be issued free, the arguments of Marxist and non-Marxist economists bring us back to the market. It is worthwhile here to try to distinguish the market we know and Professor Sik's market within socialist planning. Under social ownership of capital it need not be a market in which the pull of money is greater than the pull of people. With the help of computers, model prices can be formulated against which actual prices in the market can be tested. Capital investment may be in the hands of enterprises, but the framework of capital control will be in the hands of the government and not of private capital in giant companies. Enterprises can still act in their own short-term individual interest by consuming today rather than investing for tomorrow, but the self-governing enterprise can only realize the long-run advantage of all its members through raising productivity. Enterprises can still fail and their members become redundant, but it would then be the task of government to reorganize them with new management or on new lines of production without delay.

Under a combination of market and socialist plan, government planning might still be arbitrary and bureaucratic, but detailed knowledge of the costs and benefits of particular policies would be much more widespread where enterprises were subject to their own members' control, and to public surveillance. The allocation of resources to social services would still be effected by government taxation but without the power of the giant company to influence the choice. Government choices might still be disputed by large minorities, and even majorities, but that is a political question; and the economist can bow out after emphasizing that choice to be effective must be an individual and local affair and not just a national one.[21] Planning, like the market, is concerned with choice, now and for the future – choice for the consumer of the goods and services he prefers, choice for the worker of the conditions and rewards of his daily work; choice for the firm of different techniques and methods of production; and choice for society as a whole of the rate and path of growth of the economy. These are the four categories of economics. Choice in the last case will remain the most difficult until government at every level comes to involve the active participation of most of the people in any society.

[21] A stimulating conflict of views on this question can be found in Barbara Wootton's *Freedom under Planning* which was a reply to F. A. Hayek's *The Road to Serfdom*. A more recent critique of planning in the Hayek tradition is J. Jewkes's *The New Ordeal by Planning*, to which Maurice Dobb's *Welfare Economics and the Economics of Socialism* provides a very powerful academic reply. These studies are often difficult to master at first reading. The student will be helped if he bears in mind the four categories in the title of this book.

Bibliography

The author, title, date and publisher are given below of nearly all the books referred to in the text. They are listed in the order in which they appear chapter by chapter. There are twenty-five books which students might well consider purchasing for their own libraries. These are marked with an asterisk. The cost of these should not be much more than £10. Those which should be read but not necessarily owned are marked with a dagger. The rest are for reference only.

1. ECONOMICS, ECONOMIZING, ECONOMISTS AND ECONOMIC SCIENCE

Adam Smith, *Nature and Causes of the Wealth of Nations,* original edition 1776, Dent Everyman's Library, 1910.

S. Jevons, *Political Economy,* 1878, Macmillan.

P. Sraffa, *Production of Commodities by Means of Commodities,* 1960, CUP.

* Joan Robinson, *Economic Philosophy,* 1963, Pelican.

A. C. Pigou, *Economics of Welfare,* 1920, Macmillan.

* J. M. Keynes, *General Theory of Employment, Interest and Money,* 1936, Macmillan.

† Dudley Sears, 'The Limitations of the Special Case' in J. Knapp and K. Martin (eds) *Teaching Development Economics,* 1967, Cass.

† E. H. Carr, *What is History?,* 1961, Macmillan.

D. Ricardo, *Principles of Political Economy and Taxation,* original edition 1817, Dent Everyman's Library, 1912.

K. Marx, *Capital,* Vol I, original edition 1867, Allen & Unwin, 1946.

    † *Wage, Labour and Capital,* original edition 1849, Lawrence & Wishart, 1954.

    Contribution to the Critique of Political Economy, original edition 1859, Lawrence & Wishart, 1960.

† O. Lange, *Political Economy,* 1963, Pergamon.

* R. Freedman (ed), *Marx on Economics,* 1962, Pelican.

A. Marshall, *Economics of Industry,* 1879, Macmillan.

L. Robbins, *Nature and Significance of Economic Science*, 1932, Macmillan.

A. Marshall, *Principles of Economics*, 1890, Macmillan.

* R. G. Lipsey, *Introduction to Positive Economics*, 1963, Weidenfeld & Nicolson.

† B. Crick, *In Defence of Politics*, 1964, Pelican.

L. Hogben, *Science for the Citizen*, 1938, Allen & Unwin.

D. Hume, *Treatise on Human Nature*, original edition 1739, Dent Everyman's Library, 1911.

K. Popper, *Logic of Scientific Discovery*, 1934, Hutchinson.
   Poverty of Historicism, 1944 and 1959, Routledge.

2. THE FACTS OF ECONOMIC LIFE

J. S. Mill, *Utilitarianism*, original edition 1856, Dent Everyman's Library, 1910.

† G. Orwell, *Animal Farm*, original edition 1930, Penguin, 1965.

M. Blaug, *Economic Theory in Retrospect*, second edition 1968, Heinemann.

R. J. Gillings, *Graphs*, 1937, Harrap.

* W. J. Reichmann, *Use and Abuse of Statistics*, 1964, Pelican.

F. Conway, *Descriptive Statistics*, 1963, Leicester University Press.

† D. Huff, *How to Lie with Statistics*, 1954, Gollancz.

C. A. Blyth, *The Use of Economic Statistics*, third edition 1966, Allen & Unwin.

† G. Childe, *Man Makes Himself*, original edition 1936, Watts.

† S. Lilley, *Men, Machines and History*, 1947, Cobbett Press, Lawrence and Wishart.

W. W. Rostow, *The Stages of Economic Growth*, 1960, CUP.

† J. de Castro, *Geography of Hunger*, 1932, Gollancz.

* L. Dudley Stamp, *Our Developing World*, 1960, Faber.

* CSO *National Income and Expenditure*, Blue Book (Annually), HMSO.

3. INDUSTRY AND COMMERCE: OCCUPATIONS AND THEIR LOCATION

* G. D. H. Cole and R. Postgate, *The Common People*, 5th edition 1964, Methuen.

† M. Barratt Brown, *After Imperialism*, 2nd edition 1969, Merlin Press.

† E. J. Hobsbawm, *The Age of Revolution*, 1962, Weidenfeld & Nicolson.

B. R. Mitchell and P. Deane, *Abstract of British Historical Statistics*, 1962, CUP.

† G. Myrdal, *Economic Theory and Underdeveloped Regions*, 1957, Duckworth.

* Phyllis Deane, *The First Industrial Revolution*, 1967, CUP.

* I. Richards and J. R. Morris, *Junior Sketch Map Economic History of Britain*, 1961, Harrap.

† T. Hardy, *Far From the Madding Crowd*, original edition 1874, Macmillan.

W. H. B. Court, *Rise of the Midland Industries*, 1938, CUP.

† E. P. Thompson, *Making of the English Working Class*, 1968, Pelican.

† T. Coleman, *The Railway Navvies*, 1965, Pelican.

† E. J. Hobsbawm, *Industry and Empire*, 1968, Weidenfeld & Nicolson.

C. Pratten and R. M. Dean, *The Economies of Large Scale Production in British Industry*, 1965, CUP.

† E. M. Hoover, *The Location of Economic Activity*, 1963, McGraw-Hill.

Sir Joseph Hunt (chairman) *Report of a Committee on the Intermediate Areas*, 1969, HMSO.

* J. L. Sampedro, *Decisive Forces in World Economics*, 1967, Weidenfeld & Nicolson.

4. THE MARKET ECONOMY – I. WANTS AND INCOMES

† J. K. Galbraith, *The New Industrial State*, 1967, Hamilton.

† E. J. Mishan, *The Costs of Economic Growth*, 1968, Staples.

† G. B. Richardson, *Information and Investment*, 1960, OUP.

† R. M. Titmuss, *Choice and the Welfare State*, 1966, Fabian Society Tract No. 370.

* Alan Day, *Economics of Money*, 1959, OUP.

* A. R. Prest (ed), *The UK Economy – A Manual of Applied Economics*, 2nd edition 1968, Weidenfeld & Nicolson.

G. Routh, *Occupation and Pay in Great Britain*, 1965, CUP.

A. Sampson, *Anatomy of Britain*, 1962, Hodder and Stoughton.

† B. Wootton, *Social Foundation of Wages Policy*, 1955, Allen & Unwin.

† D. J. Robertson, *Economics of Wages*, 1961, Macmillan.

* J. E. Meade, *Efficiency, Equality and the Ownership of Property*, 1964, Allen & Unwin.

Lord Donovan, *Royal Commission on Trade Unions and Employers Associations*, 1968, HMSO.

5. THE MARKET ECONOMY – II. PRICES AND PROFITS

J. W. F. Rowe, *Primary Commodities in International Trade*, 1965, CUP.

G. W. Stocking and M. W. Watkins, *Cartels in Action*, 1947, 20th Century Fund.

J. S. Revell, *The Wealth of Britain*, 1967, CUP.

The Times, List of 500 Leading Companies 1968–9.

J. L. Hanson, *Textbook of Economics*, 1961, Macdonald & Evans

J. P. Miller, *Competition, Cartels and their Regulation*, 1962, North Holland.

† J. Burnham, *The Managerial Revolution*, original edition 1941, Penguin, 1962.

C. A. R. Crosland, *The Conservative Enemy*, 1962, Cape.

P. Sargant Florence, *Ownership and Control of Large Companies*, 1951, Sweet & Maxwell.

* K. Coates (ed), *Can the Workers Run Industry?*, 1968, Sphere.

R. Marris, *The Economic Theory of Managerial Capitalism*, 1964, Macmillan.

† M. Barratt Brown *et al. Trade Union Register*, 1969, Merlin.

† M. Harrington, *The Other America*, 1962, Penguin.

6. THE CYCLES OF ECONOMIC ACTIVITY

† R. L. Meek, *Economics and Ideology*, 1967, Chapman & Hall.

W. H. Beveridge, *Unemployment – A Problem of Industry*, 1912, Macmillan.

† *Full Employment in a Free Society*, 1944, Allen & Unwin.

† E. Mandel, *Marxist Economic Theory*, 1967, Merlin.

J. A. Hobson, *The Evolution of Modern Capitalism*, 1909, Allen & Unwin.

J. D. Bernal, *The Social Function of Science*, 1939, Routledge.

† J. S. Robinson, *Introduction to the Theory of Employment*, 1956, Macmillan.

* J. Pen, *Modern Economics*, 1965, Pelican.

US Department of Commerce, *Historical Statistics of the United States 1889–1945*, 1949.

J. K. Galbraith, *The Great Crash 1929*, 1956, Pelican.

J. A. Schumpeter, *Business Cycles*, original edition 1939, 1964 McGraw-Hill.

* E. V. Morgan, *A History of Money*, 1965, Pelican.

† R. F. Harrod, *Money*, 1909, Macmillan.

P. Deane and W. A. Cole, *British Economic Growth 1658–1959*, 1964, CUP.

7. INSTRUMENTS OF STATE INTERVENTION IN THE
MARKET ECONOMY

† G. Myrdal, *Beyond the Welfare State*, 1960, Duckworth.
DEA *The National Plan*, 1965, HMSO.
DEA *The Task Ahead*, 1969, HMSO.
* Oscar Hobson, *How the City Works*, 1959, Daily Mail.
* Samuel Brittain, *The Treasury under the Tories*, 1964, Pelican.
  J. C. R. Dow, *The Management of the British Economy 1945–60*, 1964, CUP.
† M. Barratt Brown, *Labour and Sterling*, 1968, Institute of Workers' Control.
  W. B. Reddaway, *The Effects of UK Direct Investment Overseas*, 1967 and 1969, CUP.
* T. Drinkwater, *Guide to the Balance of Payments*, 1966, Labour Research Department.
† R. Williams (ed), *May Day Manifesto, 1968*, Penguin, 1968.
  R. Titmuss, *Income Distribution and Social Change*, 1962, Allen & Unwin.
† E. J. Mishan, *21 Economic Fallacies*, 1969, Allen Lane.
† A. A. Rogow and P. Shore, *The Labour Government and British Industry 1945–51*, 1955, Blackwell.
† J. Corina, *Incomes Policy – Problems and Prospects*, Parts I and II, 1966, IPM.
† DEP *In Place of Strife*, 1969, HMSO.
* R. Blackburn and A. Cockburn, *The Incompatibles*, 1967, Penguin.

8. ECONOMIC PLANNING OR A PLANNED ECONOMY

* J. K. Galbraith, *The Affluent Society*, 1958, Penguin.
† I. M. D. Little, *A Critique of Welfare Economics*, 1950, OUP.
† E. J. Mishan, *Growth: The Price We Pay*, 1966, Staples.
† M. Lipton, *Assessing Economic Performance*, 1968, Staples.
  E. F. Dennison, *Why Growth Rates Differ*, 1967, Brookings Institution.
  United Nations Economic Commission for Europe, *Some Factors in Economic Growth in Europe during the 1950s*, Geneva, 1964.
  E. Preobrazhensky, *The New Economics*, original edition 1926, 1965, OUP.
  J. M. Keynes, *Economic Consequences of the Peace*, 1920, Macmillan.
  E. A. G. Robinson (ed), *Problems in Economic Development*, 1965, Macmillan.

W. Birmingham and A. G. Ford, *Planning and Growth in Rich and Poor Countries*, 1966, Allen and Unwin.

Ministry of Power, *Fuel Policy*, 1967, HMSO.

J. and A. M. Hackett, *Economic Planning in France*, 1963, Allen & Unwin.

E. H. Carr, *History of Soviet Russia*, 5 Volumes, 1950–60, Macmillan.

† *Soviet Impact on the Western World*, 1947, Macmillan.

† *The New Society*, 1956, Macmillan.

A. Nove, *An Economic History of the USSR*, 1969, Allen Lane.

* A. Bergson, *Economics of Soviet Planning*, 1964, Yale.

F. A. von Hayek (ed), *Collectivist Economic Planning*, 1935, Allen & Unwin.

N. Jasny, *Soviet Industrialization*, 1961, Chicago.

O. Sik, *Plan and Market under Socialism*, 1967, International Arts and Science Press, New York.

† C. Feinstein (ed), *Socialism, Capitalism and Economic Growth*, 1967, CUP.

† B. Wootton, *Freedom under Planning*, 1945, Allen & Unwin.

† F. A. Hayek, *The Road to Serfdom*, 1944, Routledge.

J. Jewkes, *New Ordeal by Planning*, 1968, Macmillan.

M. H. Dobb, *Welfare Economics and the Economics of Socialism*, 1969, CUP.

Journals and Statistics

A number of journals and statistical publications are referred to in the text and used as sources for statistics. These are listed below with the most useful ones for introducing students to the subject marked with a dagger and those suitable for purchase with an asterisk.

The *National Income and Expenditure* Blue Book should be purchased for use with this book.

Official publications may be obtained from H.M. Stationery Office, P.O. Box 569, London S.E.1. Addresses are given for obtaining other publications.

A. UK GOVERNMENT JOURNALS

* Department of Economic Affairs *Progress Report*, Monthly, Free.

† CSO *Economic Trends*, Monthly. Graphs and Tables of Current Statistics and regular articles on GNP, Balance of Payments, Company Finance and Taxation.

Board of Trade *Journal*, Weekly. Foreign Trade, Overseas Investment, Industrial Development.

Department of *Employment and Productivity Gazette,* Monthly.
Employment, Unemployment, Wages, Hours, Prices, Safety.

B. UK GOVERNMENT STATISTICS

* *National Income and Expenditure* Blue Book, Annually.
Report on Overseas Trade, Monthly.
Statistics of Incomes, Prices, Employment and Production,
Monthly.
Financial Statistics, Monthly.
Bulletin of Statistics, Monthly.
† *Annual Abstract of Statistics.*
Balance of Payments, Annually.

C. UNITED NATIONS PUBLICATIONS

Monthly Bulletin of Statistics.
Statistical Yearbook.
IMF *International Financial Statistics,* Monthly.
World Economic Survey, Annually.
Economic Surveys for Europe, Africa, Asia, Latin America,
Annually and Quarterly.

D. OTHER STATISTICAL PUBLICATIONS

† National Institute for Economic & Social Research, *Economic
Review,* Quarterly, 2 Dean Trench Street, London s.w.1.
* Labour Research Department, *Labour Research,* Monthly, 78
Blackfriars Road, London s.e.1.
Incomes Data Services, Twice monthly, 140 Great Portland
Street, London w.1.
* 'London and Cambridge Economic Bulletin', Quarterly in *The
Times.*
'Trend of Industrial Profits', Monthly in *Financial Times.*

E. BANK REVIEWS

Articles of interest by leading authorities on many problems of
applied economics will be found in the following (all issued quar-
terly and free).
† *Lloyds Bank Review,* 71 Lombard Street, London E.C.3.
* *National Westminster Bank Review,* (ex National Provincial,
District and Westminster Banks), 41 Lothbury, London E.C.2.
Barclays Bank Review, 54 Lombard Street, London E.C.3.

* National and Commercial *Three Banks Review,* 67 Lombard Street, London E.C.3.
* *Moorgate and Wall Street,* Hill, Samuel & Co., 100 Wood Street, London E.C.2.

    Bank of England *Quarterly Bulletin,* Bank of England, London E.C.2.

F. ACADEMIC JOURNALS

Economic Journal, Quarterly, Marshall Library, Cambridge.

Economic History Review, Quarterly, Peterhouse, Cambridge.

Oxford Economic Papers, Three times a year, Clarendon Press, Oxford.

Oxford University Institute of Economic and Statistics, *Bulletin,* Quarterly, Basil Blackwell, Oxford.

British Journal of Industrial Relations, Three times a year, London School of Economics, Houghton Street, London w.c.2.

† *Journal of Economic Studies,* Twice a year, Strathclyde University, Glasgow c.1.

Past and Present, Quarterly, 43 Queen Street, Oxford.

Glossary-Index of Economists' Language

L

COAL EQUIVALENT: The equivalent power or energy in tons of coal of other fuels – 1 ton of Fuel Oil = 1·7 tons of coal. 260–1

COLLECTIVE : Form of cooperative agricultural production. 264, 267

COLONY: A country either settled by people from another country or made politically (or in Marxist thinking economically) dependent. 219

COMMISSION: Payment for services of a bank or BROKER as a percentage of value of transaction. 211

COMMODITY: A good or service produced for the market, 104, 264

    AGREEMENT – To stabilize prices by managing stocks. 131

COMMUNISM: Social system under which property is vested in the community and shared alike, expected by Marx to follow after Capitalism and Socialism. 149, 266

    PRIMITIVE – similar condition among early Men. 56

COMPANY: A legal entity with the obligation to pay debts 79, 130 et with LIMITED LIABILITY, i.e. to its realizable assets. seq.

    PRIVATE – Having only thirty shareholders and no quotation. 149

    PUBLIC – Having a quotation on the STOCK EXCHANGE. 149 et seq.

COMPARATIVE COSTS: The principle under which one country specializes in producing those goods in which it has the greatest advantages relative to other countries. 82

COMPENSATION: Payment to make amends for loss, e.g. of 29, 156, land taken compulsorily for building or other social purposes. 247, 261

COMPETITION: A situation where there are several firms in 40, 00, 120 the market to supply the same goods. et seq., 272

    PERFECT – Where there are so many that no one firm's 129–31, action in entering or not entering the market or in expanding or contracting output has any effect. 138

    IMPERFECT – Where there are a number of firms in the market but perfect competition does not exist. 137 et seq.

    MONOPOLISTIC – see MONOPOLY. 137 et seq.

CONCENTRATION: Of wealth or power, the accumulation in 150 et seq. one place or firm or group of people. 215 et seq.

CONSOLS: Consolidated British Government Stock which has no repayment date. 212

CONSORTIUM: Coming together of a group of firms or governments to finance a particular project. 255

CONSUMPTION: Generally, the satisfaction of private wants by purchase of goods or services but see PRODUCTIVE CON- 46, 173–5, SUMPTION and PUBLIC SECTOR consumption. 183, 187–9

    FUNCTION – activity, e.g. level of investment depending on level of consumption. 192

CONTROLS: Administrative orders of governments to regulate money supply, consumption (e.g. by rationing) or investment or movements of funds into and out of the 9, 144,

COSTS: Expenditure in obtaining use of a FACTOR or factors of production.   32

    AND BENEFITS – SOCIAL.   29, 95, 129,
                                                        147, 161–2,
                                                        244 et seq.

    TOTAL – All expenditures in production attributable to a particular product.   87, 202–3

    FIXED – Varying little with output, e.g. plant and management, sometimes referred to as overheads, i.e. not chargeable to any unit of production.   84, 86–8

    VARIABLE – Varying with output, e.g. labour, fuel and materials.   84, 88–9

    PRIME – Including all variable and some fixed costs.   84

    SELLING – Including costs of advertising, marketing, etc.

CREDIT: Period of grace granted before payment of a debt and therefore in effect a loan or advance charged for at a certain rate.   66, 96,
                                                        105, 207

    GUARANTEES – Government guarantee of credit generally to help exporters who have to wait some time for payment.   216–17

CRISIS: A dangerous turning point used by economists of the moment when a BOOM breaks and SLUMP follows in the TRADE CYCLE, explained by Keynesians in terms of a rising SAVINGS PROPORTION plus SPECULATION and by Marxists in terms of OVER-PRODUCTION and disproportions in production. (See REALIZATION and UNDERCONSUMPTION.)   164 et seq.

    GENERAL – Of the capitalist system, seen by Marx as the inevitable result of the conflict between changing technological forces of production and the economic structure of capitalism – a conflict which reveals itself in the internal contradictions of the over-production of capital, of hastening ACCUMULATION and CONCENTRATION of capital and falling rate of profit. General crisis may take the form of STAGNATION similar to that predicted by Ricardo or of dissolution and the elaboration of new, socialist, conditions of production.   167–8

CROSS-INVESTMENT: Movements of capital between one rich advanced industrial country and another.   94, 154 et
                                                        seq., 171

CUMULATIVE CAUSATION: Central principle of economic activity that implies an increase in force with each addition, e.g. of wealth or poverty, developed by Professor G. Myrdal.   60, 62, 68,
                                                        95, 162,
                                                        183–4

CURRENCY: Metal and paper money issued by a national bank.   27, 43, 104
                                                        –6, 215–19

    KEY – especially used in international trade.   219

CURRENT EXPENDITURE (ACCOUNT): Required for day to day running which involves no addition to assets.   45, 225,
                                                        227–8

accounts to replace depreciated assets on the basis of   90, 151–2,
expected life of the asset and its historic cost (but see   155–6,
REPLACEMENT COST).   185–6, 226

DEPRESSION: A reduction in the volume of economic
activity as part of the TRADE CYCLE.   68

DERIVED DEMAND: Demand for one commodity derived
from demand for another.   119

DETERMINANT: Factor or factors that can be regarded as
causing, e.g. levels or changes in wages.   45

DETERMINISM: Philosophical theory that human action is
not free but controlled by external forces acting on the
will.   22

DEVALUATION: Fixing by a government of a new and lower   217–8,
exchange rate for its currency.   258

DEVELOPING COUNTRY: Polite phrase for an under-
developed or poor country that is trying to raise its standard   16, 56–9,
of living.   171, 253–5

DEVELOPMENT: Sustained growth in standard of living.   7, 48–55,
                                                           60 et seq.,
                                                           252 et seq.

AREA – One needing development because of high unemployment.   93–4

CHARGE – Placed on private persons who benefit from
changed use of land.

DEVIATE (verb): To move away from normal, e.g. from a
growing trend.   114

DIAGRAM: A drawing showing essential features or lines to
represent processes, movements, changes in force, etc.   32 et seq.

DIFFERENTIAL: A fixed difference, especially between
levels of wages.   128

DIFFERENTIATION: Practice used in advertising to attach   49, 110,
buyers to one particular brand of a PRODUCT.   138–9

DIMINISHING RETURNS: Idea that each new addition, e.g.
to a type of consumption or to a FACTOR in production is
less satisfying or less effective than the previous addition.   26–8, 247

DIRECTIVE: PLANNING.   261

DISCOUNT (verb): To cash a bill before it matures.   211

DISCOUNT (noun): Difference between market value of a
COMMODITY or SHARE and price charged to certain purchasers.   213

DISCOUNT RATE: Difference between price paid for a BILL
and face value, expressed as a percentage per annum.   210–12

DISCOUNT HOUSE: A bank which will accept bills at less
than their face value and hold them until they mature
(TREASURY BILL).   210–14

DISCOUNTED CASH: See FLOW.   156

DISCRETIONARY INCOME: Income available for spending
on goods and services that are not essentials.   100, 229

DISECONOMIES : Opposite of ECONOMIES.   81 et seq.,
                                                                  102–3, 246
DISPERSION: Spread, especially in range of income.   52
DISSAVE: To spend more than total income over a period,
either by borrowing or running down savings, opposite of
SAVE.   180–1, 192
DISTRIBUTION: Of populations, frequency of occurrence of   6, 10, 16,
individuals, according to some measurable characteristic   50, 52, 58,
like height, or income or wealth.   99, 231,
                                                                 246

   NORMAL – Deviating from the NORM only in a random
   manner, illustrated on a graph as having the shape of a
   cocked hat.   112 et seq.
   SKEWED – with a greater than NORMAL deviation.   114–15
DISTRIBUTION THEORY: Of resources and incomes, that   7, 15, 96,
seeks to explain their distribution in terms of the return to   105 et seq.,
scarce FACTORS OF PRODUCTION.   128
DIVERSIFICATION: Process engaged in by firms and persons who want to spread their interests among several
different activities to avoid having 'all their eggs in one
basket'.   156
DIVIDEND: Part of company's profits paid to shareholders   51, 156,
of EQUITY, expressed as percentage of nominal value of   187, 190,
shares.   198, 221
DOMESTIC: Produced at home, either of total national
product, i.e. excluding imports; or of industry, e.g.
clothing, organized so that the work can be done in the
home.   76–7
DUOPOLY : see MONOPOLY.   138–9
DURABLE CONSUMER GOODS : Those that last, like cars,   50, 54, 58,
washing machines, etc.   181–2
DUTY : A payment to the public revenue levied on imports
or sales.   94, 140
   CUSTOMS AND EXCISE – example of DUTY; ESTATE
   transfers of property another example   231
ECONOMETRICS: Branch of economics concerned with constructing mathematical MODELS, i.e. systems of equations
for computing future movements in any economy from
analysis of past movements.   16
ECONOMIC: Affairs, Relations, those concerned with human
beings associating together in getting a living.   1 et seq.
ECONOMICS: The study of such affairs and relations.   1 et seq.
ECONOMIZING: Making the best use of scarce resources,   1, 5, 6, 10,
regarded by some economists as the most important aspect   24 et seq.,
of economics.   96 et seq.
ECONOMY: Either a saving o RESOURCES, or the associa-
tion in nations or the world of human beings for the purpose
of getting a living.   1, 12

ECONOMIES
  EXTERNAL – Gains or savings outside the control of a 60, 94, 246,
    single firm, e.g. from location of other firms. 256
  OF SCALE – Gains by way of reduced COSTS of production 60, 81 et
    per unit of output arising from increasing the SCALE of seq., 102–3
    production or quantity of one item produced. 256
EFFICIENCY: Using the least resources, generally of a firm, 121, 128,
but this may not take account of SOCIAL COSTS. 129–30,
    147–8, 246

  MARGINAL – see MARGINAL. 176
ELASTICITY: Response of demand for commodities to:
  INCOME – (*a*) changes in real incomes of consumers. 38 et seq.,
    110 et seq.

  OF DEMAND – (*b*) changes in prices of COMMODITIES. 38 et seq.,
    139, 217–18
EMPIRE: IMPERIALISM. 80, 218–19,
    222 n.

ENCLOSURES: Acts, generally of Parliament, especially in
the early nineteenth century, to bring common land into
private ownership. 72–3
ENERGY EQUIVALENT: See COAL. 81
ENGEL'S LAW: A generalization concerned with income
ELASTICITIES, which says that the proportion of income
spent on food tends to decline as income grows. 39
ENTERPRISE: Another name for a firm or unit of organiza- 58, 94–5,
tion of production; also of the quality and function of those 100, 268–9,
who organize production. 274
ENTREPRENEUR: A businessman who brings the factors of
production together for profit and, particularly, takes risks by
anticipating future demand. 27, 139
ENVIRONMENTAL: Concerning the general surrounding cir-
cumstances.
  PLANNING – Concerned with all the effects on individual
    and social activity. 262–3
EQUATION: Mathematical expression of relationship. 30 et seq.
EQUILIBRIUM: A situation of balance in an economic sys- 7, 28, 30 et
tem, e.g. in prices or factor uses. seq., 242
  STATIC – When there is no economic motive for change.
  DYNAMIC–When change is in some way built into the system.
  GENERAL – For all products and their prices.
  PARTIAL – For particular products and prices.
EQUITY: The ordinary shares of a limited company, i.e.
those that carry the rights of ownership and a dividend. 136, 155
ESTATE DUTY: Tax on property passing at death, extended
to gifts made within five years of death. 231
EURO-DOLLAR: Foreign currencies mostly dollars, of
persons and companies not governments, held in European
Commercial Banks. 219–20

SPECIFIC – = cannot easily be turned to alternative uses, e.g. skilled labour and specialized machinery.

NON-SPECIFIC – can be put to alternative uses, e.g. land or unskilled labour.

FACTORY: Originally manufactory, a place where workers are gathered together for the purpose of producing goods.

   SYSTEM – Where the production of goods is based on the division of LABOUR among many workers under the same roof.   69 et seq., 81

FALSIFICATION: Proving wrong; principle of argument which according to Professor Popper requires that any theory must be able to stand up to many different attempts to prove it wrong.   18–20

FAMINE: Shortage of SUPPLY below DEMAND for COMMODITIES, especially food.   130–1

FEASIBILITY: Of tests and studies to prove whether a course of action is practicable.   262–3

FEUDALISM: Social System or Epoch, or stage according to Marx, in which holding of land gave rights to services from those on the land.   12, 56, 58, 62–4, 238n.

FIDUCIARY ISSUE: Since 1844 that amount of the banknote issue which is not backed £1 for £1 by gold – today nearly the whole of it.   209

FIG.: Abbreviation of figure, a diagram or illustrative drawing.   32 et seq.

FINANCE: Provision of money when it is needed, especially so that individuals or firms can consume more than they produce in a certain period of time, thus especially for buying major items of equipment on which repayment can be spread over months or years (CREDIT).   49, 60, 78 et seq., 209 et seq.

   INTERNAL – Funds generated for investment from profits of companies.   80, 149–52

   EXTERNAL – Funds obtained by companies from outside sources, e.g. bank loans, STOCK EXCHANGE issues, etc.   150–8

   SHORT-TERM – Through banks, Trade Credit, HP, Bills of Exchange.   155

   LONG-TERM – Through loans, Debentures, Preference and Ordinary SHARES.   155

FIRM: Unit of management to mine, or to produce, goods or services – may be a sole proprietorship, partnership, private or public, LIMITED LIABILITY company or state-owned enterprise.   137 et seq.

   THEORY OF THE – Concerns the ways PRICES are determined and RESOURCES allocated in respect of products of one individual firm in relation to others.   137 et seq.

FISCAL POLICY: Policy of Government in raising revenue either in excess of or below expenditure. (See BUDGET.)   207, 224 et seq.

crease at one pole as wealth accumulated at the other in a capitalist economy. — 124, 167

IMPERIALISM: Rule of an emperor, e.g. of the British Empire, used by followers of Marx to describe the tendency of CAPITALISM to spread out to impose its economic relations on all countries and reduce many to COLONIES of the most advanced industrial nations. In Lenin's view the highest stage of capitalism. — 61 n., 222 n.

IMPORTS: Goods or services entering a country from abroad, the value of the goods generally measured CIF. — 46, 54, 59, 74, 202–3, 217

INVISIBLE – Services provided by foreigners and dividends and interest payable to foreigners. — 223

LICENCE – Required for certain goods or all goods imported into a country. — 238–9

QUOTA – Quantitative restriction on imports. — 131, 245

LEVIES – Placed on imports of certain commodities, e.g. in the European Common Market on food imports to bring world prices up to the level of reigning prices inside the Market. — 93

DEPOSIT – Scheme to restrict imports by requiring cash deposit in payment for imports. — 217

INCIDENCE: The effect, e.g. of a tax on different groups of persons with different incomes. — 109, 229–233

INCOME: A measure of personal, firm's or national wealth received over a year or over some other period. See GROSS and NET. — 06 et seq.

TAX – A tax on personal or company income – often referred to as direct tax, e.g. PAYE in Britain. — 231

PROGRESSIVE – i.e. increasing proportionally as income increases, so that the rich pay a higher proportion of their income in tax than the poor. — 179, 229 et seq.

REGRESSIVE – the opposite of progressive. — 229 et seq.

UNIT – Definition of tax payers used by governments, defined in Britain as a man and wife combined, or single person, including children with their own income. — 105, 181

INCONSISTENCY: Keynesian concept to describe failure of SAVINGS and INVESTMENT to respond to changing interest rates. — 184

INDEX NUMBERS: Showing changes in output, prices, wages, etc. as a percentage of a BASE year, e.g. cost of living index shows changes in prices of typical purchases by householders. — 45, 250–1

INDICATIVE: PLANNING. — 257 et seq.

INDIFFERENCE CURVE: Showing the combinations of different commodities which would give a consumer the same satisfaction. — 29, 36–38

ultimate source of value and thus the determinant of 7–8, 11,
prices in production.   121, 268

DIVISION OF – The specialization of work by men and
machines which allows the best use to be made of 60, 80 et
special skills and training and specific machines.   seq.

INTENSIVE – Forms of production in which labour costs
are a high proportion of total costs, as opposed to
CAPITAL-INTENSIVE.   124, 148

MOBILITY – The ease of movement of labour between 66, 77–8,
areas and occupations.   94, 161 et
    seq.

TURNOVER – The number of workers who leave a firm or
industry or are replaced in a given period, expressed as
a proportion of the average labour force in the same
period.   162

LAISSEZ-FAIRE: 'Let be', the theory of classical political
economy that the market should be freed from state interference to allocate RESOURCES according to the free pursuit
by individuals of their own interests.   25–6

LAND: One of the FACTORS OF PRODUCTION and generally
regarded as including minerals and water. Unlike the other
factors it is fixed in quantity and unless improved by man
has theoretically no cost, although its owners may still make 6, 15, 47,
a charge for its use.   58, 62

LEADS AND LAGS: The tendency of international traders
to change their holdings of national currencies in order to
pay bills early or late according to their estimate of the
chances of a currency changing value.   219–20

LEADTIME: The time elapsing between one economic
activity and another, e.g. the placing of an order and the
receipt of goods or the making of an invention and its application.   184

LEASE: An agreement to grant the use, generally of land
or buildings, for a specified term at an agreed annual
rental.   46, 58

LEGAL TENDER: Money which a person is obliged by law
to accept as payment of a debt.   103 et seq.

LENDER OF LAST RESORT: The traditional role of the
Bank of England which does not refuse to extend credit at
BANK RATE to money market dealers, e.g. BROKERS and
DISCOUNT HOUSES, if asked to do so.   212

LETTERS OF CREDIT: An arrangement to provide early
payment for goods despatched overseas, i.e. as soon as
documents such as Bills of Lading can be presented to a
bank.   216–17

LEVERAGE: The ratio between LOANS or preferred stock and
ORDINARY or common stock. (See CAPITAL GEARING.)   155

LEVY: A tax proportional to value, e.g. on capital wealth

or, as in the Common Market, on agricultural imports at
prices below home market levels.   94
LIABILITY: Debt or financial obligation.   49, 115
LIEN: The right to retain the property of a debtor until the
debt is paid.
LIMITED LIABILITY: Of a company – provided for by law in
the UK since 1855 – that a shareholder has no liability for
the debts of a company in which he has invested beyond the
sum he has invested. This law covers both private and
public COMPANIES.   79
LIMITING POINT (VALUE OF): That to which it is practicable to go in a series or function, e.g. one that ends in in-
finity.   9
LINEAR: A relation that can be represented by a straight
line and not a curve, compare PROGRESSIVE and REGRES-
SIVE.   229
LINE AND STAFF ADMINISTRATION: Distinguishes those
line managers who execute policy 'down the line' and those
staff advisers who give technical advice.
LIQUID ASSETS: Those in the form of money or which can
be quickly converted into money, e.g. for a Bank: coin,
notes, balances at the Bank of England, money at call or
short notice and discounted BILLS.   210–13
LIQUIDITY: Ability to meet current financial LIABILITIES in
cash.   104, 184
    PREFERENCE – Preference of persons to hold money
    instead of SECURITIES.   176, 273
    RATIO – The ratio of about 30 per cent which British
    banks maintain between their holdings of Liquid ASSETS
    and their total DEPOSITS.   210–13
    INTERNATIONAL – World money, the RESERVES of GOLD
    and CONVERTIBLE currencies, including IMF funds,
    available for financing deficits in international trade.   216 et seq.
LOAD FACTOR: The number of units of output actually pro-
duced from a plant or machine in a certain period (generally
a year) as a percentage of output at CAPACITY.   86–7
LOCATION OF INDUSTRY: The place where different indus-   60 et seq.,
tries are established as a result of proximity to raw materials,   91 et seq.,
labour, markets and of transport costs, government plan-   161 et seq.,
ning, etc.   239, 262–3
LOG, LOGARITHM, LOG SCALE: Arithmetical FUNCTION
based on multiples of 10 which allows multiplication and
division to be carried out by addition and subtraction, and
which permits equal proportional increments, e.g. in a
growth curve to be shown as having equal values.   114–15
LONG AND SHORT PERIOD ANALYSIS: As defined by
Alfred Marshall, the long period is one in which there is
time for the supply of FACTORS used in production to adapt

themselves to demand whereas in the short period this is not possible (see PRICE). 52–3

LORENZ CURVE: Cumulative FREQUENCIES drawn on a graph to show degrees of inequality, see Fig. 4.3. 114–15

LOSS LEADER: Goods sold by a retailer below normal retail price in order to attract customers to buy other goods in his shop. Under the Resale Prices Act of 1965 suppliers may withhold goods from retailers who have used goods of the same description as loss leaders. 138

LUMP SUM CONTRACT: Where the contractor agrees to perform work at a given price and bears the loss if there is one.

LUXURIES: Goods or services which are given up as income falls, to allow for spending on necessities. 40

MACRO-ECONOMICS: That part of economics concerned with dynamic analysis of the economy as a whole, dealing, e.g. with such large AGGREGATES as the volume of employment, savings, investment and national income; as opposed to Micro-economics concerned with a static MODEL of behaviour of individual producers, consumers, firms and industries. 97, 164 et seq., 184n., 192 n.

MANAGEMENT: The men responsible for executing the policy decisions of the directors of a firm. These men may also join the directors on the board and in some cases managers carry out both functions of policy-making and execution and provide all the directors of the firms. 1, 48, 149 et seq.

OF THE ECONOMY – Measures taken by government to maintain a balance between capacity to produce and level of demand, between saving and investment, imports and exports, etc. 209 et seq.

MANAGERIAL REVOLUTION: The theory originating from a book by James Burnham, that the owners of capital had lost all power in business to the managers, who therefore had other interests than the maximum return to capital. 149 et seq.

MANUFACTURES: Articles made by labour with machinery especially on a large SCALE in FACTORIES. 48, 54, 85, 190, 223

MARGINAL: For one more unit at the margin as in MARGINAL COST and REVENUE where the results of adding one extra unit of a factor of production are considered. Hence. 6, 7, 26, 31, 88–91, 124–5, 141–4, 246

PRODUCT – as above. 27–8, 124

EFFICIENCY – Of capital. The earning power of the last increment of capital invested and, therefore, the anticipated rate of profit bearing in mind interest charges. 176

is consumed or saved (see MARGINAL PROPENSITY TO 164, 182 et
CONSUME). seq., 193

NATIONAL DEBT: The accumulated debts of a government
arising from its borrowing from private persons over the
years, amounting in the UK in 1966 to £31 billions, on which
£1·5 billions interest was paid.
    FUNDED – The term for consolidated funds (CONSOLS), war
    loans, etc. which carry no repayment date. 212
    UNFUNDED – Used to describe floating date or short-
    term borrowing against Treasury Bills and 'dated'
    securities including National Saving Certificates,
    Defence Bonds, Premium Bonds, and other govern-
    ment stocks. 210–14

NATIONAL ECONOMIC DEVELOPMENT COUNCIL: Or
NEDDY, set up in 1961 from representatives of government, public and private industry and trade unions to
examine the performance of the British economy and to
consider ways of improving the rate of growth. 262
    'LITTLE NEDDIES' – Since 1961 set up for many different
    industries and regions to examine and recommend on
    the problems of each. 262

NATIONAL INCOME: A measure of the money value of goods
and services available to a nation from economic activity
during any particular year, calculated in three different
ways:
(a) By adding all incomes generated including wages,
salaries, incomes of self-employed, business profits, rent and
net income from abroad – less TRANSFER PAYMENTS.
(b) By adding all expenditure on consumption (plus SUB-
SIDIES and less INDIRECT TAXES), on investment (including
increases in stocks and WORK IN PROGRESS) *plus* exports and
property income from abroad *less* imports and property
income paid abroad.
(c) By adding the values of all goods and services produced
by different industries, etc. avoiding all double counting,
e.g. of indirect taxes and raw materials used in finished
products. (See GROSS DOMESTIC PRODUCT.)
    GROSS and NET NATIONAL INCOME – are used to
    describe the money value of goods and services with and
    without CAPITAL CONSUMPTION, i.e., the REPLACEMENT 46, 52–3,
    of plant, machinery and buildings in that year. The 164, 172–3
    National Income is reckoned in current values but may 183, 225–8
    be compared with other years by adjusting for price 231–2, 250
    changes. et seq.

NATIONAL BOARD FOR PRICES AND INCOMES: Set up by
the British government in 1965 to examine claims for in-

RATE. Buying stock makes more money available; selling stock mops up money.   210

OPPORTUNITY COST: Term to describe the real cost of satisfying one want, i.e. in terms of the sacrifice of alternative opportunities.   28–9, 31, 34 et seq.

OPTIMUM: Literally 'the best', used by economists to describe the maximum satisfaction or gain for an individual, firm or nation, thus: 29

    ALLOCATION – Of RESOURCES where they are most productively used.

    FIRM – Where COSTS OF PRODUCTION per unit of output are at the minimum for any particular level of TECHNOLOGY and therefore

    OUTPUT – Where all economies of SCALE have been realized without losses occurring from falling prices or loss of managerial control.

OPTION: Right to buy or sell SHARES or property within a stated period usually at a predetermined price, often offered to higher management in addition to salary.   150

ORDINARY SHARES: The EQUITY of a LIMITED company.   136, 155

ORGANIC COMPOSITION OF CAPITAL: Concept which Karl Marx used to describe the ratio of CONSTANT CAPITAL – i.e. in his terminology, the building, machinery, plant and raw materials – and VARIABLE CAPITAL – the capital laid out on labour. Marx expected the organic composition of capital to rise, i.e. more constant per variable, and the rate of profit correspondingly to fall because surplus can be derived only from variable capital (see SURPLUS VALUE).   166

OUTPUT: Quantity of goods produced from an enterprise or an industry in a certain period of time.   45

OUT-TURN: Actual attainment as opposed to an estimate or plan.   270

OUT-WORK: That carried on in the house but on contract for a factory or merchant.   76

OVER-CAPACITY: Excess CAPACITY in relation to level of production.   193, 203

OVERDRAFT: Loan from a bank made on current account repayable on demand and of no fixed duration, generally to persons and companies, to finance short-term trading needs. Always offset in the bank's accounts by a corresponding nominal DEPOSIT. Interest charged is usually at 1 per cent or more above BANK RATE and payable only on the actual amount borrowed.   105, 210–213

OVERHEADS: COSTS which continue when no output is taking place, and which are not directly chargeable to any unit produced, to include costs of buildings, sales and research, management and capital as opposed to costs of labour and materials.   84, 86–91

OVER-POPULATION: A condition defined by economists as one where the marginal product of labour is less than average output per head in the territory concerned – a condition that might become universal as the use of labour-saving, automated machinery is extended.   123, 148

OVER-PRODUCTION: Concept of David Ricardo to describe a situation where the market for a product or products expands more slowly than the capacity to produce. Karl Marx developed the concept to describe the general tendency of a whole capitalist economy to generate ACCUMULATION of the means of production without regard for the limit of the market, i.e. for the ability to buy among the workers from whose labour the accumulation derives.   165–8

OVER-SUBSCRIPTION: Where applications for a new issue of SHARES exceeds the number offered on the market.

PAR: The value of a SHARE on the market when it is equal to its NOMINAL value.   211

PARAMETER: 'CONSTANTS that may be varied', figures that determine the governing features of a system and so are assumed to be constant for the purpose of studying certain VARIABLES. Hence in statistics the numerical characteristics of populations, e.g. MEAN, variance, etc.   32

PARTNERSHIP: Association of persons in business where each shares the risks and profits.   78

PATENT: Government grant of exclusive privilege to an inventor (or firm) or to property in his invention for a certain period, from which he may derive an income.   221

PAYROLL: Wages bill of a firm.
   TAX – Tax on wages bill of firms such as Selective Employment Tax designed to discourage 'hoarding' of labour in selected industries.   148

PEASANT: Class of persons who work as a family unit on land, which they themselves own or hold by payment of dues or rent to the land-owner.   56–8, 255

PHILIPS CURVE: Relationship of general changes in prices to economic activity – a concept developed by A. W. Philips (see INFLATION).   148

PIECE-WORK, PIECE-RATES: Payment of wages by the piece or quantity of output as opposed to payment by time.   122

PIE CHART: A diagram which shows, like slices of a pie, the distribution of a POPULATION, e.g. by occupations, as segments of a circle, the proportion of 360° in the angles of which are the same as the proportional distribution of the population.   50–51

PLANNING: In common use, considering courses of action in advance and arranging for their implementation. Hence planning by firms involves control over flows of productive factors at all stages of production. Economic planning by governments involves collection, processing and circulation of information about past performance and current trends of the economy and indications (INDICATIVE PLANNING) about future expectations. To this may be added co-ORDINATIVE and DIRECTIVE or RESOURCE planning, where governments interfere in various ways to arrange that expectations are fulfilled. 2, 207–8, 222, 242 et seq., 257 et seq.

PLANNED ECONOMY: Widespread economic planning carried to the point where government decisions at different levels largely replace the market in determining both prices and resource allocation. 8, 97, 145, 242 et seq., 250, 263 et seq., 271 et seq.

PLETHORA: Excess of blood, and so used by Marx and Lenin to describe excess of capital resulting from rising profits in relation to wages. 176

PLOUGH-BACK: Retention of profits (in RESERVES) for re-investment in a company to buy new plant, buildings and machinery (see SELF-FINANCING). 156–7

POLARIZATION: Tendency to move to opposite poles, hence used by Marx to describe tendency of wealth to grow at one extreme and poverty at the other. 167–8

POLITICAL ECONOMY: The school of economic thought originating with Adam Smith and Ricardo and carried on by Marx, Malthus, Mill and others (mostly Marxians) subsequently, which sees economic relations as so closely related to the whole social and political structure of a particular period or country as to make separate treatment of economics and politics virtually impossible. This way of thinking was ended by Marshall in 1879 because the 'body politic' was divided and political considerations reduced the exactitude of the science. 4 et seq.

POLL TAX: Literally tax on heads and therefore equal payment from all citizens – a highly REGRESSIVE tax. 230

POPULATION: Generally the number of people living in a certain area and affecting economic activity by changes in number and age composition. 70 et seq.

For statisticians the total number of any category of persons, things or events being analysed. Thus the population of IN-COME TAX UNITS is the basis for the analysis of personal income distribution in Britain. 112–15

PORTFOLIO: List of SECURITIES held by a person or INSTITU-TION, including governments; hence in relation to foreign investment the holdings of SHARES by persons and institutions in foreign stocks, as opposed to the direct investment by companies in SUBSIDIARIES and branches overseas. 154

POSITIVE ECONOMICS: Concerned with means and the

when extra supplies can be produced from the existing
plant available;

(*c*) LONG-RUN normal price – when rate of production
can be varied by extensions of CAPACITY;

RING – An association of firms or dealers to control prices
by mutual agreement. 140

THEORY – The view of non-Marxian economists that price
is determined by movements of SUPPLY AND DEMAND in
a situation of SCARCITY. 7, 15, 28, 110 et seq., 128

FIXING OR ADMINISTERED PRICES – Describe a situation where large firms can determine the most profitable price to charge, taking long-run as well as short-run considerations into account; 108 et seq., 137 et seq., 201

RESALE PRICE MAINTENANCE (RPM) – The system by
which large firms bring pressure to bear on retailers not
to cut prices for their products below the fixed figure,
the aim being to maintain control over retail outlets
and avoid price wars and threats to orderly marketing. 38

SHADOW: Computed price on basis of SOCIALLY NECESSARY LABOUR TIME. 273

PRIMARY PRODUCTS: Those which come straight from the
ground as foodstuffs, RAW MATERIALS and fuels before
further processing. 47, 62, 83, 131

PRIVATE

COMPANY: One that has no public subscription for its
SHARES but may have up to fifty shareholders (excluding
employees). It may still be LIMITED in liability as
opposed to a partnership but may not thereby be
exempt from corporation tax and publication of
accounts. 149

SECTOR: That part of a MIXED ECONOMY that is not in the
hands of central or local government or their organs. It
includes both personal and company sectors. 257 et seq.

PRODUCER GOODS: Those required for the purpose of producing other goods, i.e. machinery, plant building, etc. See
CAPITAL GOODS, INVESTMENT GOODS. 132, 154, 250 et seq., 266 et seq.

PRODUCT DIFFERENTIATION: Describes the attempts of
firms to create differences between their products and those
of others in order to attach customers to them, e.g. by brand
names, packaging, etc. 49, 110, 138

PRODUCTIVE CONSUMPTION: Use of goods in production
(see INPUT–OUTPUT). 53

PRODUCTIVITY: Efficiency in use of FACTORS OF PRODUCTION, generally measured in output per man hour, but as
such liable to mislead, since output may depend on level
of sales (which may be deflated by general government
action) as much as on the level and efficiency of input. It need

M

QUANTITY THEORY OF MONEY: States that if the velocity of circulation of MONEY and the number of trade transactions are given, then an increase in the amount of money in circulation by governments must raise prices, and a decrease must lower prices. In fact velocity is not constant and the amount of money does not depend entirely on government action but moves up and down with the levels of economic activity.   196–7

QUANTUM: Measure of value, e.g. of trade or output over a period, taking into account changes of price (VOLUME).   44

QUARTILE: The result of dividing a population into four equal groups in order of some value, e.g. of income. The value at each quartile will mean that a quarter, a half or three-quarters of the population respectively have less. The middle division will be the MEDIAN, the others the upper and lower quartiles.   52, 127

QUASI-RENT: A DIFFERENTIAL payment for a commodity or service in temporarily limited supply beyond what should be necessary for maintaining the supply. A concept developed by Marshall from Ricardo's theory of RENT.   146, 246

QUOTATION: The right granted to a company to have its SHARES quoted on the STOCK EXCHANGE. Hence QUOTED COMPANY, of which there are some 2,000 on the London Stock Exchange.   101–2, 132–6, 151–2

QUOTA: An agreed quantity or value of goods permitted to be imported into a country from another country over a certain period of time – used to limit imports which are in competition with home production.   131, 245

RANDOM: Left to chance; of SAMPLES, unbiased and so permitting the same mix to appear in the sample as in the population it represents.   113–14

RATCHET EFFECT: Concept of J. S. Duesenbery, that consumption moves up and down in steps as incomes rise and fall.   192

RATE OF INTEREST: A measure of the payments due per year on borrowed money expressed as a percentage of the sum borrowed.   176 et seq., 198–9, 212–14

  BANK – The rate at which the Bank of England, acting as what is called 'LENDER OF LAST RESORT', will make advances to DISCOUNT HOUSES against bills of exchange, TREASURY BILLS, etc. when the DISCOUNT HOUSES find themselves short of cash. Thus the bank rate governs the market rates of discount (which remains somewhat lower than bank rate) and also all other administered rates such as the rates on bank deposits, rates of lending by the Exchequer to local authorities, nationalized industries, etc.   205, 209 et seq.

RATE OF RETURN: A measure of the ratio of PROFIT over a certain period to the capital employed in a business.   109–10, 145 et seq.

RATES: Local taxes raised by local authorities from occupiers of premises according to an assessment of their value – hence   199, 231
>RATEABLE VALUE – Of premises on which a fixed tax per £ is levied each year.

RATIONALIZATION: Of an industry – measures adopted by companies or enforced by banks or governments to improve EFFICIENCY (profitability) by reducing the number of units of production and concentrating output in the most efficient (profitable) ones.   128, 150 et seq.

RATIONING: An allowance, e.g. of food, fixed by governments, to deal equitably with scarce resources.   142–4
>BY THE PURSE – Really the opposite of rationing, where goods in short supply go to those who are prepared to pay most for them and therefore in some economic theory those that have most need of them.   145

RAW MATERIALS: Unprocessed mineral, animal or vegetable products for use in manufacture.   8

REALIZATION: REPRODUCTION.   165–7

REAL-TERMS: As opposed to money terms, are measures of value taken over a period of years which allow for changes in price, so as to provide a comparison which is not distorted by price changes, generally based on the prices in a certain year to which all other year's prices are adjusted. Thus: 41, 43–5
>WAGES – Movements of wages where money wage changes have been adjusted for price changes.   8, 190, 200

REBATE: A reduction in price of a COMMODITY or service or FACTOR OF PRODUCTION allowed for prompt payment, BULK PURCHASE or special circumstances of the customer.   90

RECIPROCAL: An INVERSE relationship; in mathematics, where the product of two numbers is unity, each is the reciprocal of the other.   31, 183

REDEPLOYMENT: Organized change in employment of men or resources; hence the justification for encouraging REDUNDANCIES.   183

REDUNDANCY: State of excess labour to a firm's requirements caused by introduction of new labour-saving machinery or by decline of demand.
>PAYMENT FUND – Compulsory contribution from firms to meet compensation for those made redundant, and therefore designed to encourage firms to save and release labour for other requirements.   148, 183

RE-EXPORT: Goods imported only for sampling and sale on the commodity markets which do not leave the customs sheds until exported.   54

REFLATION: Process whereby governments make money more easily available after periods of DEFLATION.   194–5

REGRESSION: The relationship (either positive or negative)

governments and other bodies until needed for replace-   156–7,
ment or extension of CAPITAL EQUIPMENT.   187, 198,
   226, 274

RESIDUAL ERROR: The difference, especially in national
statistics, between the results of calculating AGGREGATES in
two ways, e.g. as income and as expenditure.   199
RESOURCES: The economist's term for all FACTORS OF   1, 34–5,
PRODUCTION and primary, INTERMEDIATE and finished   47 et seq.,
goods available at any time for production of goods or services.   61–2, 82–3
   144, 164,
   172, 243–5

UNEMPLOYED, UNDEREMPLOYED – Or unutilized and
under-utilized resources, those which are available but   172, 258–
are not being used or fully used.   60
RESTRICTIVE PRACTICE: (a) agreement among firms to
restrict output, fix prices, divide up markets, collude in
tendering, etc. Hence Restrictive Practices Court set up in
1956 to examine and pass judgment on such practices as to
whether they are in the public interest. Government may
then require that such practices should cease.   139–40
(b) Regulations by trade unions restricting persons who
may do certain work, intake of apprentices into certain
trades, closure of shops to non-trade union members, etc.
RETAIL: Sales to final customers. Hence: 137–8
  PRICES – Those charged to consumers. See PRICE
  MAINTENANCE.
  PRICE INDEX – An INDEX of price changes over time
  based on the mix of goods consumed by a SAMPLED
  typical household.   45, 250–1
RETURN ON INVESTMENT: Methods of comparing profitability of alternative investments according to income
expected over years of expected life of an ASSET.   109–10
REVENUE: Income of firm over a period of time or from
sale of a single unit (MARGINAL); income of government from
taxes.   32
RIGHTS ISSUE: The offer to shareholders of a BONUS of
SHARES in relation to shares held – when issued free it is on
the grounds that the real capital value of the company has
increased; otherwise shares issued below the current market
price as a cheap and convenient way of raising new capital.   156
RING: PRICE RING.   140
RISK: Implies chance of loss, e.g. by fire, burglary or death,
which may be insurable; or by bankruptcy or loss of earnings which may not be insurable. Hence:
  CAPITAL – That part of the capital invested in a company
  on which there is no guarantee of repayment, i.e.
  ORDINARY SHARES.   155

prices of the products of the industry in which the wages
were earned, as in the coal and steel industries.

SCARCITY: The basic concept of most analysis of SUPPLY
AND DEMAND whose inter-action results in prices reflecting   5, 15, 106,
scarcities and therefore in optimum allocation of RESOURCES.   146

SCATTER DIAGRAM: A statistical term for points representing two aspects of a POPULATION, e.g. price and sales of a product, which are marked against CO-ORDINATES on a diagram
to discover the relationship between them.   31

SCHEDULE: Tabulated statement of detailed times or, in
economics, points on a diagram, e.g. relating movements of
SUPPLY AND DEMAND to PRICE.   31–3

SCIENCE: Study of the world or a part of the world in a
systematic manner to discover relationships, which can be
tested and may lead to generalizations and predictions. See   14, 17, 19,
DEDUCTIVE and INDUCTIVE, SOCIAL SCIENCES.   20–2, 167

BASED INDUSTRY – One that is based on new products,
e.g. chemicals, invented by scientists.   55–6, 93

SCISSORS: Of price movements which cut into earnings of
PRIMARY PRODUCERS as primary product prices fall and
manufacturing prices rise.   47

SCRIP: Short for subscription, a provisional SHARE
certificate of a company and hence scrip issue or RIGHTS
ISSUE.   156

SEASONAL ADJUSTMENT: Alterations made to statistical
INDICES and other comparisons over time to iron out regular
seasonal changes and reveal only the changes from other
than seasonal factors, e.g. in unemployment figures.

SECONDARY: Industry or employment concerned with
processing PRIMARY PRODUCTS.   47

SECULAR CYCLE: TRADE CYCLE.   192

SECTOR: Major part of an economy, e.g. agricultural, PUBLIC.   45, 259

SECURITIES: General word for all STOCKS AND SHARES, but
especially long-term and short-term government stock.
Also other claims to property which can be offered as
COLLATERAL for a loan.   210–14

SELECTIVE EMPLOYMENT TAX (SET): A tax on all employees imposed on firms but subject to a rebate or PRE-
MIUM in the case of manufacturing plants and of those in
regions of high unemployment.   148, 236

SELECTIVE CREDIT CONTROLS: MONETARY MEASURES by
governments to limit credit to specified activities, e.g.
exports or HIRE PURCHASE controls or CAPITAL ISSUES CON-   207 et seq.
TROL.

SELF-FINANCING: That part of new capital found by
firms from their own earnings (see RESERVES, PLOUGH BACK,
RETENTIONS).   150–7

SELF-REGULATING: Of an economy whose movements are

SLUMP: Falling off in economic activity (compare BOOM,   164 et seq., TRADE CYCLE).   197–9

SOCIAL

ACCOUNTS: NATIONAL INCOME.

CLASS – Distinction made among members of a community according to the kind of work they do or their ways of behaviour – generally in Britain as follows: 63

UPPER – Old landed aristocracy;

UPPER MIDDLE – Better-off businessmen and members of professions;

LOWER MIDDLE – Less well off professional and businessmen, shopkeepers;

LOWER OR WORKING – The rest.

Compare Marxist division of economic CLASSES by relation to means of production, e.g. owners of CAPITAL.

CREDIT – Concept of Major Douglas, a Canadian, in the 1930s, in which unemployment was supposed to be the result of inadequate MONEY SUPPLY to be remedied by SUBSIDIES to retailers.   196

COSTS – Those which fall on the community at large and are not taken into account by companies in making decisions about allocation of RESOURCES.   95

FORMATION – Concept of Marx's embracing all levels of social STRUCTURE in his MODEL of society, including FORCES OF PRODUCTION, RELATIONS OF PRODUCTION and SUPERSTRUCTURE.   13

INSURANCE – Collective insurance of members of a community through the State by taxing individuals and companies according to employment, and paying benefits to cover sickness, old age and unemployment.   200–2, 275

SCIENCES – The sciences which treat of human beings in society, viz; ECONOMICS, Politics, SOCIOLOGY, Anthropology, Criminology.   14, 19–22

SECURITY – State assistance to persons whose insurance benefits in sickness, unemployment or old age are below a certain standard.   107, 177

SOCIALISM: A society in which the means of production are owned and controlled socially in the interests of society as a whole, rather than by a few private persons in their own interests.   12–13, 15, 56, 146, 243, 264, 274–7

UTOPIAN – Term used by Marx to describe early socialists, like Robert Owen, who believed that society could be changed into a socialist one by the strength of their own convictions.

SCIENTIFIC – Term used by Marx to describe his own view that socialism would result from the working of certain laws of social change which required the corres-

PAYMENT – Cash for immediate settlement.

PRICE – For immediate delivery as opposed to forward PRICE for delivery at some later date.

PURCHASE – Of commodities, or currency, immediately available as distinct from 'forward' or 'future' transactions.

SQUEEZE: In Stock Exchange parlance a situation where BEARS are forced into losses.

CREDIT – Where government MONETARY MEASURES reduce available credit.   214–15

STABILIZERS: Government measures designed to offset economic instability, specifically, e.g. by deliberate creation of BUDGET SURPLUS or deficit to counter TRADE CYCLE movements or by building in automatic devices such as price-support policies – e.g. for agricultural products.   164 et seq.

STAGES OF ECONOMIC DEVELOPMENT: Concept of Marx of a succession of SOCIAL FORMATIONS based on man's advancing control over nature.   56–7

STAGNATION: Absence of growth in economic activity.   168, 176–7, 200–1

STANDARDIZATION: Making products or parts of products to conform to a standard for the purpose of MASS-PRODUCTION.   144

STANDARD-DEVIATION: A measure of the DISPERSION around the average of a statistical POPULATION.   253

STANDARD OF LIVING – The material well-being of a community measured per head, e.g. NATIONAL INCOME divided by the population and measured in comparable prices.   2–3, 42, 49, 52, 58, 234

STAPLE PRODUCT: Principal product of a country, especially for export.   59

STATE OWNERSHIP: Property owned by the state, e.g. nationalized industries, the basis of state SOCIALISM.   226–7, 264, 271–2

STATIC THEORY: A part of EQUILIBRIUM THEORY in which equilibrium is assumed to have been achieved; dynamic theory being concerned with change or with the path by which equilibrium is achieved.   30

STATISTICS: The collection and arrangement of numerical facts, originally those concerned with the state – population, income, etc. – with the purpose of making clear the relations between them.   18, 42 et seq., 250, 265

STATIST INDEX: An INDEX covering the PRICE movements of certain foodstuffs and RAW MATERIALS over a long period.

STERLING: Originally standard value of English coin, now used of the CURRENCY of the UK.   4, 215

AREA – Certain countries, mainly present or one-time Commonwealth countries, which hold their RESERVES in London and may make payments between each other, generally without control.   215 et seq

BALANCES – Term used for national reserves and other funds banked in London, which are in effect short-term debts which may be used for long-term investment.   215 et seq.

STOCK: SHARES.

BROKER – Acts on behalf of investors as buyer and seller of shares – in London there are about 350 firms of brokers (1969).   210–11

JOBBER – Buys and sells certain groups of shares in dealings with brokers – there are about 80 firms of jobbers (1969).

EXCHANGE – The market for stocks and shares. In London the market value of shares in 1966 was about £70,000 million, £20,000 million of which was Government stock.   79, 132–6, 150–2, 155–9, 191

STOCKS: Supply of materials held or of goods produced but not yet sold which are generally valued at the beginning and end of each year.   43, 49, 178–9, 198–200, 270

APPRECIATION – Refers to the increase in prices of stocks over the year and must be discounted by the price increase to find the value of the physical increase in stocks.

STRUCTURE: Organic relationship of parts, e.g. of the economy or society, so that the whole hangs together in a SOCIAL FORMATION.   12–13, 16

SUBSIDIARY: A company wholly owned by a larger company in the same country or abroad.   152–61, 238

SUBSIDIES: Grants of money made by the state to particular industries or groups of persons, with the purpose of keeping prices of food, housing, exports, etc., below economic COST.   94, 177, 198–9, 231–2, 261–2

SUBSISTENCE: Means of livelihood, generally implying a minimum.

ECONOMY – One in which production is wholly for use by the producers with no margin for sale in the market.   58–9

THEORY OF WAGES – Assumes that wages will tend always to be driven to minimum SUBSISTENCE level (WAGES).   11, 117 et seq.

SUBSTITUTE: A COMMODITY or FACTOR that can be used in place of another, especially if the price of the other rises.

SUBSTITUTION: Replacing one FACTOR or one COMMODITY by another so that the owner or consumer obtains the highest return from his expenditure.   25, 27

SUBVENTION: Grant of money in aid by the State to particular industries or regions to make up for certain weaknesses they may suffer from.   221

SUMPTUARY LAW: Limiting private expenditure in the interest of state expenditure.

SUPER-PROFIT: Extra profit obtained from MONOPOLY positions, used especially by Lenin in his book on IM-PERIALISM to describe profits from colonial labour.   222

SUPERSTRUCTURE: Concept of Marx's of the political and legal forms corresponding to a certain MODE OF PRODUCT-ION.   12, 13

SUPPLY: Amount of a COMMODITY or FACTORS of PRODUCTION that a person or firm is willing to offer on the MARKET at different prices, the assumptions in economic analysis being:

(a) that as prices rise more is offered.

(b) that as more is offered the cost of providing each unit rises, depending in both cases on the ELASTICITY of SUPPLY.

   AND DEMAND – The relationship in a market of sellers and buyers that determines prices in the SHORT-RUN and allocation of RESOURCES in the LONG-RUN according to EQUILIBRIUM analysis.   7, 31–3, 88, 97 et seq., 178

SUPPORT PRICE: A minimum price guaranteed by the state, e.g. for agricultural produce where home producers' costs are higher than foreign producers'.

SURCHARGE: An addition to a price or tax, e.g. the 1964 tax on imported manufactures imposed by the British Government.   217

SURPLUS: An excess of income over outgoings, e.g. (a) In nationalized industries' accounts, where the word profit is not used; (b) In the Central Government annual accounts where a surplus or deficit is budgeted for; (c) In a nation's foreign payments account, where there may be a current, capital or overall surplus or deficit.   46, 220–2

An excess of output over demand at existing prices, e.g. a world wheat surplus.

SURPLUS VALUE: A concept of Marx's to describe that part of the VALUE added in production by Labour and not received by the labourer, i.e. newly created value less wages; hence the source of rent, interest, dividends, profits ploughed back, etc. (cf. VALUE). Thus: 11

   RATE OF – The relationship of that part of value added, received by the labourer, to the part not received.

SURTAX: Additional income tax payable on personal in-comes, in 1968 roughly where husband and wife's joint income exceeded £5,000.   230

SWITCHING: Changes of investor's PORTFOLIO among different SECURITIES or of a firm among different mixes of capital and labour.   158

SYMBOL: Conventional sign or mathematical expression used to represent an object, idea, relationship or process.

SYNDICATE: A group of firms associating together for a

INDIRECT – Comprises taxes imposed indirectly or
through purchases of alcohol, tobacco.   177, 198–9,
                                                            229 et seq.
PROGRESSIVE – Increasing more than proportionately   180, 229 et
with increases in income.   seq.
REGRESSIVE – Increasing less than proportionately with
income, the aim of progressive or regressive taxation   207, 229 et
being to redistribute income between rich and poor.   seq.
TAX RESERVE CERTIFICATES: Form of investment of
personal or company funds which enables them to earn
interest before tax payment is due.   198
TECHNOLOGY: State of technical or industrial development.   5, 12, 13,
See FORCES OF PRODUCTION.   22, 56, 62–
                                                            63, 103,
                                                            153, 162,
                                                            164, 167,
                                                            169, 183,
                                                            192, 243–4

TENDER: Any offer, but especially a written offer, to carry
out work at a certain price or to buy STOCK at a certain
price. Thus:
    ISSUE BY – Treasury bills offered to the DISCOUNT HOUSES
    according to the quotas tendered by them and also to
    other private tenderers in the money market.   211–12
TERMS OF TRADE: Shortened form of gross or net barter
(or commodity) terms of trade, i.e. a measure of the terms
on which commodities are exchanged between countries or
groups of countries or more usually the changes in those
terms.   59, 222
    GROSS – Changes in quantity relationship of EXPORTS and
    IMPORTS.
    NET – Changes in price relationship of exports and im-
    ports.
    FAVOURABLE – Movement for any country in which the
    ratio of export prices to import prices has risen.
TIED HOUSE: A house provided with the job, and to be
surrendered when the job ceases.
    PUBLIC HOUSE, SHOP, GARAGE – One which receives
    finance from a company on condition that it retails only
    company products. Where a house is not so tied, it is
    called a 'free house'.
TIME: A crucial factor in economics in relation to INTEREST,
SUPPLY, social accounts, etc., where time may be considered
not as continuous but discrete, that is broken up into
defined periods, e.g. of a day, a month or a year, etc.
    LAG – A lapse of some defined period before the effects of
    some economic action are seen.   184, 219
    AND MOTION STUDY – Analysis of methods of work with

N

materials, tools and machinery to determine the most
economical method, with the aim of standardizing this
and laying down times required for norms of task com-
pletion.

RATE – Payment according to hours worked, cf. PIECE-
RATE. Hence: 122, 201

AND A HALF AND DOUBLE TIME – Higher rates of payment at different periods of the day or week.

SERIES – A number of observations over time often shown
on a GRAPH or in the form of an INDEX.   45, 250

TIMES COVERED: Phrase used to describe the relationship
between NET PROFIT and DIVIDEND paid by a company.

TITHE: A tenth part, originally that part of the produce of
the land paid to the clergy. After 1836 changed into money
RENT and in 1936 into annuities.

TOKEN: A symbol and hence:

MONEY – Which has more NOMINAL value than its in-
trinsic material value, e.g. paper money.   27

TRADE ASSOCIATIONS: A number of firms in an industry
formed to further their common interests, e.g. by fixing
prices, QUOTAS, etc.   140

TRADE CYCLE: Alternating periods of BOOM and SLUMP, dis-
cernible at roughly eight year intervals since the last quarter
of the eighteenth century; successively supposed to have
been due to sunspots and their effect on harvests (W. S.
Jevons, 1880); friction in the labour market as new
machines were introduced (W. H. Beveridge, 1908); the
tendency of capitalism to OVERPRODUCTION (Marx, 1867);
monetary changes (R. G. Hawtry, 1928); the rising PRO-
PENSITY TO SAVE income (J. M. Keynes, 1937); UNDER-
CONSUMPTION as profits increase and consuming power is
cut in a boom (J. A. Hobson, 1920), relationship of saving
and investment (neo-Keynesians like A. H. Hansen, 1940).
Some writers like J. A. Schumpeter (1939) have discerned
a longer cycle of some 25–30 years, first suggested by N. D.
Kondratieff (1920) and sometimes called a KONDRATIEFF   165 et seq.,
CYCLE.   208

TRADE GAP: The gap in a country's payments between
exports and imports.   54, 59

CRUDE – Where imports are measured CIF and exports
(plus re-exports) are measured FOB.

TRADE UNIONS: 'Continuous association of wage-earners   3, 47, 121
for the purpose of maintaining and improving the con-   et seq.,
ditions of their working lives.' (Sidney and Beatrice Webb, 148, 168,
1920.)   240–1

CRAFT – Organized by occupation and relying much on
regulation of entry into the trade.

INDUSTRIAL – Organized by industry, and relying on

collective bargaining at national and plant level over
wages and conditions.
GENERAL – Organized in various ways, and relying
mainly on national negotiation.
TRANSFER-COST: In the concept of 'OPPORTUNITY COST'
the term for what must be offered to attract a supply of a
FACTOR OF PRODUCTION from one use to an alternative use.
IN THE BALANCE OF PAYMENTS: Those direct transfers
between governments. 220–1
  PAYMENTS – Those made by public authorities from taxation levied mainly on one group of persons – the
  middle-aged and better off – for meeting the needs of
  others, e.g. in pensions, family allowances, sick and
  unemployment benefit; but also includes payments on 125, 177–8,
  the NATIONAL DEBT. 198–9, 228
  PRICES – Special prices charged for transfers of goods between firms and their foreign SUBSIDIARIES when they
  want to move capital between them. 219–20
TRANSFORMATION CURVE: A graphical representation
showing the alternative combinations of two FACTORS OF
PRODUCTION within given resources. PRODUCTION POSSIBILITY
BOUNDARY. 34–8
TRANSPORT COSTS: An important element in costs depend- 67, 72–3,
ing largely on bulk to value or weight to value ratios. 77 et seq.,
91 et seq.

TREASURY: The central department of the British Civil
Service, responsible for supervising the rest of the civil
service, for controlling the spending of government departments and the rest of the PUBLIC SECTOR, and for national 209 et seq.
ECONOMIC PLANNING.
  BILL – See BILLS OF EXCHANGE. 209 et seq.,
226–7

TREND: A general tendency in a certain direction, e.g. of
observed changes in demand for a product over time. Such
a line of change may be extended by EXTRAPOLATION to
indicate guesses about future demand. 243, 247
TRUCK: Payment of wages by means of orders on a shop
(generally owned by the employer) instead of payment by
money wages, forbidden by Truck Acts in the nineteenth
century, which for long made payments of wages by cheque
illegal.
TRUST: Combination or MERGER of large firms so as to provide a MONOPOLY position in the market, limited in the USA
by various anti-Trust Acts.
  INVESTMENT – Holding of capital on behalf of a number
  of private persons. 159, 209
  UNIT – Financial intermediary for small private investors. 156
TURNOVER: Literally of stocks over a certain period of time,

MASS – Affecting many trades and industries, as in TRADE
CYCLE SLUMPS, sometimes called cyclical, e.g. over ten
per cent rate during 1930s in Britain.   164, 168,
177, 183

SEASONAL – In agriculture and sea-side resorts.

STRUCTURAL – Due to technological changes in industries requiring labour or to permanent failure of exports.   93, 177

TEMPORARY – Those like school leavers who may be
expected to find employment soon.

UNEMPLOYABLE: Those who cannot find employment even
in a BOOM either because of mental, physical or psychological
disabilities or because of lack of education – not generally
included in statistics of unemployment.

UNION: TRADE UNION.   121 et seq.

UNIT: Individual thing or person.   31

UNIT OF CURRENCY: The standard monetary unit used in
reckoning CURRENCY exchange rates e.g. £, $, franc.

OF OUTPUT – One part of output, e.g. a ton of steel or a
car, in terms of which costs are measured.   32–5

COSTS – Average cost of one unit of output.   32–5, 84–5,
88–90

UNIT TRUST: An Investment TRUST for small investors,
where the investor has a share in a portfolio managed by the
Trust mainly in ORDINARY SHARES.

UNITY: The number one.   114

'UNREQUITED' EXPORTS: Where exports of goods and
services exceed Imports and are used for payment of debts
due to foreigners.

USANCE: Time allowed by custom for payment of a BILL OF
EXCHANGE.   212

USE VALUE: Satisfying wants, as opposed to EXCHANGE
VALUE, in classical and especially Marx's economic thought –
the VALUE of COMMODITIES taking into account the actual
labour and materials incorporated in them rather than the
generalized or ABSTRACT LABOUR.   8, 103–4

USEFUL LIFE: Of an ASSET having regard to both deteriora-
tion and OBSOLESCENCE, taken into account in making provision for DEPRECIATION.

USURY: The practice of lending money, especially at exor-
bitant rates of INTEREST; British laws limited this to 5 per
cent up to 1854.

UTILITY: Concept of the capacity of a good or service to
satisfy human wants; hence.   25–6

MARGINAL – The extra satisfaction from one more unit
of a good or service, supposed in economics to diminish
with each extra unit (see MARGIN).   26, 246–7

Concept largely abandoned now in favour of OPPORTUNITY
COST.

'UTILITY' GOODS: Those produced cheaply to standard
specifications at fixed prices during the Second World War.   144

VALORIZATION SCHEMES: Phrase used to describe attempts
by producers of PRIMARY COMMODITIES, e.g. of coffee, to
maintain selling prices by destroying part of the crop.   131
VALUE: The worth of a good or service or FACTOR OF PRO-
DUCTION or CURRENCY measured in money terms to the
user. An ultimate concept in what economists call Value
Theory.   5
   ADDED – What is added in the process of production,
   hence value added tax.   46, 53, 268
   EXCHANGE – MARKET VALUE distinguished from USE
   VALUE by Marx and classical economists in terms of   8, 103 et
   abstract or actual labour incorporated.   seq., 273–4
   LABOUR THEORY OF – Concept of classical economists
   and of Marx, according to which COMMODITIES exchange
   in the proportions of general or ABSTRACT LABOUR incorporated in them.   7, 8, 273–4
   COST OF PRODUCTION THEORY OF – a restatement of
   labour theory in money terms to measure the costs of
   various FACTORS entering into production.
   MARGINAL THEORY OF – Of W. S. Jevons and L. Walras
   at the end of the nineteenth century who rejected
   Labour theory in favour of a concept of value being
   determined by marginal utility.   26, 246
VALUE JUDGMENT: A decision based not on alternative
means judged in relation to ends (the subject of POSITIVE
ECONOMICS) but on alternative ends according to the importance attached by each person judging to concepts of
equality, liberty, etc.   97, 248
VARIABLE: A FACTOR influencing any situation which can
often be isolated and measured at different times and places,
to discover the relation between its variations and those of
other factors.   32 et seq.
VARIABLE COSTS: Those which vary directly with the
changes in the volume of output, e.g. labour and material.   84, 88–9
   CAPITAL – Marx's term for that part of capital laid out in
   buying LABOUR POWER which reproduces its own value
   plus SURPLUS VALUE, as opposed to CONSTANT CAPITAL
   (machinery and raw materials) which is used up in production.   166
VARIANCE OF A SAMPLE: Measure of dispersion, the mean
square of deviations from the average;
Square root of variance = Standard DEVIATION.   253
VARIATION AND COVARIATION ANALYSIS: Used by
statisticians to assess the relative importance of different

possible sources of sample variation and thereby to distinguish the effect of different factors. 253

VELOCITY OF CIRCULATION: The average number of times that any unit of money changes hands in the course of a certain period, usually a year (see QUANTITY THEORY OF MONEY) where money is regarded as a STOCK but income as A FLOW. 183

VERTICAL: INTEGRATION. 90

VIABLE: Capable of maintaining life. Applied to firms = able to meet financial obligations. Applied to countries = able to pay their way.

VICIOUS CIRCLE: Action and reaction that intensify each other in a harmful way, applied especially to the poverty of a country, where RESOURCES are not adequate or are not used in such a way as to provide investment for developing more resources. Applied particularly by G. Myrdal (1957) to the failure of poor countries to attract capital. 1, 105–6, 183–4

VISIBLE TRADE: The export and import of goods in the BALANCE OF PAYMENTS. 54, 221–3

VOLUME: Measure of quantity after allowing for PRICE changes. 44, 169–71, 223

WAGES: A general term covering all forms of payment to labour but often limited to labour paid weekly, SALARIES being used to describe payments made monthly for non-manual workers. 25, 51–2, 117 et seq., 190, 200

THEORY – Concerned with accounting for the level of wages in an economy at any time, e.g.: 117 et seq.

SUBSISTENCE, THEORY OF – held by classical economists, especially by Malthus that wages would tend to be driven down to SUBSISTENCE level by population increases, or by Marx by the RESERVE ARMY of unemployed; sometimes called Law of Wages. 120 et seq., 167

FUND: Theory that the total amount of wages will be limited by the amount of capital available, assuming the return to capital is fixed and PRODUCTIVITY unchanging. 120 et seq.

MARGINAL – Productivity Theory – that wages will tend to equal not the average NET PRODUCT of labour but the MARGINAL NET PRODUCT. 120 et seq.

RATES – Basic minimum payment for a job, generally expressed per hour. 125, 201–2

DRIFT – The gap between movements in nationally negotiated wage rates and actual average earnings in any industry, including overtime, bonuses, piece-rate payments, etc. 125, 200

COUNCILS – Replaced in 1945 the Trade Boards established by legislation to determine minimum wages for

WORKER: Person who works for his living.   47, 116,
  MANUAL – Mainly with his hands.   126
  SKILLED – Having a certain training.
  UNSKILLED – Having no training.
  SEMI-SKILLED – Having some training.
WORKING CAPITAL: The LIQUID resources of a business, generally the current ASSETS less the current LIABILITIES.
WORKING CLASS: Concept now used mainly by Marxist and other socialist economists to describe those persons in a community having no other means of livelihood than their LABOUR POWER.   77, 167
WORKING DAY: The number of hours worked on average in any society, of importance in Marx's analysis of the intensification of EXPLOITATION.
WORTH: Measure of VALUE. NET.   115
WRITE-OFF: In company accounts to cancel the value of   158, 167–
ASSETS.   168, 192-3

YIELD: The return on CAPITAL invested at any time, i.e. the annual amount received in dividend or interest as a percentage of the purchase price (not the NOMINAL VALUE) of the share.   210–13
  NET – Yield after deducting tax due at the standard rate.
ZENITH: Highest point, of sun in the sky, or of an economic series.
ZERO: Figure 0, lowest point.   141
ZONE: Area of the earth or a country, e.g. one allocated to a particular firm for sales. Hence Zoning.   138

Index of Names